Henry's

WONDERFUL

Model T

1908-1927

Books by Floyd Clymer

Henry's

WONDER

1908-1927

BONANZA BOOKS · NEW YORK

Floyd Clymer

FUL

MODEL

Library of Congress Catalog Card Number: 55-10405

Printed in the United States of America

DESIGN BY JOSEPH J. BINNS

This edition published by Bonanza Books,
a division of Crown Publishers, Inc.,
by arrangement with McGraw-Hill Book Company, Inc.
F G H

HENRY FORD

1863-1947

This book is dedicated to the memory of Henry Ford. To enumerate the qualities and to attempt to describe the foresight and ability of Henry Ford would be wasted effort at this late date. So many words have already been devoted to his achievements.

The production of automobiles in tremendous quantities and at low prices so that millions of people the world over could enjoy them was his essential contribution. For the vision, perseverance, and tenacity that ultimately brought him success, he will go down in history as one of our greatest industrial leaders.

Though he passed away April 7, 1947, the record of his life and work will live on for future generations. And perhaps the fondest Ford memories that his contemporaries will always cherish concern his own favorite car, the Model T.

ACKNOWLEDGMENTS

In compiling a book such as this, it is always necessary
to secure material from sources outside one's own library.
I therefore wish to thank the following persons and firms
for their kind cooperation and assistance in supplying
portions of the material used in this book: The Ford
News Bureau, Henry Edmunds and his staff at the Ford
Motor Company Archives, Les Henry, Antique Automo-
bile Club of America, Dick Shaw, Marvin Townsend,
Ford Owner and Dealer Magazine, U.S. National Mu-
seum, *True* magazine, *Motor* of England, Jerry Duryea,
A. 'L. Dyke, Victor W. Page, the *Ford Times,* General
Petroleum Corporation, *Automobile Topics, Motor Age,*
Art Twohy, M-G-M Studios, Hal Roach Studios, Walt
Woestman, Albert Brouse, and any other contributors
who may have been unintentionally overlooked.

Contents

Model T Memories

A country woman and her small son were driving to town when a clanking flivver bore down upon them. Their horse was badly frightened and began to prance, whereupon the old lady leaped down and waved wildly to the flivver driver, screaming at the top of her voice.

The driver stopped his Ford and offered to help get the horse past.

"That's all right," said the boy, who remained composedly in the carriage, "I can manage the horse. You just lead Maw past."

This was an endearing and rib-tickling kind of humor that infected vaudeville jokes, the master of ceremonies' speech at dinner parties and wherever citizens and fellow townsmen got together. They couldn't resist including a joke about Ford or the "Tin Lizzie" in their kit of humor or their stage act or their after-dinner conversation over cigars and brandy. Thousands of witticisms, too, were printed on post cards and valentines. But the jokes about the Model T

amused no one more than Henry Ford himself. He often said that every Ford joke sold a car.

Ford was an institution; Ford was also a hardheaded, practical builder of automobiles dating back to the infant Ford Motor Company of Detroit. Time: 1903. I remember when, aside from this hilarity over the quirks and habits of the Model T, Henry Ford coined the slogan "The Universal Car," and it truly was. Indeed, one of the advantages of the man with a Ford over the buggy rider with a horse in 1908—the year the first T was offered—was that he could modify his car to plow the fields with it on weekdays and still go country-riding in it on Sundays. Legions of owners used their Fords to saw wood, pump water, store grain, run stock shears, generate electricity, and in ways and for jobs that the most imaginative had never dreamed of. A Ford gave the owner transportation along with a utility power unit that was excitingly versatile in the hands of the man who liked to invent new rigs.

A 2-ton load of hay on a Ford truck and trailer. The Model T was almost indispensable on many farms.

It was so "universal" that Ford owners and salesmen, before they had even cranked up their engines, were positive beyond a shadow of a doubt that Ford's Model T was better than the elephant or the horse or the steamboat. Millions of former owners of the T still hold the "Lizzie" in affectionate esteem. For the Ford, besides guaranteeing a ride through snow and rain, a means for the "go-getter" to increase his sales and the doctor to do his calling, contributed more than any other car to the welding together of the towns and cities of this country. The Model T, although it was to share the American market with approximately 2,200 other makes of cars, from the earliest Duryea to Ford's new Continental, was an automobile that helped to revolutionize a people's way of life. Ford's jalopy, as the "common man's car," was a unique contributor to the history of transportation in America.

What sort of contraption was this car? First of all, it was a car of contradictions. It was imperfect, and its imperfections were a part of its fascination. Sometimes she wouldn't start on cold mornings, or she burned too much oil, or she got poor mileage over the muddy roads, or she wouldn't outrun a jack rabbit. And once started, would the Ford engine keep running? One farmer even vowed that the potatoes on a piece of his hilly farm land could hold her back. The blamed thing was always a subject of complaints. These became the fertile soil for the accessory manufacturers who, over the twenty years of Model T life, were to turn out some 5,000 gadgets to dress up and cause to run "with the surest ease and invincible power" that rattling T that stood out in the woodshed.

For many years, the Model T came equipped with only the barest necessities—no speedometer or starter, no temperature gauge or bumpers. And even though Ford was one of the first car manufacturers to place the steering wheel on the left side, steering the T was a whole lot like driving a truck—or at least so said many complaining owners of the flivver.

The T, however, was supposed to be the

Midwest farmers used the Ford for pulling stumps, threshing grain, sawing wood, and pulling hayracks. In this 1912 photograph, Frank Atcherson, of Mapleton, Minnesota, used his Model T to fill a silo.

"Ma wants to know—will it change the babies' diapers?"

latest word in automotive engineering. It took you where you wanted to go. Parts were cheap and available in almost any small town or farmer's barn, and if you could drive it you could fix it yourself. That was real design. And with his use of vanadium steel, Henry Ford succeeded in building a quality and dependability into his car which many other higher-priced cars did not possess.

In the early scramble for sales in the automotive field, many salesmen and representatives for a tire-puller or a tractor-attachment firm drove Model T's. Furthermore, sporting a bow tie and speaking in a mechanical jargon, the salesman would take out your clutch before your very eyes to show you that his tool kit for clutch and related parts on the T Ford was the very best on the market. The greater part of Ford owners at one time or another tinkered on their cars, removed a transmission band here, cleaned the spark plugs there, greased, hammered, wiped and pampered. They were a high-spirited, interested bunch and forever talking about their T's. They learned of necessity how to repair their own cars. They represented the

mechanical America that was on its way. It was easy enough to exchange brake bands, or to take off the head and the pan to put in a new piston. Because there were few mechanics as we know them these days, situated on every other corner in our cities, the man who owned a Ford often did most of his mechanical work himself. The motorist accepted his roadside grief with his joy. For this reason, Ford had more dealers by far than did any other maker.

The driver of this top-heavy jalopy knew, too, when his T was hitting on three instead of four cylinders. Many a car owner of today can't tell whether his V8 is hitting on seven or eight. And if you were to suggest that he clean his spark plugs, he might throw up his hands in helplessness. His auto is a piece of precision machinery, and a far cry from Ford's first Model T's. That is one reason for the average driver's disinterest in his car's engine; he feels that he could not possibly understand it. But the fact of the matter is that people today would rather let George do it. Neither could they repair their engines, nor do they care much about how they work. That is evolution. Yet it's hard to forget the days when,

"Do you have to drive in town today, Ma? I was planning on using the car for plowin' the north twenty."

Would she keep running?

to survive on the road, a man had to be a mechanic. With "The Wedding of the Sunshine and the Rose" running merrily through his head, and while Sarah opened her fringed parasol in the midsummer's heat, he had to get out and get under if he wanted to put his car back on the road. Ford dealers prospered in that do-it-yourself climate.

At the tender age of eleven, I was a dealer for Reo, Maxwell, and Cadillac cars in the little town of Berthoud, 50 miles north of Denver, and at the foot of the Colorado Rocky Mountains.

In two years of hard bargaining and with surprising regularity in both fat and lean seasons, I sold 26 cars. Ford was not very stout competition then, although in 1905 he built the Model N Roadster at the competitive price of $500. That sum, in crop money or celluloid-collar sales, was almost unheard of for a four-cylinder car at that time. I had been selling one-cylinder Reos, silent two-cylinder Maxwells, and one-cylinder Cadillacs. But four cylinders for half a thousand, though a considerable sum, was a recognizable bargain that began to make a dent in my sales.

Ford built the improved R and S four-cylinder models in 1906 and 1907, and then he reached for high fruit with his large Model K

six-cylinder job. Its sale price was $2,750. My little one-cylinder Cadillac at that time was selling for $750. His "big six," however, with the 120-inch wheelbase didn't go over as successfully as he expected, and as a consequence Ford decided that the K was his last venture into the high-priced-car field. The "big six" was the last six-cylinder automobile he would build. So long as Henry Ford held the guiding reins in the Ford Motor Company, he never did change his mind.

I'll never forget the day I met Henry Ford. It was in 1907 in Denver when the late Charles K. Hendy, a Ford salesman who later became one of Ford's closest friends and manager of Ford's Denver assembly plant, introduced me to the car builder. Hendy told him I was the youngest auto dealer in the world, so called by no less than President Theodore Roosevelt. Mr. Ford agreed. "You are surely a youngster to be selling automobiles. Someday I hope you will be selling Fords." I saw him several times in later years, and he always remarked, "And how is the young auto agent?"

It was not until 1908 that the land-office Model T business began to starch up the sales competition in my district. The local Ford dealer

Model T owners were tinkerers.

Young auto agent demonstrates Maxwell

The 1908 Model S—Ford's last model before the T

NOTICE TO USER

To obtain best Results this car should not be driven faster than 20 miles per hour for the first 500 miles.

Oil should be changed after first 400 miles and every 750 miles thereafter.

IMPORTANT

Always insist on genuine Ford Parts

This is a copy of the original sticker placed on the windshield of all early Model T's.

was a fellow by the name of George Nall, and he drove a T. That T of George's was a machine. When it got a leak in the radiator, which was quite often, he would put a handful of oatmeal or cornmeal in it to plug the leak at least temporarily. He was trying to do the same thing to my sales, and it was hard to keep up with him.

George was so enterprising in those early days that he even went in for trade-ins. He'd take a horse and buggy from a prospective customer or allow him a generous discount on a Model T.

In those days, a man needed only to buy a manufacturer's car and, if the territory was open, he could have the dealership thrown in. This was the situation in the territory around Berthoud. I had rung up some sizable profits for myself selling one- and two-cylinder cars at prices higher than what the four-cylinder T sold for. Ford's flivver, at that low price, seemed just short of sensational when it first appeared.

In order to meet this new competition, I flushed the farmers' sugar-beet and wheat fields and the Main Street stores for new buyers. Then I took on the E.M.F. "30" and, a few months

later, the Flanders "20," both built by the E.M.F. Company in Detroit, and distributed by the Studebaker wagon people of South Bend. They were fair sellers, good hard-rock bargains in looks, dependability, and savings in boot wear. They had a fairly large "refinement" clientele, also. It was only natural that the Studebakers, well-known builders of horse-drawn vehicles, should attempt first to sell a name car already known for its quality.

The first Model T, if it lacked elegant style and mohair cushions, did boast improvements over the earlier Ford models as well as competitor makes of cars. A mysterious howling, jerking mechanism called the planetary transmission came installed on the 1908 T. All enclosed except for the sound, and with two speeds forward and a reverse, it was the epitome of the gearbox of the day. If the planetary was cranky and anything but quiet, it still made motoring a sport. Only when the 1928 Model A appeared, equipped with sliding gears, did T drivers, some grieved and others relieved, realize that Ford had abandoned his famous gear scramble called the planetary.

One of the 1908 T improvements, and an innovation of course that would stay, was the steering wheel and wobbly column on the left-

"We'll give you more trade-in for your old horse and buggy than any other dealer in town."

hand side. A few of the off-brand models before the T had left-hand steering, but Ford was the first manufacturer of any consequence to stick the driver in the left front seat in order to accommodate the ladies and oncoming traffic. Passengers could climb down off the high leather seats onto the board sidewalk instead of the gumbo of the mud street. And it was possible for two lonely motorists, way out in the country somewhere 20 miles from town, to pull their jalopies up alongside each other and inquire as to weather and road conditions and "Have you a patch or two you can spare, brother?" More

and more customers began to take to Ford's left-hand-drive Model T.

There were certain other notable features about the flivver of 1908. The engine had a low-tension magneto, built into the flywheel. The timer and coils gave plenty of trouble, as did the oil line, which had a habit of becoming clogged. Many inventions appeared on the market designed for cleaning the line once it became plugged up. The new flivver was cooled by the thermosyphon system rather than by water pump. Ford did continue the transverse spring suspension of his former models, both front and

Tourists in a 1908 Model T stop to watch a farmer's steam traction engine pass. Note duster and goggles of man leaning against side mount. They protected him against clouds of dust on the open roadway.

rear. The drive shaft was enclosed, and the T had radius rods from the rear axle to the rear of the transmission, and from the engine to the front axle. Henry cast his four-cylinder 20-horsepower engine *en bloc* on his "Tin Lizzie," which meant that you could have all cylinders cast in one piece instead of in pairs as had been the custom on his four-cylinder N, R, and S models.

Any blacksmith or T driver knew about the improved T engine and the *en bloc* feature. George Nall, in Berthoud, was an expert. Even though we were shop and curbstone competitors in the car-selling field, George and I remained good friends. Intrigued by the new Ford model, I took many a ride with him into the country while he explained the fine points of the T on his demonstrator. Because selling ethics were not so firmly set in those days, George wisely left me out when he went on a demonstration ride with a prospective customer. He knew that when we got back to town I would be calling

A blowtorch to heat the intake manifold, a bucket of boiling hot water, and a strong arm always helped a T owner get going on a cold winter morning.

on his Ford customer to sell him an E.M.F. or Maxwell. Yet I admired the car that people, even then, were beginning to call the flivver. Also about this time the word "jitney" was coined, probably because many Model T's were used in rental service.

I remember one extremely cold morning when we started on a short trip to Loveland in George's jitney. Six miles of snow-covered road lay ahead, and the thermometer had dropped below zero. George had put antifreeze into the radiator, a home-made solution of alcohol and water. The Model T was notoriously hard to start on cold mornings, but George had learned that if he jacked up one of the rear wheels, released the hand brake, and gave the crank a few turns, it would start more readily. We went through this ritual that morning, but his T was balky and refused to start.

George had plenty of Model T savvy. The proper manner of starting the T was to crank the engine, using the battery ignition first, and once the engine started, flip the switch for magneto ignition. My ingenious friend put a kettle of water on the kitchen stove. Meantime he drained the radiator. When the water came to a boil, he unscrewed the radiator cap and poured it in. I can still hear that crackling sound as the hot water hit the ice-cold metal of the cylinder block. Once the engine was started and the rear wheel was again on the ground, the car crept forward slowly and almost crushed George between the radiator and the wall of the barn that was his "garage." George was not always light of foot.

One of the quirks of Henry's "heap," as some called the car on those cold mornings when there seemed to be no life in her, was that the T had the "creeps." Many is the time I cranked and pulled out the carburetor choke and then reset the hand spark and throttle levers and cranked again. Usually the engine would commence to hit on two or three cylinders, then cough and break out into a glorious, deafening roar. She would really sound sweet—like a thresher trimming the nap off an acre of barbed

"Help!"

wire. But when she shook and shivered and was running, she also had a tendency to crawl forward, so that I had to put both hands on the radiator and push until I could make a dash for the front seat to adjust the gas and spark levers before the engine conked out. The throttle lever was located under the steering wheel; until a few gadget makers offered one, the T had no foot throttle.

The T was a car that rared to go, a challenge to every driver. Once the engine had run for a few minutes and the crankcase oil was warmed up, the T settled down, and there never was, in the twenty years of its life, a finer piece of automotive machinery, as dependable as a pack mule if you carried a tool kit and checked your gas regularly. And never can I recall my friend George taking a horse and buggy out of town to bring in his flivver.

I can still recall how my friend George taught me to check the oil. There was no dip stick in those days. I got down on my knees, and, with a pair of pliers, turned one of two petcocks located in the lower half of the flywheel housing. If oil ran out of the top petcock onto the ground, the oil supply was okay. If no oil came out of the lower petcock, we were headed straight for

bearing trouble if oil was not added. This was a primitive method for testing the oil supply, but any ten-year-old kid could learn how to do it. George was a stickler for simplicity, and the Ford was a simple car.

Returning from that same trip to Loveland that day, we journeyed through some hilly country west of town and found that our T climbed nearly every grade. We ran into one hill, though, where the car sputtered and almost stopped. George knew right away what the trouble was. With the gas tank under the front seat, the gravity flow to the carburetor would not work on hills too steep. Equal to the emergency, he swung the car around so that we headed downhill, and we backed up the remainder of the hill to its crest.

Indeed, many folks claimed that the Model T worked better in reverse than in low gear on a sharp grade, and doubtless this quirk of the gravity fuel system was what they referred to. The gravity flow was positive and constant in hill backing; also the gear ratio for reverse was lower than for low gear, and this gave the car added power.

"Hey, George, she needs oil!"

I recall a similar event that took place outside of Berthoud in those few years before the T had caught on. There was a fast-talking old farmer in the area who had taken to the "gas buggy" and was dealing out Fords for Henry. One of his neighboring farmers was looking for just the right automobile, and the old codger proceeded to give his friend and prospective buyer a demonstration. The buyer had heard down at the barbershop that several drivers, gripping their wheels for dear life, had tried to crawl up a steep quarter mile of hill from the road to his house. He promised to buy a Ford if he could be shown that it would climb the hill. "Be glad to," said the farmer-salesman, and he started up the hill, the customer alongside of him in the front seat and hanging onto a top strut. The jalopy did fine until about halfway up the hill, when it began to buck and cough. The quick-witted salesman cramped the wheels over and swung into a side lane. He pushed the reverse pedal and backed into the hill road again, remarking with great pride, "You see, this hill is really nothing. I can even back up it." At the

"I understand he can afford a new car, only he doesn't want to give up that mother-in-law seat in his 1909 model."

top of the hill, the buyer, in great wonderment, signed the order. The salesman had some tall explaining to do when the irate owner later found that he could not pull the entire quarter mile in low gear. For over a year that farmer had to back up the last 200 yards of hill to his house. Soon the farmer got the hang of his hill, though, and was boasting to his friends about sighting along the fence post and the scrub oak for accurate back-up aim.

In 1909 Ford brought out a slick roadster. It was one of the most unusual models in the whole T line, made so, above all else, by a one-passenger bucket seat, exposed to the weather, that was bolted on just behind the double front seat. This rear commode, shaped like a bucket half, was often referred to as the "mother-in-law" seat. Also in 1909, Ford mounted a brass gas generator on the running board, and by use of carbide it furnished gas for the headlights. Water, carried in the upper part of the generator, would drop onto lumps of carbide, and the gas so formed would flow through rubber or copper tubing to the lamps. Kerosene cowl lights and taillights—and a bulb horn—were kept highly polished and were pointed out with pride by the

"I can even back up this hill."

T owner. With lights, the city-bound man could drive at night, and when he squeezed the bulb horn, a raucous blast would inform other drivers and pedestrians of his presence.

This year, too, Ford made much to-do about his use of vanadium steel in some high-stress parts, especially axles. For years his advertising and dealer displays played up that feature, often showing a vanadium-steel axle twisted like a pretzel but unbroken to prove the toughness of the material forged into the T.

By 1910 the Model T Ford was on the up-swing in popularity, gaining more customers every day over my E.M.F. and Flanders "20." I was in fact, losing loyal customers simply because the Ford was a cheaper car. Though the E.M.F. factory was producing in the Flanders a fast, stylish machine in the low-priced field, repair and operation costs were not on a thrifty par with the Model T's for the average buyer.

The Ford owner had clincher tires and no spare. He always carried a spare tube and a tire-repair outfit. Sometimes he strapped an extra tire casing on the rear, on the side, or over the hood for a long journey. This was one of the many ways that the Ford owner could save on tires. But the true dyed-in-the-wool flivver man needed only to say he drove "a plain jalopy and bought two gallons of gas three days ago" to convince many folks away from my cars. Ford, as a product and a name, was becoming a by-word, as native to the American scene as Boston baked beans and Georgia grits and gravy.

Henry Ford, too, was becoming a well-known figure. By repute, he was a stubborn and inde-pendent man who built the car he felt most like building. He claimed, and sincerely believed, that his T was the car people *ought* to own. In a few years—1913 to be exact—he was to ad-vertise a cure for insomnia with the slogan: "Open your eyes and watch the Fords go by." The Ford owner swore by his car, as well as at it. In a favorite cartoon of the period, the Model T was marked as the last in seven stages of transportation—from a primitive man climbing a tree, riding a dinosaur to market, and perched on a mammoth elephant, to travel by way of camel, covered wagon, and railroad. The stub-born Mr. Ford had brought the end product in transportation to the American scene.

The Model T's success in the first half-dozen years of its existence was partly due to the tem-

The seven stages of transportation

per of the day and the desires of the motorist. The following is a good example of the exuberance with which many people truly admired, bought, and drove their T's. This ad, which appeared in the early *Ford Times*, a propaganda publication if ever one existed, spoke for the exuberant consumer as well as the producer.

"It leads the way; it blazes the trail; it sets the pace. To the utmost corners of the earth the *Ford* journeys. It is the pioneer car in many lands. Many sections of the Canadian Northwest knew no other car but the Ford. The first car on the Island of Jolo, Philippines, was a Ford.

A Ford was first to scale Scotland's Ben Nevis. The first pleasure car across the Gobi desert of Mongolia was a Ford town car destined for the Living God of Urga. And the Ford has countless other firsts to its credit. Even here in the United States there are many places where Ford has led the way for the rest—it has been the first automobile owned in the country, the first to cause pride to the village, the first to traverse the rough trail. . . ."

We didn't go in a Ford, but in 1910 my father, Dr. J. B. Clymer, decided we ought to hit the rough trail for the Pacific Northwest and

Loaded with 50 boys weighing a total 3,492 pounds, this Model T chugged in high gear through the streets of Payne, Ohio, in 1912. The publicity stunt, staged by

Payne's Ford dealer, Joseph Miller, Jr., proved the Model T's "ability to take it" at a time when durability was a car's chief selling point.

sample life in Walla Walla, Washington. It was at this time that adventure in the guise of "competition against the Model T" entered our house. My younger brother, Elmer (nicknamed Bill), and I, eleven and fourteen respectively, cooked up a scheme that was approved by a Mr. Porter, the manager of the Studebaker branch in Denver. He saw valuable publicity in a trip by two kids from Denver to Spokane, Washington, in a Flanders "20." This was a stunt the Ford crowd had not hit upon to push their Model T. Bill and I were to take the car on this hazardous journey, without a mechanic or spare parts, over plenty of rough terrain, mountains, and desert strewn with sagebrush, with only a load of trust in a comparatively new make of car. We started on our journey with the jovial blessings of the derbied governor of Colorado and a letter from Denver's genial Mayor Robert W. Speer to Mayor Pratt of Spokane. Among our special equipment we carried a collapsible canvas bag for filling the radiator from irrigation ditches and two 100-foot-long strips of canvas sewed together by my mother for use over sand roads.

Well along the route, everything was going fine. Our engine sounded invincible, even when

Thousands watched in amazement as a 1911 Model T climbed the steps of the Tennessee capitol. Largely as a result of this stunt by Harlan W. Major, Nashville Ford dealer, Ford's Tennessee sales rose from 35 per cent of the market in 1911 to 47 per cent in 1912. Major's mechanic stands on the rear of the vehicle, giving greater traction to the churning wheels.

confronted with the dry terrors of the desert and the worst imaginable roads. We refueled and oiled up at small towns along the way. The Far West stretched out ahead of us. We hoped to reach our new home before too long. The applause and cheers of crowds of Spokane natives lining the main streets and pointing to our car, gaping and filled with awe, already rang in our ears.

Out in the open country to the west of Cheyenne, Wyoming, jack rabbits played in the beams of our headlights as we neared the Continental Divide. At night the sheepherders would pass us in their covered wagons, if they weren't busy pulling us out of ditches, or a cowboy would stop to talk or wave at us. One night we slept in the wagon of some sheepherders. Most of the time, though, we rolled out our blankets in the open beside a clump of sagebrush, and two scared kids settled down for a lonely night.

West of Laramie in Wyoming our transmission, located just in front of the rear axle, gave

out, grinding and howling and finally locking up. We were two tired and disgusted kids but we couldn't just sit there and rust, our Flanders a speck on the great open prairie. We found the railroad tracks leading west and walked to the nearest flagging station, where we sent a frantic telegram to Studebaker in South Bend, Indiana. Posthaste, the factory dispatched to us by train a mechanic with a new transmission, and there on the loading platform of the prairie railroad station at Walcott, he installed it in the Flanders and tuned the engine for us. We were off once again.

Another 100 rocky miles west, the transmission broke down on us a second time. This time a Flanders mechanic came out from Denver and fixed our car. When the third transmission broke a gear, Studebaker calculated costs against publicity value and decided it was just too expensive to keep a couple of kids in transmissions. Sadly, we had to abandon the project. Feeling bedraggled and a bit let down by our sponsor fac-

1910 Flanders "20"

tory, we shipped the Flanders "20" back to Denver and went on to Walla Walla by train. Thus ended the ambitious publicity stunt in the name of the Flanders by which two youths tried to stem the tide of the Model T.

In Walla Walla I went to work for the John Smith Company, Studebaker dealers, as a salesman for their E.M.F. and Flanders cars. In the fall of 1910 I got the speed urge. I removed the body from a stock E.M.F. car and, attaching a couple of bucket seats on the top of the gas tank, I put together an early-day "hot rod." I hoped, by dint of practice outside of town, to become a down-stretch freewheeler and establish local records and reputation in racing. At that time, pioneer aviators Walter R. Brookins with his Wright biplane and Charles F. Willard, flying a Curtiss biplane, had come to Walla

Walla and were to fly at the County Fair celebration. When I heard about this event, I arranged through my boss a stunt which would advertise the E.M.F. and bring me some fun. Briefly, I would race the daredevil fliers. My employer furnished me with a mechanic and we worked feverishly to tune up the car. All was ready. When the fair opened, each day I churned around the 1-mile dirt track with one or the other of these planes hovering over me, zooming and roaring precariously close to my racer. Each day their dip of death or my skid on a turn brought the crowd to its feet. Our daring event at the County Fair brought customers flocking into the agency and a big hand at the racecourse. Of the four races, I won two and lost two. On the third day, in appreciation for my competition, Brookins took me for a ride. At fifteen

A Model T on a typical country road in 1909

of local ads and repeated personal calls on prospects, we managed to sell all but one of the seven cars of the first carload. That last model was a coupé. It stood on the showroom floor for at least six months. Nobody wanted to ride in a coupé at the risk of getting diced up by glass and roof posts in that accident that was sure to happen. And people were too accustomed to the raw weather in open buggies and wagons to bother much about getting cold and wet in bad weather. They wanted nothing to do with "showcase" models, as they called the coupé. More than one customer came into our store positive there was no future in the closed car.

Despite "home-town" resistance to the coupé and to the T model generally, people who owned the T drove it and liked it. Meanwhile I kept a sharp eye out for a sale and/or a motoring trip. In those days there were traveling stock companies playing in the small out-of-the-way towns in the Midwest and Far West. Dahlen was a very liberal man, and he furnished me with a T demonstrator. One afternoon when a troupe of actors and actresses, playing in a local stock company, came around to the store and asked me for a ride in a T, without Dahlen's authorization I loaded them into my jalopy and we

years of age, I became the first passenger ever to be carried aloft in the state of Washington.

Late in 1910 I decided that if I was ever going to get anywhere in the car business, I had better join up with a fast-moving company to sell a make whose popularity had staggered the lovers of quiet and the connoisseurs of the horse and buggy. The Model T Ford, I felt, would be a rich vein. With little trouble I secured a job selling Fords for a couple of brothers in Walla Walla. Harold Dahlen, a former lumberman from Bellingham, Washington, had just opened a Ford agency in town with his brother. Three or four other Ford agencies had failed in Walla Walla before Dahlen hung out his shingle. But our predecessors had sold the previous N, R, S, and K models, not the T.

I helped Dahlen unload from the boxcar the first railroad shipment of T's to come to Walla Walla. In the face of buyers' bias and their disgruntlement over previous Ford models, we had to pitch a strenuous line of sales chatter. By dint

"I don't care if you do like the pretty posies, I'm not going to get killed if that 'glass showcase' turns over!"

"She don't handle so good when you hit a deep rut."

set out for the country.

We were bumping along fine on a long stretch of Washington's straw-covered dusty road. The throttle was wide open; about 40 miles per hour was a good top speed in the old T. I reached over to "lean up" the mixture by turning a knob extending through the cowl on the right-hand side; the knob controlled the adjustment of the carburetor needle. At the instant I took my hand off the wheel, the car struck a deep rut, crossed the road, and ploughed into the ditch. It rolled over and over before coming to a stop. One of the actors suffered a broken arm, another a broken leg, and all of us were skinned and bruised. One had a bloody nose and his pants were torn off. My only injury resulted from the back of the seat roughing up the nape of my neck. As for the car, the fenders were crumpled, the top bashed in, windshield folded, glass broken, and the upholstery torn loose. My T demonstrator was ready for the scrap heap.

Dahlen considered the ride a "joy ride" in-stead of a demonstration. He was ready to fire me, but he decided against it in order to protect his investment. I would pay him for damages to the car on my $12-a-week salary and $5-per-car commission. And although it wasn't easy to pay for an almost completely wrecked Model T when new ones were selling for $700, I scraped together and borrowed enough money to pay off my debt in a year's time. In nearly fifty years of motoring, this was to be my only serious accident.

Competitive makes of cars were vying against each other in endurance, speed, and performance contests. The Northwest was considered one of the badlands spots for the automobile. At about this time I witnessed an interesting hill-climbing contest between a Ford and an air-cooled Franklin. The race was up a long, winding hill in the Blue Mountains of southwestern Washington, not far from our town of Walla Walla. R. P. Rice, then manager of the Ford branch in Seattle, sat at the wheel of the stripped-down Model T Ford that day, and as the car curled up the mountain leaving the dust flying under its wheels, he really brought out the heart in that little flivver. The crowd was scattered along the length of the race hill, and, much to their amazement, they saw the popular big air-cooled Franklin fall behind and Rice's T top the hill an easy winner.

In order to push sales, Ford never failed to editorialize upon the fact that his Model T could often outperform larger and heavier and more expensive cars. Through his advertising and cartoons, which the motorist could find in the lobby of the remotest hotel in the smallest American town, he acquainted the public with the car with a unit-power-plant type of engine with a mind of its own. One such ad showed the earth as seen by Martians; the earth is ringed, like Saturn, but by Ford Touring Model T's. Another cartoon of the same year, 1913, shows a big car stalled on a stubborn hill, pushed by the sweating menfolk and pulled by a team of straining plow horses. Nearby a gay foursome in an open Model T airily whiz up the hill. The caption reads,

"Too big."

In a way, such exuberant ads as these, coupled with my own personal experiences with the T, helped to sway me in one direction. About 1911 the family returned to Colorado, and, seeing with my own eyes that Fords were gaining in sales on other makes of cars, I decided to devote my energies to the leg work of selling Henry's Model T. The branch manager of the Denver Ford Motor Company was still the same Charles K. Hendy who had introduced me to the T in-

ventor in 1907. With Hendy's help I signed up to handle the Ford agency in Louisville, Colorado. There was some delay and considerable beating around the bush, for the plain fact of the matter was that Ford factory officials at Dearborn did not approve of a sixteen-year-old kid selling their cars. I had to settle for a job selling Model T's for Ford dealers as a sort of curbstone broker.

Some of my happiest Model T memories are of the days in 1912 when I was a curbstone

broker in Loveland, Colorado, for Jim Lanham, the local Ford dealer. One of my oddest sales was to a famous old Indian, Louis Papa, born in Snake Creek, Utah, in 1844. Louis's father, Joe Papa, had traded his family (wife, son, and daughter) to a Spaniard for four ponies. Such colorful stories were a part of Louis's reputation, and he was rightfully considered the "local character."

A friend of mine, a great practical joker, told me that someone had left Louis $5,000 in his will. I hurried to the mountains west of Loveland only to be told by Louis that the most he'd ever in his life received from a white man was $5 for posing in full regalia for a photograph

The beloved Indian of the Rockies, Louis Papa

with an Easterner. Surprisingly enough, however, he had saved enough money from cattle raising to buy a car, so all day long I sang the praises of the Model T and taught him how to drive it. Not only did Louis give me an order that evening but he told me of a vacationing family from the East on the other side of the mountain that wanted *two* Model T's, one each for father and son. Louis drove me over in his newly acquired Ford and I made the quickest triple sale of Model T's on record—all because of an innocent practical joke.

A friend of Louis's told me later that he saw Louis a few days after I'd sold him the car. He asked Louis how he liked his Model T and the Indian replied, "Ugh—him no go straight." But he never complained to me, and I've always assumed that Louis Papa was a satisfied Ford owner.

Soon afterward I sold a Model T to a Seventh Day Adventist, Elmer Hankins, by carefully abiding by Adventist custom. I'd heard that the Overland dealer from Berthoud was going to pay Hankins a visit on Sunday, so I scooted out to the Adventist colony at Campion on Saturday afternoon in a Model T. Saturday is the Adventist day of rest, which meant that Elmer wasn't going to talk business with anyone until after sundown. I waited around patiently, gossiping with his family, with one eye on the sun and another on my unsuspecting client. As soon as that orange ball dropped over the horizon, I cornered Elmer and let him have both barrels of Model T sales talk. He bought the car, and invited me to dinner too.

The man I sold Model T's for, Jim Lanham, was pretty strict about my using his flivvers for other than demonstrating purposes, but he did not blame me for one "errand of mercy" I did for my father, Dr. J. B. Clymer, a small-town physician and surgeon for forty years. One morning Dad rushed over to the Lanham garage with the news that his two-cylinder Maxwell was balky and that he was urgently needed at the Jackson farm 10 miles out to deliver a baby. He hopped in my T demonstrator and rattled out to the farm. Dad decided to try to get Mrs. Jackson to the hospital, so we all piled back into the car—the nervous father and I in the front seat, Dad and Mrs. Jackson in the back. I had driven halfway back to Loveland, trying to avoid the bigger bumps and ruts, when Dad suddenly ordered me over to the side of the road and told me to sit on the running board and put my hands over my ears. I did hear Mr. Jackson swear to name the child "Henry if he's a boy, Lizzie if she's a girl." A few minutes later Dad delivered a sturdy son and Mr. Jackson kept his promise. Henry Ford Jackson, weighing about 200 pounds, walked into my store in Los Angeles about five years ago and reminded me of the circumstances of his birth so many years ago in the back seat of my T demonstrator. Truly, Henry Ford had accurately named his jalopy the "Universal Car."

In 1942, thirty years after Henry Ford Jackson made his first appearance, Dad received payment for this back-seat delivery. A letter arrived, and with it a $20.00 money order. The letter read:

Dear Dr. Clymer:

Surely you will recall in 1912 delivering a son to my wife in the back seat of a Model T Ford. Soon after that time we left Colorado due to bad crops and not enough rain, and I had hard financial times for many years. I never paid your fee but I did not forget it and recently I joined Father Divine's church. One of Father Divine's strictest requirements is that all honest debts be paid. I appreciate your patience all these years and am enclosing $20.00.

Yours for health, peace, happiness, and prosperity,

(signed) H. R. Jackson

"Doc, if it's a boy, I'm going to name him Henry; if it's a girl I'm going to name her Lizzie."

Not long after this incident, a prospective car buyer who enjoyed a good argument said he would buy a Model T or a Stanley Steamer, whichever could win a road race from Loveland to Greeley—a distance of 22 miles. The following Sunday morning two cars lined up for the race. I was driving a Model T and Lew Hertha, the Berthoud Stanley dealer, drove the Stanley, a 20-horsepower model. Word of the race spread quickly and some 500 people gathered at the start, an equal number at the city limits of Greeley to see the finish. The straight road was dry and dusty, and at the start the Steamer left me far back in her dust. Driving the Model T wide open in hot pursuit, even over the chuckholes and deep ruts, I managed a speed of about 45 miles an hour. Gradually I started to gain on the Steamer, and about 5 miles from Greeley, Lew began to slow down. I drew closer, and finally came alongside, well aware of the fact that Lew's steam pressure was running low. Lew had a disappointed look on his face as he slowed down to build up his steam pressure. As I neared the finish line, he was gaining very fast, but his pressure didn't rise quickly enough and I beat

him across the finish line by about 200 feet. The advocates of the gas car were elated, and Mr. Lanham gave me an extra bonus of $10 for the sale.

While still working for Lanham, I developed a car product of my own, a soap I called "Skid-du-Dirt" to clean the grease and dirt from the hands of mechanics. It is a Model T memory of mine only because I used the "Universal Car" to make it. I poured the ingredients (castile soap, corn meal, oatmeal, and a little oil of wintergreen) into a big meat grinder. I raised a rear wheel of my Model T, at that time housed in a

barn, with a wooden jack and coupled the grinder to the hub of the wheel with a steel shaft. With the engine in high gear, the "Skiddu-Dirt" flew out of the grinder faster than I could feed the ingredients into its mouth. But my Model T helped me make more "Skiddu-Dirt" than I could sell, and my infant industry folded.

In the early days of the automobile business it was not unusual for car dealers to take horse-drawn vehicles, a horse or team of horses, a cow or pig, and occasionally even farm machinery in trade as part payment on a new car. In a small farming community it was often customary to

"Hey, Lew, I knew you would run out of steam."

take all kinds of products in trade to make a sale.

I had made a few such deals, and had been told by Mr. Lanham that he couldn't use any more livestock in trade during that particular month. But a farmer named Oscar Johnson, who lived about 5 miles out in the country, said he would buy a Model T Ford if I would take his 2-cylinder Maxwell, a horse, and a bicycle which his son had outgrown, in trade as part payment. Always the eager salesman, I decided to take a chance and made the deal on the spot, knowing that I could sell the Maxwell easily. The trip back to Loveland was made slowly, in low gear, with the horse tied back of the Maxwell. I was counting on the local auctioneer to sell the horse, car, and probably the bicycle at his sale the next day. When I drove up to the garage in the Maxwell, Jim Lanham was mad as a wet hen. He didn't mind so much about the Maxwell but that old nag really upset him—and when he saw the bicycle tied on the rear deck he nearly blew a fuse. At first he was going to fire me, but when Auctioneer Warnock got more for the horse, the Maxwell, and the bicycle than I had allowed Mr. Johnson, he cooled off considerably—in fact he gave me $5 extra commission for the sale!

Most drivers needed a gas gauge, but the manufacturer supplied none. As a result, it was standard practice for the flivver to run out of gas about five miles from the nearest gas station. Instructions were that the driver should cross the field to the farmer's house. His only option was—which farmhouse? He should then hope against fate that in the middle of the night the farmer would have either a can of gasoline around the premises, or a telephone for calling home. If he was really stuck and the sun hadn't gone down, the T motorist should stand beside his car along the deserted road and wait until the next infrequent motorist came along. The latter, with a knowing glance, would siphon a little gas for him from his tank.

To forestall these emergencies, the motorist could buy one of several kinds of gas savers and select one of at least fifty different types of gasoline gauges. One such gauge sounded a bell under the seat when the gas supply was low. This eliminated guesswork. The flivver driver of course had the black ruler to stick in the tank to measure the gas he had left. These little rulers were handed out by dealers, service stations, and merchants with their ads printed on them, and almost every Ford owner carried one under the front seat cushion. The only trouble was that these little rulers were very easy to lose.

"I told you, no more livestock this month!"

"Darn that bell!"

I recall one instance of running out of gas when I was driving a Model T. I went to a farmhouse, but the owner had no gas. He did have a gallon of kerosene—"coal oil" they called it then—in a can with a potato stuck in the spout. Making the best of the situation, I rushed back to the car and emptied the can into my tank. I managed to reach town by using coal oil for fuel, and with a haze of blue smoke from the kerosene coming out of the exhaust pipe. This could be done only if the engine was still hot, and by spinning to start the engine. A driver had to keep the engine "speeded up" or running fast for kerosene to work.

Along with this out-of-gas inconvenience came another that Model T owners will always associate with Henry's T. The gas cap and tank were under the front seat, so that, if a fellow was out with his best girl, he had to ask her apologetically if she would please get out for a minute because they needed gas. This was one of the commonplace scenes of Sunday driving, driver and passenger climbing down from the stratosphere so that the gas tank could be filled. Chances were that they made of their gassing-up party a social occasion.

To crank the engine and get it started again could also be a cooperative affair; Mabel sometimes learned how to work the spark and gas levers for her boy friend. Fords were temperamental, and if the young man had just the right touch he could tell by the feel of the "innards" and almost by ear how the engine was perking. And if he was smart, he never wrapped his thumb around the crank handle. Because of the frequent "kickbacks," it required a light touch to avoid the sprained wrist and skinned knuckles.

In the mid-1920's a ratchet-type non-kick device was put on the market which disconnected the crank from the engine shaft after the engine fired. Even more interesting was the manually operated starter; it typified the lengths to which some owners went to put their cars into up-to-date shape for the new motoring year. The Hunter Starter ($10) was a clever item that looked like a Rube Goldberg invention. It turned the engine over quickly by a chain operating from a combination of levers which finally ended up inside the car with a handle located within reach of the driver. All he needed to do was to pull the handle, as he would that of a slot machine. Sometimes it actually worked.

A Buffalo, New York, firm put out an electric starter for the driver of a jalopy. At about that time (1913–1915) the electric starter became generally popular, and with the electric self-starter came the storage battery.

"Sorry to disturb you, honey, but she needed gas."

"Old Dobbin never *kicked like this critter."*

Around the middle of the decade, the Model T came equipped with electric headlamps, although the old kerosene side lamps mounted on the dashboard were still factory equipment. When the T driver slowed down, as he had to at the square field-boundary corners in the road, the headlights would dim and flicker. Sometimes he preferred to drive his car in low gear with a fast-turning engine. Then he could read the signs and see the ruts and chuckholes, saving his springs and tires.

The car actually sold itself, however, and at prices that were then unbelievable. For example, the Ford Runabout in 1916 could be had for $390 and the elaborate Sedan for $740. But Ford stated stubbornly and specifically that no speedometer came with these cars, otherwise fully equipped. And if his factory furnished a full set of tools, it ignored the sales possibilities in offering a variety of colors. His 1916 catalogue read: "No option is given on color, tires, or equipment." In other words, "Take it or leave it." And Henry Ford made millions of Americans take it and like it.

As early as 1913, though the automobile business was still in its infancy, the high-pressure Ford sales psychology had developed to the point where the company's sales manager, N. A. Hawkins, prophesied that the sales of Fords simply must increase substantially every year. He claimed that fully 2,000,000 families *needed* Fords that year, and he cited the reasons for their need: picnics, road comfort, sales in circuit riding and telephone testing, pleasure, and general utility. "At the rate of 200,000 yearly," he concluded, "ten years would be consumed supplying those who already need and have not bought." It was heady talk, but the most optimistic estimate of future business turned out to be the most accurate.

To illustrate the power of his entrenched position in 1914, Ford devised one of the greatest sales promotion stunts in automobile history. On July 31 of that year, he offered a fifty-dollar rebate to every Ford buyer if sales during the following year topped 300,000. The year's total was 308,218, and accordingly $15,410,650 was mailed out to Ford buyers. That was probably one of the first instances of profit sharing

"It's nothing—they're just waiting to see me work the new self-starter."

Naturalist and poet John Burroughs behind the wheel of a 1913 Model T Henry Ford gave him. Note the kerosene dashboard lamps and elegant tonneau.

under our capitalistic system.

Ford's T had reached the crest of its popularity. His Coupélet was one of the best bargains in 1916, and signified Ford values. Wrapped up in one package, here was an "all-year-around" car for two passengers. Ford ads stated that with the top raised, the driver had a "snug, comfortable, enclosed car," and with the top rolled—an effortless two-minute job—he had a "runabout of distinctive appearance." I remember the Coupélet for its sleek lines and its gleaming paint and brass finish. If you had $590 for a car, you could buy this dandy right off the showroom floor.

Ford, in 1919, had inaugurated the moving assembly line in his River Rouge plant for the assembly of magneto flywheels for the T. It was an important invention for our factories, the same development that Charles Chaplin was later to burlesque as symbolic of American life in *Modern Times*.

Unlike the gaiters and skirted bathing suits of those times, the assembly line was here to stay. One anecdote I recall had the Ford line belts moving so fast that the worker who one morning dropped his hammer on the floor lost his job because three Fords went by before he could pick it up. This apocryphal tale at least suggests the mood of a new age devoted to speed.

On the models of 1920, Ford made styling and equipment changes that showed automotive progress. The kerosene dashboard lamps were gone. The angular look of the hood was streamlined and, being higher, blended in with the body top. The radiator sat inside of a shell, and the front fenders were rounded over the wheels. Ford's Fordor Model T of 1922 was a splendid all-enclosed car for its day. It was powered by an improved four-cylinder 20-horsepower engine, and if the driver fully opened the accelerator and "leaned up" the mixture just a bit, he could get 45 miles an hour out of it.

Ten gallons, or a full tank, would take him almost anywhere he wanted to go. A joke of the time put this T economy in a pithy way.

FILLING-STATION MAN: "Yer car needs gas, mister."

MR. GROUCH (who has stopped for free air): "Say, that flivver had five gallons of gas day before yesterday, and that's every darn drop it's going to get till tomorrow."

The following year Ford turned out an all-enclosed Ford T with new styling. Probably the most outstanding features were its low, straight roofline, high radiator, and a large oblong windshield that offered maximum visibility. On the practical side, in one hour, if the motorist didn't

The Model T was born October 1, 1908, and when the last of more than 15,000,000 was produced 19 years later it had become the most famous car in history. Henry Ford's specifications were simple: the T was easy to operate and repair, low-priced, and durable. This model (late 1915) carried through the 1916 season.

pinch the tube or mind barking his hands, he could buff up and patch his tube on the front fender, allowing another ten minutes for pumping up the tire with the hand pump.

In 1924 Ford offered what his ads called a "jazzy Runabout," a trim Roadster with the same standard four-cylinder, 20-horsepower engine capable of the usual T speed on the ordinary dirt road. This was one of the last radically new body styles in the Model T line. Although the 1926 Touring Car met with great popularity, the T was nearing the end of its day. This Tour-

ing Car had steel-wire-spoke wheels, but only two-wheel brakes. Though most other makes had changed over to four-wheel brakes, Ford was still adamant against the use of brakes on the front wheels. He contended that they weren't practical. Their upkeep was too costly, they were dangerous because they grabbed, and almost useless on the road from an engineering point of view. No Model T ever had four-wheel brakes. The first Ford to have them was the 1928 Model A.

In 1927 Ford made one last big effort to keep

With Ford's ten-millionth Model T produced in June of 1924, a new milestone was passed in the automobile industry. Edsel Ford is between the cars, his father Henry at right.

the Model T on the road. With the gas tank back of the hood, and with balloon tires as standard equipment, he offered a choice of colors and gave the customer wire-spoke wheels. He was still convinced, however, that the planetary transmission and two-wheel brakes were what the mass of motorists ought to have.

Adults of the 1920's who knew their stuff when it came to driving a car more than likely had first learned on Henry's three-pedal T. When the avalanche of new makes appeared in those exciting days of prosperity, those who had grown up with the "Tin Lizzie" were having to change their method of shifting the gears in their new cars. Chevrolet, Studebaker, Buick, Dodge, and other makes already had three-speed standard transmissions. Although Henry clung to his two-speed planetary transmission, accessory manu-

facturers were offering three-speed transmissions to the owners of Fords.

I've got a hunch that Henry might smile a bit if he could look over today's automatic transmissions, which basically employ the old planetary gears he used for so long. He might even say, "I told you so." Today the bands of the planetary unit are operated by hydraulic oil pressure instead of manually, but the principle is essentially the same.

In the twenties Henry Ford's son Edsel became president of the company, although Henry still ruled with an iron hand. Edsel, a brilliant man, could do little with his father, but he did see the handwriting on the wall—that the famous old Model T was beginning to sputter and run out of popularity. Other makes had progressed with great strides, but Mr. Ford wanted,

No goat was too large for the Model T. T owners carried almost everything on the running boards.

Henry might smile a bit. . . .

still, to force the T on the American motorist. Edsel at last convinced his father that the T would have to give way to a more modern car with a three-speed transmission and four-wheel brakes.

So Henry, almost alone, set out to design his Model A—a car to replace his beloved T. The job took months to get under way. The change-over from the T to the A was a long-drawn-out, painful, and dramatic process. As brilliant as Henry Ford was, he took so long to make the conversion that many Ford dealers, who for years had been geared for volume selling, nearly went broke while waiting for the new Ford Model A car to appear in 1928. Yet despite the loss of at least five months' time, the A went over with a bang. In the final analysis, the public had great confidence in Henry Ford, a confidence engendered by his "Tin Lizzie."

No automobile can ever take the place in the hearts of so many motorists that the Model T occupied for the nineteen years it was manufac-

Henry Ford (in derby hat) and friends taken at a race track during his racing-driver days.

In Mr. Ford's office, December, 1914. Left to right: William Livingston, prominent Detroit banker; former President William H. Taft; and Henry Ford.

World-famous personalities were Ford's friends. Shown here left to right are Harvey Firestone, President Calvin Coolidge, Henry Ford, Thomas A. Edison, and Mrs. Calvin (Grace) Coolidge.

Three chums who are, left to right, John Burroughs, Thomas A. Edison, and Henry Ford. The "Lizzie" is 1914 vintage. Note the carbide generator on running board for supplying gas to the headlights. Kerosene dash lamps were used.

tured. We can attribute many forward steps in our industrial history to its inventor, a man of great vision, Henry Ford. He accomplished amazing and unheard-of feats, such as establishing the eight-hour workday, and guaranteeing in 1914 a minimum wage of $5 for every employee, including those who only swept floors. He built an organization which, through mass production, placed millions behind the wheels of a contraption called the "horseless carriage." One of my favorite auto gags in the 1920's went something like this: "A part of a magician's act is to make a horse vanish. That's nothing, though. Henry Ford did it." There can never be another Henry Ford or another Model T. Millions regretted the passing of both, and in the generations to come the legend of Henry Ford and his famous "Tin Lizzie" will never die.

Farewell, my lovely

2. The Ford in Photos

During the first ten years of the life of Henry's Model T, the automobile business in the United States sprang to life and gave the first indications of momentous things to come. And no better gauge of that early industrial growth can be found anywhere than in the production figures of the Ford Motor Company. In 1908–1909, the first year of the T, 10,067 Fords were sold. Only eight years later, in 1916–1917, this figure was multiplied some seventy times to 730,041 cars sold.

People tend to forget, in this day and age of new models every few years, that the T's reign lasted an unprecedented nineteen years, from 1908 to 1927. Though the very first T was a notable success immediately hailed for its general utility and fine performance, Ford and his engineers continued to improve the car each year. On the following pages are photographs representing each of those nineteen Model T years, clearly showing the changes in design which the car underwent. Interspersed with the car photos are memorable Model T trucks and scenes from various Ford plants.

To underline the immediate success of the T, one need only recall that in 1909, one year after its initial appearance, William Durant, who later put together the General Motors empire, was said to have offered Ford $8,000,000 for his company.

This 1908 Touring Car was the first of the Model T's and was offered in red and the Roadster in pearl gray, which contradicts the story that all Model T's were black, although that statement was attributed to Henry Ford and for most of the years of peak production it was true.

This unusual Model T is one of the first 1908 Models (with two hand levers) which Henry Ford used on a ten-day trip from Detroit to Chicago, Illinois, to Iron Mountain, Michigan, and return to Detroit.

This is an unusual photo of a Model T because it has two hand levers which were used on the first 1,000 Model T's produced. One lever operated the emergency brake and the other lever engaged high gear—there were only two foot pedals used on this model.

This car engine number 17,771 was the 1909 pro-
duction car priced at $850. The basic design of the
Model T remained with few changes for some nineteen
years.

Among the first users of the Model T Ford were the
doctors of America located in cities and small towns.
This photo shows a typical doctor and members of
his family in his first car, a 1909 Model T.

One of the first closed Model T's was this 1909 Landaulet. This body type was popular at that time and Ford fell right in line by offering a lower-priced Landaulet than his competitors were offering.

This Ford chassis produced almost without change for a number of years was offered to the customer so that he could construct upon this chassis a body of his own design.

One of the early pictures of Henry Ford in his office was taken at the Piquette Avenue plant about 1910. Interesting features are the large safe shown at left—probably because Mr. Ford could still keep an eye on his own money—the old-fashioned telephone shown on the arm of the chair, the derby hat and duster shown on the leather couch, the duster hanging on the hatrack. It is said the unique wastebasket with wooden slats was made and sent to Mr. Ford by a Model T enthusiast.

One of the niftiest of Ford's Model T cars was this 1909 Roadster with bucket-type rear seat, sometimes referred to as the "mother-in-law" seat. Note the bulb horn, kerosene dash and tail lamps. Carbide generator located on running board supplied gas for headlights.

Water dripped from upper half of generator into carbide carried in lower half. This dripping water created gas fumes which were piped through either rubber or brass tubing to the headlights.

Contestant cars near start of transcontinental race, a novel event in 1909. Ford racer No. 1 driven by Frank Kulick, mechanic H. B. Harper. Ford racer in second place driven by Bert Scott, his mechanic C. J. Smith. Races such as this helped to improve roads and the automobile.

No. 2 Model T during the 1909 race. Bottomless gumbo greatly reduced speed on the open highway.

Same racer, No. 2 Model T, in the 1909 cross-country contest. Driver has doubtless gone to the near- *est farmhouse for the farmer and his team. Mud made travel by car difficult.*

Hotfooting it down the road between towns. Rear view of No. 1 and 2 cars, stripped-down T's, during *1909 transcontinental race. Bucket seats were special. Kerosene lamp on rear end was standard equipment.*

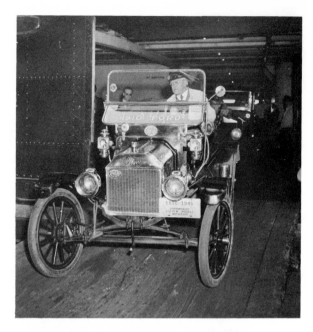

Walter Matter, a Pennsylvania Dutchman, who until his death in 1954 participated in many tours conducted by various clubs, is shown here with his 1910 Ford Torpedo Roadster during the 1946 Glidden Tour to commemorate the automobile Golden Jubilee held at Detroit in 1946. Note the gas headlights, kerosene dash lamp, and bulb horn. Matter completed his journey from Albany, New York, to Detroit with no trouble. The photograph at top right shows Matter coming off the Cleveland-Detroit boat.

Sportiest of the early Model T's was this Torpedo Runabout of 1910 and 1911. Gas-tank location at the rear instead of under the seat enabled the seat to be lowered, thus giving the car a "racy" appearance.

Employees at the Highland Park plant are shown upholstering Model T bodies in 1911

This 1910 Roadster was offered with a demountable third-passenger seat. This seat was sometimes referred to as the "mother-in-law" seat.

Second-floor body assembly room of Highland Park plant, then in Detroit suburbs. Here 1910–1911 touring bodies are being fitted with appurtenances.

Special 1911 Model T Torpedo Runabout, one of ten built for use by fire chiefs. They were finished in bright red and polished brass. Chief's model included rear box for fire extinguisher, coil of rope, and other implements; also a fire bell and front bumper, and a spare tire inflated for emergency use. Fire Commissioner Waldo, New York City, is on left. Note demountable rims, "special" equipment on these fire-department cars. With four lugs they were optional equipment at extra cost on 1920 or later models.

1911 Model T five-passenger Touring Car with bulb horn and gas headlights

In 1954 E. B. McCormack of Mission, Kansas, restored this excellent 1911 Ford Torpedo. This racy runabout had the gas tank located back of the seat. Shown in the car, which has won several prizes for best restoration, is Mrs. McCormack. Collectors now are restoring hundreds of Model T's to their original condition.

Ford was again right when he referred to the Model T as "The Universal Car," for this unique vehicle was used by McKay's as a special transportation vehicle between Daytona Beach and Deland, Florida. It was called McKay's Daytona-Deland Express. The picture was taken about 1912 and the original body was a Ford Torpedo Model. This happy-looking crowd is apparently seeking a new life at the start of the first Florida boom.

Many Model T's were used for rail transportation and this 1912 model with steel wheels once provided transportation for J. P. Murphy, right, superintendent of the Little River Railroad, with headquarters at Townsend, Tennessee.

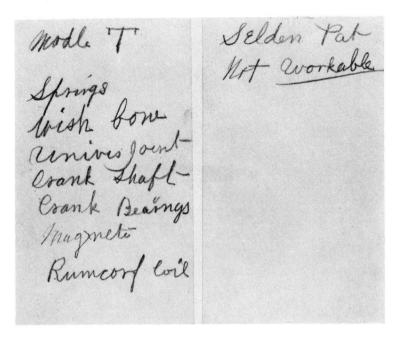

This is Henry Ford's notation in his own handwriting of some of the features claimed in the historic Selden Patent which he believed unworkable.

Henry Ford at his office desk in 1913 with a copy of Iron Age *magazine in his hand*

Glenn H. Curtiss, like Henry Ford, was a pioneer. Shown here in 1912 are Curtiss and Ford alongside the famous Flying Boat. The photo was taken near the Curtiss factory at Hammondsport, New York.

58

In 1913, C. I. W. Smith and his wife, of Omaha, Nebraska, completed a 10,000-mile tour in this Ford Runabout (left) through the West and Southwest. The entire expense, including gas, oil, and minor repairs, averaged less than two cents per mile, and the car averaged over 25 miles per gallon.

First mass-production line in automobile production was set up by Henry Ford. Here are bodies being lowered on Model T chassis in 1913 at the famous Dearborn, Michigan, plant.

Mr. and Mrs. William Kales of Detroit drove a Ford about Bombay, India, in 1913 (left). Kales reported that the Indians considered him a "spinner of tall tales" when he tried to convince them that Ford was building more than 900 cars a day.

This 1913 Model T is in the collection of the U.S. National Museum, Washington, D.C. Probably some- *one installed electric dash lamps, as 1913 models still had kerosene side lamps.*

1913 Ford Model T Town Car, a six-passenger, four-cylinder, 20-horsepower car. Price, $800, included speedometer, two 6-inch gas lamps, generator, three oil lamps, horn, tools, including jack—f.o.b. Detroit.

1913 Ford Model T Runabout, a two-passenger, four-cylinder, 20-horsepower car. Price, $525, included top cover, folding windshield, speedometer, two 6-inch gas lamps, generator, three oil lamps, horn, and tools—f.o.b. Detroit.

A 1913 view of the new Ford craneway between the new gigantic buildings then being constructed. The bridges are exactly in the center—450 feet from either end. Two 5-ton cranes operate on each side of the bridges.

Chassis assembly at the dashboard station in Highland Park plant. Earliest American assembly line for *mass production in full operation September, 1913, turning out the next year's Model T's.*

A side view of the 1914 Model T. The buildings in the background are the Detroit streetcar barns, across from the Highland Park plant.

Another view of the 1911 Model T with runabout body converted to a pickup style. The driver with short trousers and button shoes was right in style.

This lad with the fire in his eyes is apparently teaching his lady friend to drive a 1914 Runabout. The Prest-O-Lite tank on the running board was used by many drivers before electric lights became standard equipment in 1915.

Touring in 1914 required hardy souls and durable automobiles. This Model T carried a group of hardy pioneers from McPherson, Kansas, to California. Note the equipment included: a washtub, folding seats, a cookstove, a tent, a rope for emergencies, an extra can of oil, and a gallon can with a funnel.

End of the chassis assembly line at Highland Park, circa 1913–1914

In 1914 Henry Ford (at the wheel), naturalist John Burroughs, alongside, and Thomas A. Edison, in the rear, made a journey from Detroit to Florida.

Sir Harry Lauder shown here in a 1914 English Model T Roadster. Note that the steering wheel is on the right-hand side, and a folding windshield (evidently a British accessory) has been added. British license plate is shown.

In 1912 Ford made a bid for the light delivery market with this special pickup truck model. Notice the emergency lantern hanging on the side.

These three photos show the method used by many Model T owners to convert the touring car into a light delivery truck. Photo at top right shows the standard 1914 Touring Car; at center right, the same car after the rear seat had been removed; at bottom right we see how the car appeared with a homemade delivery body.

These are the final assembly lines of the Highland Park plant in 1914, for by this time Ford had made great strides in mass assembly of the Model T.

In 1914 Model T chassis were rolled along outside the Highland Park plant to the point where the body installation took place.

This photo showing a portion of the day's production of Model T's was a common sight for many years.

Henry Ford in H.P. office, 1915. Picture of Edison is easily recognizable above Henry Ford's desk.

In 1915 Edsel Ford and party were driving to the Panama Pacific Exposition held in San Francisco. This shows a sample of the roads encountered.

Test-running the 1915 engines, next step after chassis assembly. Note crude jack under differential for lifting wheels from their wells. Position of gas tank was standard until 1926 models.

When the driver and passenger entered the Model T, these controls were what they saw in 1915. About the only thing that has been added since the first Model T's were built is the speedometer located at the right of the dashboard.

This first Two-Door (Ford spelled it Tudor) Sedan was offered in 1915 for social, shopping, and general uses. Note split windshield and high-hung fancy lamps at rear. Price was $975 f.o.b. Detroit.

Front view of the 1915 Coupé-let. Note small rear window.

In 1915 curved rear fenders appeared on most of the Model T body styles for the first time, including this Model T Tudor.

Another view of the 1915 Model T Coupélet produced in the late fall of 1914

In 1915 this Town Car was popular with the ritzy crowd. Some taxicab buyers also preferred this model.

In 1915 this Coupélet was offered. It could be that this car was the forerunner of the present-day car known as the Convertible.

In 1915 most of the taxicabs used in cities and towns throughout the United States were Model T Fords.

The 1915 Roadster had a rear deck which was sometimes removed to build a special type of body.

The 1916 Model T Convertible. The driver had almost the privacy of a darkroom in a photo laboratory. Note the size of the side windows. A man with good eyesight could easily peek out and learn what was going on in the outside world.

Employees in the frame department of the Highland Park plant about 1916

This 1916 Model T went on many a voyage of mercy for the Western Pennsylvania Humane Society, usually to offer succor to the horses it was scaring off the road and fast supplanting.

A dependable 1916 Model T, carrying passengers, mail, and light freight through the wilderness, crosses Ptarmigan Creek on the trail from Valdez, Alaska, to Copper Center, a distance of 102 miles. There were no bridges on this stage route but the City "Day & Night" Express apparently did not need them.

Left, front end of a 1917 Model T Coupé. Black was Ford's best color.

The Model T car of 1917, below, was referred to as a Town Car or Landaulet and was sometimes used as a taxicab. It offered plenty of fresh air and privacy for the elite. Note that the driver, sometimes a taxicab driver, and other times a chauffeur, was completely cut off from the rear-seat passengers. Truly a royal model with a low price for its day.

A 1917 Coupé with body reminiscent of a carriage

Model T's were sold throughout the world. This is a photo taken in 1917 of a Ford agency at Aden, Arabia.

This 1917 Model T Touring Car was the first model with the black radiator shell. This gave the hood a higher and more massive appearance.

An overhead view of the 1917–1918 Model TT 1-ton truck. This car was popular because buyers could purchase the chassis and build any type of body desired for their specific needs.

A 1917 Coupé in full dress, 'lectric lights 'n everything, but still with kerosene dash lamps

Throughout the world famous people depended upon the Model T; shown here in 1918 is British General Elsemie in a Ford converted truck which was the first power vehicle to cross Perizan Pass.

Employees in 1918 shown assembling the flywheel magneto on a moving conveyor belt.

This 1918 1-ton Model TT truck equipped with solid rear tires and worm-gear drive offered some semblance of protection for the driver through the use of detachable storm curtains.

By 1918 the Ford truck was using a worm-gear drive, solid rear rubber tires, and making a bid for use in many different lines of business, such as the delivery of bottles of distilled water.

In the days when the United States Postal Department decided that automobiles should replace the horse for mail delivery, the Model T Ford was among the first makes to be used. This photo taken in 1917 or 1918.

This classy Coupé was offered during 1918.

This 1919 Ford Motor Company Pickup Truck with the long toolbox on the running board was designed to more efficiently service Model T owners when they encountered trouble.

Introduction of the new Fordson Tractor in 1919. The Ford tractor was named Fordson in honor of Edsel, son of Ford. Left to right: Edsel Ford, E. G. Liebold, Ford official, unidentified, Henry Ford, engineer Charles E. Sorenson, Japanese government official, F. E. Klingensmith, Ford official, and publicity man.

The 1919 Touring with deep-chair comfort. Note kerosene side lamps.

In order to improve fire-fighting apparatus, many cities such as Jackson, Tennessee, used a lengthened Ford chassis on which to mount such fire-fighting equipment as this chemical tank. Truck also had collapsible ladders.

One of the many special bodies mounted on the Model T chassis was this fire truck used by the North Syracuse, New York, Fire Department.

Still another version of a Model T chemical and hose truck, this one used by the Montpelier, Vermont, Fire Department.

Another early piece of fire-fighting equipment is this chemical and hose truck mounted on a Model T chassis.

1920 Model T Runabout. Here is a two-passenger 1920 Ford Runabout produced in the derby hat era. It was powered with a four-cylinder, 20-horsepower engine and had a maximum speed of about 40 miles an hour. An electric starting and lighting system came as optional equipment. The car had a 100-inch wheelbase and used tires 30 x 3. The gasoline capacity was 10 gallons. The car sold for $550.

A snappy, dashing 1920 Runabout for the playboy spirit. Salesmen, doctors, farmers favored its convenience and adaptability, while the younger set enjoyed its sporty lines.

Model TT 1-ton Truck of 1920. The ideal hay wagon. Ford sold the chassis only to buyers who wanted to build their own special bodies for their own farming or hauling purposes.

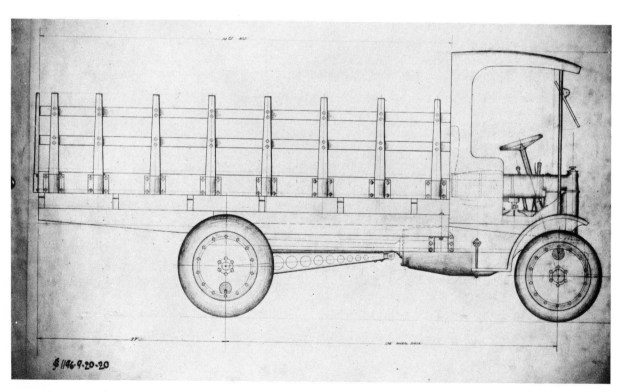

Pencil sketch of a proposed 3-ton truck; on the drawing board in 1920. It never was produced. A rare photo of a rare car that was to be Ford's answer to builders of large trucks.

By 1920 the Model T was taking on some semblance of streamlining, although the mechanical units of the car were basically the same as when Ford first started building the Model T.

1920 Model T Ford Tudor Sedan

Henry Ford shown with a Model T demonstrator. Taken at Grand Central Terminal, New York, 1921.

The 1921 Model T Sedan had an unusually placed door, allowing easy entry for front or rear seats.

An optional self-starter was a boon to the comfort and convenience provided for Milady.

A Runabout of 1921 with a high gloss and white-rubber tires—perfect for the traveling salesman.

Experimental body of Model TT Truck chassis, 1922. Early-day version of snow-tread tire on rear wheels (holes in tire tread to prevent skidding).

Florence Bryant behind the wheel of her 1922 Sedan with special wire wheels. Her flivver had charm.

The fabulous Ford River Rouge plant of 1922 with Ford ships in dock

Special wire wheels grace this 1923 Coupé. Snubbers just under the headlights eased bounce-backs over rutted roads into cloudlike ripples—or did they?

The 1,000,000th Model T was produced in December, 1915. No. 8,000,000 was assembled July 11, 1923, and No. 15,000,000 on May 26, 1927.

This 1923 model featured a "one-man" top, no center bows. Windshield is slightly tilted backward.

Note detachable rims which permitted removal of the tire, held onto the wheel by four bolts.

This 1924 Model T Roadster was powered by a 4-cylinder, 20-horsepower engine and was capable of speeds of 40 to 45 miles per hour.

A 1924 1-ton T Truck with side curtains and kerosene lamps. Trucks like this took a real beating on the rutted roads of the day.

On October 15, 1924, Edward, Prince of Wales, and the present Duke of Windsor visited Edsel and Henry Ford. This photo was taken on the terrace of Henry Ford's residence, Fairlane.

Display of 1924 models in front of Highland Park plant. Rear to front: Roadster, Touring, Fordor Sedan, Tudor Sedan, and 1-ton Truck. By its sixteenth year, the Model T had developed considerable variety.

From front to rear: Touring Car, Coupé, Tudor

1925 Model T with metal pickup body. Dairy milk collectors, grocerymen, and grain merchants found this model just right.

This 1925 Model T used demountable rims and was priced at $290 f.o.b. Dearborn. The tapered rear luggage compartment back of the seat was removable.

1925 Coupé with cowl ventilator

Looks like a dogcatcher's truck. It was the new 1925 TT 1-ton screened panel Truck.

Frontal view of new (1925) 1-ton TT Truck with rear 8-ply high-pressure (80 lb.) 30 x 5 tires and two-wheel brakes. Photographed near Engineering Laboratories, Dearborn. Still 20 horsepower with transverse springs.

Ford's own new 1-ton TT Truck of 1925. Accessory makers had long enough converted Ford car chassis. For drayage and the farmer's summer hay.

A close-up of Ford's air transport luggage-carrier truck of 1925. Made of polished aluminum with balloons on rear wheels.

The British have always gone in for special carriage work, and this photo shows the British version of a 1925 Model T to which front-wheel brakes and *drum* headlights have been added.

Polished aluminum air transport truck and Ford plane, "Maiden Dearborn," at Michigan State Fair in 1925. The plane was built in Model T days, a fore- runner to the all-metal Ford Trimotor plane built later on.

1926 Tudor Sedan had nickel radiator shell.   *Tudor was a very popular model for small families.*
Appurtenances included roller shade on rear window.

1926 photo showing the body drop station on the chassis assembly line at Highland Park

At the country club in 1926. The following year this Coupé was available in gray, maroon, or green.

Nickel radiator shell was high-class, as was the lady's chic hat.

This heavy-weather Coupé of 1926 represented the T as it neared the end of its illustrious life.

A 1926 Sport Touring that included such conveniences as electric starter, balloon tires, windshield wiper, bumpers, five steel-spoke wire wheels, and side curtains. The T driver's dream.

A Fordor Sedan body shell, 1926. Note use of wood for flooring and top.

By 1926 Ford was offering this 1-ton Model TT Truck. A variety of bodies was offered by many body builders throughout the nation.

The Model TT Truck of 1926 equipped with dump body, one of the numerous special bodies accessory makers would build for Ford truck or T car chassis.

1926 light delivery T truck with new-style body and disk wheels. Note battery under the door.

This snappy 1926 Sport Roadster with gray wire-spoke wheels, isinglass wing panels, and a top cover was a favorite among Saturday golfers and college boys. Note hand-operated windshield wiper.

This 1926 model with nickel radiator shell and bumpers had steel-spoke wire wheels and top cover. However, Mr. Ford was still against four-wheel brakes, which were then popular on most other makes of cars.

Ford's last effort to bolster a sagging Model T market is this 1927 Fordor. It featured balloon tires, self-starter, steel-spoke wire wheels, and a choice of body colors.

During the 1927 bus strike in New York City, the Model T Ford (sometimes called the jitney) shown here helped reduce the transportation problems of millions of workers.

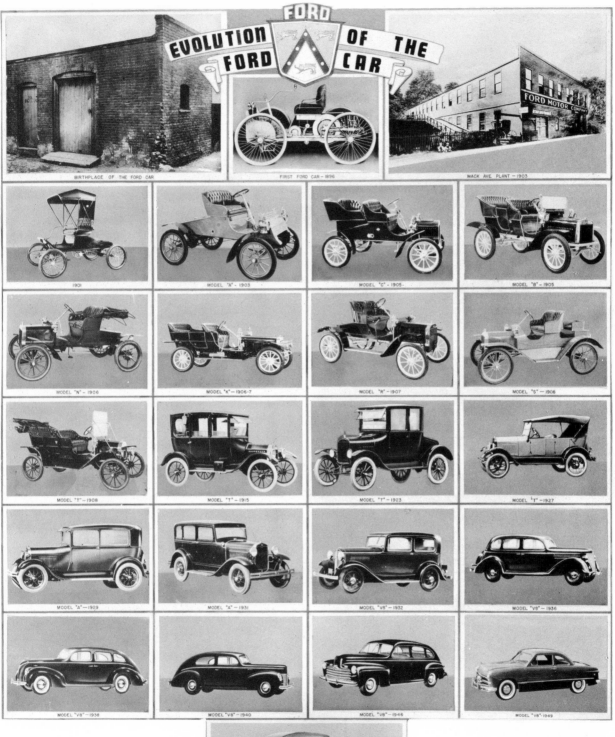

1954 FORD SKYLINER

This group photo taken in 1913 shows officials and employees of the Ford Motor Company. Second from the left in the front row is Edsel B. Ford. In the center row are famous racing driver Frank Kulick and Ford engineer C. H. Wills, who later built the Wills-Sainte Claire. Second from right, back row, is Henry Ford.

A rare photograph of Henry Ford, holding his grandson, Henry Ford II, taken in 1928

Thomas A. Edison appears amused as Henry Ford talks to him. Mr. Edison was hard of hearing, which accounts for the closeness of Mr. Ford to Mr. Edison's ear.

For many years these three cronies—Henry Ford, Thomas A. Edison, and Harvey Firestone—frequently met, sometimes in the industrial cities of the nation, and at other times in rural communities.

Three famous people in conference in Mr. Ford's office. Left to right, Harvey S. Firestone; C. Harold Wills, and Henry Ford.

Three generations of Fords. In the portraits, Henry (right) and son Edsel. At the table, Edsel's three sons who now control the destinies of the Ford industries: Benson (left) and William at the table and Henry II standing.

The three grandsons of Henry Ford and sons of Edsel started their motoring careers early. Shown driving the British M-G is Henry Ford II, with his brother Benson as his passenger. In the midget car is the youngest brother, William. The photo was taken in front of the Ford home, Fairlane, in 1934.

3. The Ubiquitous Model T

by Les Henry

So much has already been written and so much is still remembered from firsthand experience concerning the Model T Ford that there seems little of value left upon which to expound; but, with no pretense to be either encyclopedic or yet entirely original, this writing is humbly dedicated to those of us now interested in Model T Fords who never before knew them, or having known, forgot.

PART ONE: THE PARADOX

Remember Model T! While mundane, it was never mediocre. In its day it commanded honest respect for the service it rendered and for the revolution it wrought, and in our day, it commands a place of honor in our museums and private collections of venerable motorcars. Uncompromisingly erect, unquestionably ugly, funereally drab, Model T combined the web-footedness of the duck with the agility of the mountain goat; it could go anywhere—except in society! And though seemingly conceived in madness, there is somewhat of immortality in this strange car.

It is now exactly a quarter century since the last Model T rolled off the assembly line; yet it seems surely here to stay, all laws of nature to the contrary notwithstanding. Lee Strout White thought to mark its passing in 1936 with his humorous and knowing article, "Farewell My Lovely"; and he marveled then that Sears, Roebuck's catalogue listed parts for the 1909–1927 Fords—well, it still does! Statistically the "T" is with us yet; for as late as 1949 there were more than 200,000 registered in the United States; more than *all* the automobiles registered in the country when Model T was created, just forty years before.

From October, 1908, until May, 1927, there flowed an almost unbroken flood of Fords, all of a mold but not identical, to the number of fifteen million. No other automobile model even began to approach such tremendous volume and only the Rolls-Royce Silver Ghost (1907–1927) enjoyed such duration of production. During most of this time Ford produced as many or more than all other American motorcar manufacturers combined, and during all of this time, the Model T, often modified, *was never basically changed.* It is these myriad and often subtle modifications which interest many of us today; it is these that spark many a debate and bring strong men to their knees before the Model T to prove a point in question. Let us look into the seeming paradox of change in the changeless Model T.

While it is not usually difficult for those knowledgeable to establish the age of a Model T by certain features peculiar to a particular "style year," no generalization concerning the Model T is ever safe; too many minute changes were constantly being worked upon it for the purposes of speeding production, cutting costs, or—to a very limited degree—increasing customer appeal. Many arguments are engendered today by such simple facts as the appearance of plain hoods on some Fords in 1915 (which "style year" featured the first louvered hoods), and the appearance of both plain and lipped front fenders on the pre-1917 Fords (compare Figs. 1 and 6 with Figs. 7 and 10). Actually, Model T cars during a given production year did vary in many points and were not so much alike as "peas in a pod" as legend would have us believe. Variations also resulted from the necessity of having parts made by several different contractors whose particular tools and methods dictated such; it was not until the 1920's that Ford attained his goal of producing one hundred per cent of the car in his own factories.

Typical of Ford's cost-cutting program was the fate of the full-leather upholstering prevalent through 1912; this gave way to leatherette door panels in 1913; was followed by leatherette back cushions in 1914; which yielded to all leatherette with leather patches only at the doors in 1915–1916; and finally led to replacement of even this vestige by cheap, pressed steel caps at the doors in late 1916. While these are indeed generalizations, they serve to exemplify the many changes evolved in the interest of econ-

Fig. 1. The first Model T—1908 Touring (from Ford catalogue 1908). "The Universal Car": new, light, fast, agile, with a 22-horsepower, high-compression engine.

Note the two pedals and reverse lever which appeared only on the first 1,000 of these Fords. Basic design and many parts were unchanged for nineteen years.

Fig. 2. The Last Model T—1927 Tudor Sedan (from Ford catalogue, 1927). The "Universal Car" grown old; heavy, slow, sedate, with 20-horsepower, low-compression engine. Note such advanced features as

nickeled radiator and lamp rims; long, smooth hood and cowl; large windows; demountable wire wheels with balloon tires, all of which were standard equipment then.

Fig. 3. 1909 Touring—No. 8367. Formerly owned and restored by Clifford W. Moyer; now owned by Dr. Paul W. Morgan. Winner of "Best Model T" Trophy, 1948 Glidden Tour. This well-known car is remarkable for its aluminum body, believed to be experimental in the era of wooden bodies. Note the front fenders and compare with the plain in Fig. 1. The steel running board was an innovation early in 1909.

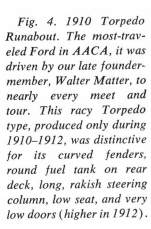

Fig. 4. 1910 Torpedo Runabout. The most-traveled Ford in AACA, it was driven by our late founder-member, Walter Matter, to nearly every meet and tour. This racy Torpedo type, produced only during 1910–1912, was distinctive for its curved fenders, round fuel tank on rear deck, long, rakish steering column, low seat, and very low doors (higher in 1912).

No battery to run down, no windows to wash or tires to check

omy during that period when Ford had the whole industry in a dizzy spin; this was the time when Ford introduced the five-dollar day, the five-hundred-dollar car, and the fifty-dollar refund to purchasers.

Cost-cutting did not result in loss of quality in Model T, except in the sense that luxury appointments not affecting serviceability were lost. Simple in the extreme and lacking in many comforts, Model T seemed always to run despite adversity. Into the vital parts went vanadium alloys, new to the automotive industry in 1908. While the structural, mechanical and economic advantages of *en bloc* cylinder casting had been seen by others before, Ford extended this idea to include also the upper crankcase with main bearings as an *en bloc* casting, with a removable cylinder head. Although the principle of mass production had been practiced for half a century by arms manufacturers, Ford applied it to the automotive industry in a successful and spectacular way. And then, years ahead of the times, Ford seemed to sit back to watch and to listen as the Model T clattered over the entire nation—the continent—the world.

Doubtless the greatest controversy among Ford devotees centers on the alleged "1908"

Model T; but—let there be no doubt left on this point—there never was such! The Ford car for 1908 was the Model S; for 1909 it was the Model T born in the new Piquette Avenue factory (Detroit) in October, 1908. True, there were actually 308 Model T cars built during the last quarter of 1908, but these were acclaimed the new 1909 style and were always referred to as such in contemporary Ford literature and parts catalogues. For the purpose of dating *any* automobile we can accept only the model or "style year," rather than the actual date of manufacture of an individual car. This is in line with the long-established practice by nearly all automobile makers, including Ford, to introduce a new style at some time other than on New Year's Day—an entirely understandable practice.

It would be much less confusing for us today if the Model T had actually been presented as the 1908 style, for those produced after mid-April differed so vastly from the earlier 1909 Fords as to constitute an evident, though not acclaimed, style change. Ford always referred to these as "the 1909 Fords under number 2500"; we cannot now do otherwise. Rarest of the 1909 Fords were—and are—those of the first 1,000, which were characterized by having the wheel brake and reverse band actuated by individual and distinctly different hand levers, as illustrated in Fig. 1. Ford quickly abandoned

Handles easily in emergencies

this system in late February in favor of the well-known three-pedal system and encouraged conversion of all outstanding Fords to the three-pedal system by offering owners the new parts at cost ($15), but requiring the return of all original parts to the factory. So thoroughly was the hand reverse lever thus eradicated that in later years Ford, wishing to restore a very early Model T for his museum, had to reinstall a reverse lever, unfortunately, however, using for this a brake lever and failing to remove the ratchet release handle! Parenthetically, publicity being what it is, this car is erroneously claimed to be a "1908" Model T Ford. It would indeed be interesting to know just how many Model T cars numbered under 1,000 are in existence today, and of these how many still have the two-lever system intact.

The first 2,500 Model T Fords were equipped with centrifugal water pumps (Fig. 21); had slightly shorter engine blocks and crankshafts; and had very small commutators (Fig. 18), commonly called "timers" by contemporary owners in their profane moments. These and other such features meant that the later-style Ford parts, excepting pistons, rods, and oil pan with transmission case, were not interchangeable with the earlier parts. Thus today a col-

Absolutely burglar-proof

lector fortunate enough to find an early Model T will be unfortunate in a search for parts.

As the demand for gasoline increased, particularly during World War I, its quality was decreased in favor of volume until the late twenties; this held back automobile engine performance. Under these circumstances, while the Model T progressed in style, size, appointments, and weight, it retrogressed in engine performance. The early Model T engines had the highest compression, 60 pounds per square inch, with approximately 4½ to 1 ratio, which permitted development of 22 horsepower. These characteristics were first reduced for 1912, again for 1915, and, finally, were set in 1917 to a compression of 45 psi at 3.98 to 1 ratio, with a resulting 20 horsepower.

Figure 20 shows the horsepower curve for all Ford engines starting with the 1917 style to the end of production. Maximum horsepower was developed at 1,500 revolutions per minute with a road speed of 37 miles per hour, at which point the "pulling power" or torque had dropped off to 70 foot-pounds.

With a few notable exceptions, the bodies were of wood until the 1911 style was advanced

Instantaneous stops—upon application of brake, clutch, and reverse pedals

with sheet steel applied over a wooden frame. Some few touring cars in 1909 had sheet aluminum bodies, one of which is pictured in Fig. 3. It is of interest to note that the 1913 style was the first Ford touring car to have front doors designed in the bodies (see Fig. 8) and that the left front door was a dummy and remained as such (except in the Canadian Fords) until 1926. In 1912 a "Fore-Door" version of the touring car appeared with factory-fitted front door units; these were actually removable and could be purchased as parts for adding to the 1911–1912 touring cars already in use.

All radiators of the Model T "brass era," ending September, 1916, were dimensionally the same, but differed in that the first 2,500 had a leading and a trailing stroke (often called "wings") on the *Ford* script pressed into the radiator tank, while some very few of these bore no name at all. The later brass radiators displayed the *Ford* script in its familiar form (Fig. 4).

The winged script and the block lettered *Ford* hubcaps were but carry-over details of the previous 1908 Model S. The V-shaped radiators sometimes seen were not genuine Ford products, but were simply a dress-up item, as were wooden top trim on doors (Figs. 6 and 9), coil-spring shock absorbers, demountable rims, electric conversion units for gas lamps, lined wheel-brake shoes, "30-minute" transmission bands, and mechanical starters. Whole industries sprang up and prospered in supplying gadgets to overcome real and imagined deficiencies of Model T, under the theory that anything would be an improvement! And some *were* improvements which Ford later recognized and adopted.

In this vein, it is interesting to note that a "Hind-View Auto Reflector" was offered as a *new* accessory made expressly for Fords by Kales-Haskel Company in August, 1911—interesting because this was only three months after the 1911 Indianapolis Race wherein Ray Harroun innovated the rear-view mirror on his winning Marmon "Wasp."

The 1914-style Ford, while similar to the 1913 except for door shape (see Figs. 6 and 8), was the last exhibiting the truly "antique" appearance afforded by the straight fenders front and rear, the acetylene gas lamps, and the bulb horn.

Then came the transitional form of Model T which, while holding somewhat to the old, reached out toward the new. Two enclosed body types were presented for 1915 in the preceding November; the Sedan with two central, side doors and the Coupélet, the first "convertible" coupé. The open-body types were continued unchanged until April, 1915, and must even now be considered as 1914-style Fords, though built in 1915. The new-style cars were characterized principally by the magneto-powered electric head lamps, the straight front but curved rear fenders, the louvers in the little boxlike engine hood, the hand Klaxon and the pressed-steel cowl fairing sharply out to the body and mounting an unbraced windshield. No significant change appeared in 1916, except for the elimination of brass from lamp rims and tops. For taillights, the little round-bodied, black oil lamps remained standard for yet a decade on the lowest-cost types of Model T, side lamps having been eliminated in 1921.

But a completely "new look" came to Model T with the 1917 style. Front and rear fenders both were curved and crowned, the engine hood was enlarged, fairing smoothly from the higher, smarter (and cheaper!) pressed-steel radiator shell right up to the sharply curved cowl. This comparatively tremendous advance in styling (illustrated in Figs. 12 and 17) served to set a pattern for most of the succeeding decade.

Unchanged in size or appearance, Model T gained mechanical improvements in 1919 (Fig. 13) in the form of the electric starter and demountable rims as limited optional equipment.

The year 1923 brought refinements of lines and trim (see Fig. 14), featuring lowered bodies and the introduction of the one-man top and the four-door sedan.

Like Ford himself, Model T was a paradox. Ford continually resisted change—yet changed.

He professed scorn for history—yet spent millions to perpetuate it in the Edison Institute and in Greenfield Village. To demands for a change from Model T, Ford always replied, "Why change when we can't make enough as it is?"; so, basically, Model T continued in the pattern of its original conception. Even in 1924–1925, when Model T floated out of Dearborn on "balloon" tires, some types were still offered sans starter and defiantly wearing the little oil tail lamp as a badge of Ford's resistance to change!

It has often been stated that Ford maintained two production lines, one for the cars and one for the jokes, but this is apocryphal. However, both were legion and Ford, quick to appreciate the free advertising value of such jokes, actually promulgated them. He was more interested in their effect than in their veracity, of course; witness his own jest apropos color for Model T, "The customer may have any color he wants— as long as it is BLACK!" This the public heard and remembered, forgetting the colorful Fords of 1909–1913 and shrugging off those of 1926–1927.

Then, in a final splash of color, and after an heroic essay at glamour, Model T was finally stricken from the Ford production schedule in June, 1927. For a while parts were stockpiled; then the 1908 molds were discarded as Ford enthusiastically produced the equally famous Model A.

But the inertia of fifteen million model T Fords is not yet spent!

PART TWO: THE CHRONOLOGY

Toward the goal of more positive identifications and to aid in more authentic restorations of antique Fords, this résumé of progressive change in Model T is hopefully directed. Some information which might have been included here was not for want of its complete verification or because of its availability in Ford handbooks.

As a supplement to manuals which tell the "how" of Model T, this summary attempts to tell "what" and "when." Listed only are new items and changes peculiar to each production year and, where no further reference is made, such items may be considered as continued unchanged during the ensuing years. Typical of the "antique" styles of Model T are Ford specifications published January, 1912, and reproduced here in Fig. 16.

1909

The newly designed Ford, Model T, was introduced in October, 1908.

TYPES AND PRICES

Touring	Runabout	Coupé	Town	Tourster
$850	$825	$950	$1,000	——

SALIENT FEATURES: "Winged" *Ford* name on radiator tank; one-piece oil pan; flat, rectangular door on transmission cover; open valve chambers.

ENGINE

Engines under No. 1000 (late February) had a very low, flat cylinder head drilled for fifteen $\frac{3}{8}$-inch cap bolts. Compression was 60 pounds per square inch, and ratio was about $4\frac{1}{2}$ to 1. No name appeared on head or on transmission cover door.

Engines under No. 2500 (mid-April) had a slightly higher cylinder head for greater water capacity; the head remained flat but was drilled for fifteen $\frac{7}{16}$-inch cap bolts and bore the name *Ford Motor Co.* in block letters. All these engines (see Fig. 21) were further characterized by the absence of a front water jacket and by the inclusion of a water pump, gear driven from the camshaft and carrying an eight-bladed fan on the end of the pump shaft. A long oil-fill pipe was attached on top of crankcase at left front; the engine number appeared on a boss near bottom of front cylinder at the right. The crankshaft was only 25 inches long; the very heavy connecting rods were bronze-bushed for a wrist pin held tight in piston.

The *Ford* name appeared in script on transmission cover door.

Engines above No. 2500 had no water pumps but were cooled by thermosyphon effect. There-

fore, the cylinder head was again given greater water capacity with a jacket dome sloping forward to a vertical hose connection (see part 3001, Fig. 23). The block was altered because of elimination of the water pump, and the water jacket was extended around the front. The crankshaft was increased to $25\frac{5}{32}$ inches and fitted with a pulley for a flat belt drive to the four-bladed fan. The timing-gear cover was altered and included an integrally cast oil-fill spout (part 3009, Fig. 23). The commutator was enlarged (part 3200, Fig. 18) and remained as standard size thereafter. Connecting rods were lightened slightly, and the bushing was omitted; shaft end was bored to $1\frac{1}{2}$ inches with $\frac{1}{8}$ inch or babbitt thickness. Cylinder bore and stroke remained at $3\frac{3}{4}$ x 4 inches with a displacement of 176.7 cubic inches.

The cam was designed to open exhaust valve $\frac{3}{8}$ inch before bottom center and to close $\frac{1}{64}$ inch past top center. Intake opened $\frac{7}{64}$ inch past top center, closed $\frac{3}{8}$ inch past bottom center.

BODIES

Colors were optional; black, red, green, blue, pearl gray, and French gray were available. Wood was the standard material of construction (Fig. 1), but a very few Touring Cars had sheet aluminum bodies, presumably experimental (Fig. 3). For this year only, the Tourster body was offered having no doors at all and having identical front and rear seat assemblies. The Coupé was distinguished by having the doors hinged at rear.

Running boards were of wood covered with linoleum on cars under No. 2500, but were later of pressed steel with several rows of interrupted ridges running lengthwise, as shown in Fig. 3; no *Ford* script appeared on any of these. Fenders were steel, flat-topped and rimmed, and were generally square-ended (as in Fig. 1), though often lipped in front (as in Fig. 3). Fender finish was always in black japan. Engine hoods were 24 inches long for Runabouts, 22 inches long for all other types . . . until 1917.

STEERING GEAR

This 50-inch assembly was fitted with a wooden wheel of 13-inch outside diameter, had a brass spider and had a brass case for the planetary steering gears mounted directly under the spider. Steering ratio was 3 to 1 reduction.

RUNNING GEAR

Standard tread was 56 inches, with 60 inches optional for the Southern trade, where wagon ruts were wider. Peculiar to the early Fords was the pressed-steel, riveted differential and axle housing which contained straight (untapered) axles and drive shaft running in bronze bushings; only the outer axle bearings were roller. On cars above No. 7500 (mid-July) the pinion-gear end of the drive shaft was increased in diameter from 1 inch to $1\frac{3}{16}$ inches, and was fitted with a longer bushing. The steering knuckle and spindle unit was forged in one piece and radius rods were socketed into the spring perches atop the front axle.

IGNITION

Alternating current was generated by 16 V-shaped magnets $\frac{9}{16}$ inch wide clamped to the flywheel and rotated past a ring of 16 coils fixed to the inside of the transmission case; voltages up to 28 were obtained, varying with engine speed. This low-tension current was distributed by the commutator, or "timer," to four vibrator spark coils contained in a wooden case on the dashboard, thence as high-tension current to the spark plugs. These were either Heinze coils, size $2\frac{5}{16}$ x $3\frac{1}{16}$ x $3\frac{1}{16}$ x 5 inches, or were Kingston coils, size $2\frac{5}{16}$ x $2\frac{9}{16}$ x $5\frac{3}{4}$ inches.

LAMPS AND ACCESSORIES

The all-brass lamps were made by E. & J., Brown, or Victor and included two 8-inch acetylene-gas head lamps, with a brass generator, two square oil side lamps, and a square tail lamp. The bulb horn and all other such accessories were of polished brass.

1910

Essentially identical to late 1909 Fords, the 1910 style was announced in October, 1909.

TYPES AND PRICES (AUGUST)

Touring	Runabout	Coupé	Town	Torpedo
$950	$900	$1,050	$1,200	——

SALIENT FEATURES: *Ford* name appeared in script along with the diamond designs pressed into running boards.

ENGINE

Changes were not obvious, consisting principally of an alteration in the method of fastening magnets to the flywheel starting in March

Fig. 5. Model T engine. Close-up view of world's most famous power plant—the Model T engine. Note gas headlights and kerosene dash lamps, the brace for windshield. Rod from carburetor needle valve extends up through dashboard for easy adjustment while driving. This is one of the very first Model T's, as two hand levers can be seen. Only a few hundred cars with two levers were made. All others had only one hand lever.

Fig. 6. 1914 Touring—No. 516498. Formerly owned and restored by Chris Hannevig; now owned and rebuilt by Thomas Hespenheide. Another AACA prize winner, this Ford was similar to the 1913 except for rounded door corners. Note particularly the plain but slightly rounded ends on front fenders compared with the plain but straight ends in Fig. 1, and with the lipped fenders in Fig. 9. Front wheels on this car were genuine Ford accessories, fitted with clincher rims for 30 x 3½ tires to match the rear.

Fig. 7. 1911 Touring—No. 56769. Formerly owned and restored by Robert C. Laurens; now owned by T. Clarence Marshall of Yorklyn, Delaware. This car won the "Best Model T" Trophy, 1949 Glidden Tour. In it are embodied some of the first major engineering improvements in Model T; the tapered axles and drive shaft, larger sloping transmission cover (Fig. 22), and an oil pan (Fig. 23) removable without taking out the entire engine, radiator, dashboard, and steering gear!

Fig. 8. 1913 Touring—No. 168839. Owned and restored by W. Harrison Hall, Jr. Winner of the Ford Motor Company Trophy, 1951 Glidden Tour. Here was the first Ford touring body designed with front doors (left one was a dummy) and integral tonneau, and the last offered in colors with striping until 1926. Note the angularity of the doors. Lamps were then iron with brass trim only.

Fig. 9. 1915 Touring—No. 762316. Owned and restored by Leslie R. Henry. Winner of the Ford Motor Company Trophy, 1950 Glidden Tour. This was the transitional design; first to have magneto-powered electric head lamps, curved rear fenders, and sharply faired metal cowl. Note the brass trim on all lamps, which serves as a distinction between 1915 and 1916 styles. The toolbox was a Ford factory accessory; the wooden door trim was not.

(engine No. 17500) and a second alteration of the flywheel itself to accommodate the larger ⅝-inch magnets installed in May (engine No. 20500) to increase magneto power.

The standard carburetor was the Kingston Model L-2.

BODIES

No changes were offered except for the new Torpedo Roadster; a racy looking car (Fig. 4) which featured very low doors, curved front and rear fenders, and a 16-gallon fuel tank and a toolbox mounted on rear deck. The long, 61-inch steering column and the windshield were set at a very rakish angle to carry out the suggestion of speed. And, with its high compression engine, light flywheel (including magneto), and very light, low body, this car had undoubtedly the best performance and greatest speed of all Model T Fords ever produced.

At this time the doors on the Coupé were hinged in front.

On New Year's Eve cars were shipped from the Piquette Avenue (Detroit) plant for the last time; on the first day of 1910 deliveries were made from the new Highland Park plant.

1911

Many new engineering advances appeared in

Its unusual lines command courtesy and respect.

the 1911-style Fords, .brought out in October, 1910.

TYPES AND PRICES (AUGUST)

Touring	Runabout	Coupé	Town	Torpedo
$780	$680	$1,050	$1,200	——

SALIENT FEATURES: Removable connecting-rod pan; larger steering wheel; larger transmission-cover door; metal bodies.

ENGINE

Most welcome was the inclusion of a removable connecting-rod pan (part 3100, Fig. 19), obviating the necessity of removing the entire engine—and all forward body parts—to adjust rod bearings. With this change came a larger, sloping access door for easier adjustment of the transmission bands (part 3376, Fig. 18) and the clutch pedal was altered to fit this enlarged transmission cover. The engine number was relocated to a boss over the water hose connection on left of block.

Enclosure of the valve chambers, entailing a second alteration of the engine block casting, was introduced later in the year. Along with this came steel valve push rods replacing the former brass.

A *Ford* carburetor, Model G, was issued on many cars; Kingston remained standard.

BODIES

During this year sheet metal bodies became standard but resembled the former wooden bodies closely.

STEERING GEAR

This assembly was lengthened to 56 inches and the steering-wheel diameter increased to 15 inches.

RUNNING GEAR

The drive shaft and the axles were each tapered at one end and were carried entirely on roller bearings instead of partly in bushings; a malleable-iron spool piece was inserted between the shaft housing and the differential housing to

Replacement parts easily obtainable—anywhere in U.S.A.

contain the new roller and ball thrust drive-shaft bearings.

The front-wheel steering knuckle and spindle unit was assembled of two pieces to simplify forging and remained unchanged until 1917. A larger ball and socket was fitted to the front radius-rod unit.

IGNITION

Spark coils made by Jacobson-Brandon were furnished on many cars this year.

LAMPS

Magneto-powered electric conversion units were offered for the first time by K-W Company for Ford gas head lamps; Ford warned that the magneto was not powerful enough for lights and ignition too. Side-lamp brackets were changed from round brass to flat iron.

1912

October, 1911, saw the first of the new 1912-style Fords.

TYPES AND PRICES (AUGUST)

Touring	Runabout	Town	Torpedo
$690	$590	$900	——
Fore-Door		Commercial Runabout	
——		——	

SALIENT FEATURES: Enclosed valve chambers.

ENGINE

For the first time, the engine compression ratio was slightly lowered by enlarging combustion space in the cylinder head.

A third change in timing-gear cover plate introduced the unusual timer with a built-in oil-fill spout, as shown in Fig. 18; this was soon abandoned in favor of the fourth-type cover plate more nearly like the earlier but having an adjusting screw for fan-belt tension just above the integrally cast oil-fill spout which itself was pierced by a cap screw (see part 3009B, Fig. 23).

BODIES

New in styling was the "Fore-Door" Touring Car, unique in that front, or fore, door units were factory equipment. These units were subsequently made available as Ford accessories for shop installation in the regular 1911 or 1912 Touring Cars already in use.

A Torpedo Runabout was officially offered and for the last time this year, but it had not the rakish appearance nor yet the performance of the previous 1910–1911 Torpedo. It was really the regular Runabout except for the curved fenders, and the toolbox and 16-gallon round fuel tank mounted on the rear deck. It had the standard 56-inch steering column, the 23 x 34¼-inch cherry dashboard, and the regular high doors. The Commercial Runabout was yet another modification, possessing a flat rear deck for light freight with a single, detachable bucket seat on the toolbox for the mother-in-law.

After 1912 the erect, brass-bound, and brass-braced windshield was seen no more on new Fords; neither were the all-brass horn and lamps, nor the all-leather upholstery. Ford had begun to economize and to *produce!*

STEERING GEAR

This was the last production year to have a cast-brass steering-wheel spider, though the brass steering-gear case remained until 1917.

Ford Coupelet—2-Passenger—4-Cylinder—20 Horsepower—fully equipped, except speedometer. Inviting trimness of appearance with the highest degree of utility. Top raised or lowered in two minutes. Price $590 f. o. b. Detroit

Fig. 10. 1915 Coupélet. First of the convertible cars, it was offered only four years, then replaced by the Coupé. Today an excellent example of this rare style may be seen in the collection of Henry Austin Clark, Jr.

1913

With a definite note of austerity came the 1913-style Model T in November, 1912.

PROFITS: $25,000,000 for the fiscal year ending August 1, 1913.

TYPES AND PRICES (AUGUST)

Touring	Runabout	Town
$600	$525	$740

SALIENT FEATURES: First Touring with front doors and integral tonneau; first Runabout with rear "turtle-back" compartment; steel replaced most of the former brass units.

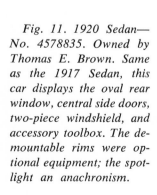

Fig. 11. 1920 Sedan— No. 4578835. Owned by Thomas E. Brown. Same as the 1917 Sedan, this car displays the oval rear window, central side doors, two-piece windshield, and accessory toolbox. The demountable rims were optional equipment; the spotlight an anachronism.

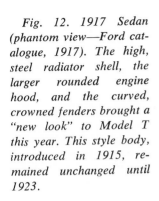

Fig. 12. 1917 Sedan (phantom view—Ford catalogue, 1917). The high, steel radiator shell, the larger rounded engine hood, and the curved, crowned fenders brought a "new look" to Model T this year. This style body, introduced in 1915, remained unchanged until 1923.

(See 1909 data for engines above No. 2500.)

ENGINE

The exhaust manifold and camshaft alterations were the only changes in the engine. The exhaust valve was made to open 5/16 inch before bottom center and to close at top center. The intake valve was made to open 1/16 inch past top center and to close 9/16 inch past bottom center.

BODIES

Last to be offered in colors and with factory striping, these were the first to have front doors designed into smooth-sided bodies; the tonneau was no longer a distinct division. A handle projected through the top edge of each door which

Fig. 13. 1919 Runabout —No. 3000028. Owned by Marvin W. Moyer. The "new look" introduced two years earlier is displayed by this AACA prize winner in the curved, crowned fenders, the high, pressed-steel radiator shell, and the more graceful hood. Starters and demountable rims, offered for the first time as optional factory equipment, were reserved for the closed Fords.

was sharply rectangular in shape and which extended below the floor level to the top of the splash apron (see Fig. 7). Except for the Fords produced in Canada, and which are not considered in the scope of this treatise, the left front door was a dummy, access there being obstructed by the brake anyway.

The cherry dashboard was continued though reduced in size to 21½ x 32¼ inches, better to fit the new body style. At this time the windshield frame was changed from brass to steel, was mounted with the bottom section sloping backward, and was braced with short steel tubes to the top edge of the cowl (see Figs. 7–8). *Ford* script on running board was changed from a longitudinal to a crosswise position.

Leatherette was employed for door panels only, while the upholstering remained in leather.

STEERING GEAR

Cast steel replaced the brass steering spider, but the wooden wheel remained 15 inches in diameter.

IGNITION

Far outnumbering the wooden coil boxes this year were the new, angular, pressed-steel coil cases bearing the *Ford* name and containing K-W spark coils, size 2¼ x 3¼ x 5⅜ inches.

LAMPS AND ACCESSORIES

Here, too, brass was largely replaced by steel, and black-painted lamps were furnished in the following makes and models:

HEAD LAMPS

E. & J., Model 66	Brass top and rim
John Brown (1913–1914)	Brass rim only
Victor, Model 1	
Corcoran (1913–1914)	Brass top and rim

SIDE LAMPS (SQUARE)

E. & J., Model 30	Round front lens; brass trim
John Brown (1913–1914)	Brass trim
Victor (1913–1914)	Brass trim
Corcoran (1913–1914)	Brass trim

TAIL LAMP (SQUARE)

E. & J., Model 10	Round green, round red, square white lenses; brass trim
Standard (1909–1914)	Same as above
Victor	Same as side lamp with one red lens
Corcoran	Same as above

The gas generator was made of black iron instead of brass. The bulb horn, while still made of brass, was painted black except for the belled end, and was mounted to project through the dashboard. A Stewart speedometer, chain driven in a flexible housing from the right front wheel, was included at no extra cost. This too was black with a brass bezel.

1914

Ford greeted the new year, January, 1914, with a new-style Model T.

TYPES AND PRICES (AUGUST)

Touring	Runabout	Coupé	Town
$490	$440	$750	$690

SALIENT FEATURES: Black was the only color offered; doors had rounded corners; back cushions were leatherette and only the seats were leather.
PROFITS: $30,000,000 for the fiscal year ending August.

Prices were actually lower than posted for all Fords sold between August, 1914, and August, 1915, at which time Ford announced a flat fifty-dollar refund to each customer in line with his profit-sharing plan. Yet during 1914 profits soared to $30,000,000 despite Ford's introduction of the five-dollar minimum payment for an eight-hour day. Competitors were paying an average of $2.34 for a nine-hour day!

ENGINE

The intake manifold was cast of iron instead of aluminum. Transmission-cover door was a plain sheet-steel stamping; no name appeared thereon. For the last time, pedals were initialed, and the crank was fitted with a curved, aluminum handle.

BODIES

This was the last year in which Ford held to the truly "antique" styling. The bodies resembled those of 1913, having the small cherrywood dashboards and the straight, flat fenders. However, each door had rounded bottom corners and did not extend below the floor line; the latch handle extended through the inside panel rather than through the top of the door.

For the first time, front fenders were stamped with a strengthening rib across the widest portion. Up to and including 1914, windshields were similar in design though different in materials and mounting, and were made by any one of three Detroit suppliers: the Diamond Manufacturing Company, the Vanguard Manufacturing Company, or the Rand Manufacturing Company.

RUNNING GEAR

The rear cross member of the rectangular frame was lengthened, thereby eliminating the riveted attachment of brackets formerly used. Wheels were available in black or dark blue until 1920.

IGNITION

Ford spark coils were introduced and the K-W and Heinze coils were altered to conform to the new standard size of 2⅛ x 3½ x 5 inches. All coils were housed in a pressed-steel box.

LAMPS AND ACCESSORIES

Acetylene-gas head lamps and square oil lamps were furnished for the last time with this style. All lamps and accessories were the same as offered in 1913, except for some lamp model changes as noted:

HEAD LAMPS

E. & J., Model 656   Brass top and rim
Victor, Model 2

SIDE LAMPS

E. & J., Model 32   Round lens front; brass trim

TAIL LAMP

E. & J., Model 12

1915

The transitional styling of Model T for 1915 appeared first in November, 1914, with the closed cars, then in April, 1915, for all types. Car No. 1,000,000 was completed December 10.

TYPES AND PRICES (AUGUST)

Touring	Runabout	Town	Sedan	Coupélet
$440	$390	$640	$740	$590

WEIGHTS

1,510	1,395	—	1,730	1,540

SALIENT FEATURES: Electric head lamps; louvered hood; curved rear fenders; metal cowl; round oil lamps.

ENGINE

Compression ratio was again lowered slightly. To supply the extra power required for lighting head lamps, the magneto coils were enlarged and the magnets were again increased in size to ¾ inch. The transmission pedals were no longer initialed but had vertical ribs on the surface.

A medium-weight connecting rod was introduced having a bore of 1⅜ inches and a babbitt thickness of 1/16 inch.

BODIES

Starting November, 1915, the new styling was offered only in two entirely new body types, the Sedan, having two central side doors, and the Coupélet (Fig. 10), having the first convertible top; the Coupé was discontinued. Gone was the cherrywood dashboard, supplanted by a metal cowl sharply faired down to the original style, boxlike engine hood which was still made of aluminum and was inletted with louvers. Until April, 1915, the Touring, Runabout, and

Town types remained in the styling of 1914 and must be considered as such. Rear fenders were curved for the first time on all body types; front fenders remained straight, flat, and, without exception, lipped. The windshield again became erect and was mounted without braces atop the cowl, immediately ahead of the doors (Fig. 9).

Upholstering was entirely of leatherette on the open cars, except for a patch of leather at each door where wear was greatest. The closed cars were upholstered in cloth.

IGNITION

For the first time all spark-coil boxes were made exactly alike of pressed steel with smooth corners and sloping top.

LAMPS AND ACCESSORIES

Since the gas lamps were retained on some Fords until April, all cars until then had the forked lamp brackets even when fitted with electric lamps. But, when all types were at last equipped with the new 8½-inch electric head lamps, these were then mounted each on a single, flanged post. The light bulbs were of 9-volt capacity and were wired in series because the magneto voltage ranged from 8 to 28 volts or higher, depending on engine speed. This arrangement was never entirely satisfactory, for at low speeds the lights were dim, and, occasionally, at high speeds were so bright they would burn out.

Fig. 14. 1923 Coupé. Owned and assembled by Herbert J. Singe. Featured for 1923 was this lowered body with integral rear compartment, the large rectangular rear window, and rotary window controls. The Touring Car sported a one-man top and sloping windshield (as in Fig. 15).

Side lamps no longer differed as to right or left, but were interchangeable, being rounded and symmetrical. The tail lamp was similar to the side lamps, except for the ruby lens and a white side lens. All lamps were trimmed in brass.

The bulb horn appeared no more, but was replaced by a hand Klaxon with a polished-brass belled end. In August the Stewart speedometer was discontinued as standard equipment but was available as an optional item.

1916

The transitional styling of 1915 remained for 1916, which style year may be considered starting in January.

TYPES AND PRICES (AUGUST)

Touring	Runabout	Town	Sedan	Coupélet
$360	$345	$595	$640	$505

PROFITS: $59,000,000.

SALIENT FEATURES: After April, all lamps and the horn were entirely black and the engine hood was made of steel.

BODIES

This transitional style was the last to have the semblance of antiquity afforded by the straight front fenders, the small brass radiator, and the little boxlike engine hood, now made of steel instead of aluminum. Later, even the patches of leather on the upholstering at the doors were re-

Fig. 15. 1925 Touring. Owned new in 1925 by Paul H. Cadwell, this Ford was one of the first to have "balloon" *tires, size 4.40 x 21, as optional equipment. Body lines were the same as introduced in 1923.*

SPECIFICATIONS
For all Ford Model T Cars

Motor—Four (4) cylinder, four cycle. Cylinders are cast en-bloc with water jackets and upper half of crank case integral. Cylinder bore is 3¾ inches; piston stroke is 4 inches. The Ford Motor is rated at twenty (20) horsepower. Special Ford removable cylinder head permits easy access to pistons, cylinders and valves. Lower half of crank case, one-piece pressed steel extended so as to form bottom housing for entire power plant—air proof, oil proof, dust proof. All interior parts of motor may be reached by removing plate on bottom of crank case—no "tearing down" of motor to reach crank shaft, cam shaft, pistons, connecting rods, etc. Vanadium steel is used in all Ford crank and cam shafts and connecting rods.

Unit Construction—There are four (4) complete units in the construction of Ford Model T—the power plant, the front axle, the rear axle and the frame. Any of these may be removed or replaced as a single unit.

Three-Point Suspension—Each of the Ford Model T units is suspended at three points of the chassis. This method of suspension insures absolute freedom from strain on the parts and permits the most comfortable riding of the car body.

Transmission—Special Ford spur planetary type, combining ease of operation and smooth, silent running qualities. Clutch is so designed as to grip smoothly and positively and when disengaged to spring clear away from the drums, thus assuring positive action and maximum power. Transmission cover is of aluminum.

Magneto—Special Ford design, built in and made a part of the motor. Only two parts to the Ford Magneto, a rotary part attached to the flywheel and a stationary part attached to the cylinder casting. No brushes, no commutators, no moving wires to cause annoyance on the Ford Magneto.

Lubrication—Combination gravity and splash system. Oil is poured into the crank case through the breather pipe on the front cylinder cover. All moving parts of motor move in oil and distribute it to all parts of the power plant.

Cooling—By Thermo-Syphon water system. Extra large water jackets and a special Ford vertical tube radiator permit of a continuous flow of cool water and prevent excessive heating. A belt-driven fan is also used in connection with the cooling system.

Carburetor—New design, float feed automatic with dash adjustment.

Clutch—Multiple steel disc, operating in oil. There are 27 discs in the Ford Clutch.

Fenders—Large and graceful in design, enclosing the entire length of car.

Gasoline Capacity—Touring Car, Commercial Roadster, Town Car and Delivery Car, cylindrical gasoline tanks of 10 gallons capacity and mounted directly on frame under front seat. Torpedo Runabout, cylindrical tank of 16 gallons mounted back of seat.

Steering—By Ford reduction gear system. Steering knuckles and spindles are forged from special heat-treated Vanadium steel and are placed behind front axle.

Valves—Extra large, all on right side of motor and enclosed by two small steel plates, making their action absolutely noiseless. Enclosed valves are dust proof, thereby saving wear on valve stems and push rods and giving perfect valve setting.

Control—On the left side of car. Three foot-pedal controls, low and high speeds, reverse, and brake on the transmission. Hand lever for neutral and emergency brake on left side of car. Spark and throttle levers directly under steering wheel. Ford cars may be stopped or started without removing the hands from the wheel.

Brakes—Dual system on all Ford Model T cars. Service brake operates on the transmission and is controlled by foot pedal. Expanding brake in rear wheel drums serves as emergency brake. It is controlled by hand lever on left side of car.

Springs—Both front and rear springs are semi-elliptical transverse, all made of specially Ford heat-treated Vanadium steel. Ford Model T springs are the strongest and most flexible that can be made. Model T rear springs are extra large, giving easiest riding qualities to car body.

Wheels and Tires—Wooden wheels of the artillery type with extra heavy hubs. Only tires of the highest grade are used on Ford cars. Front 30 x 3 inches. Rear 30 x 3½ inches.

Final Drive—Ford triangular drive system with all shaft, universal joint and driving gears enclosed in dust proof and oil proof housing. Direct shaft drive to the center of the chassis; only one universal joint is necessary. All shafts revolve on roller bearings; a ball and socket arrangement in the universal joint relieves the passengers of all shocks and strains caused by the unevenness of the road. The Final Drive of the Ford Model T is patented in all countries.

Axles—Front axle of I-beam construction, especially drop-forged from a single ingot of Vanadium steel, insuring the highest quality of axle strength obtainable. Rear axle also of Vanadium steel and enclosed in a tubular steel housing. The Ford Differential is of the three-pinion bevel type; all gears are drop-forgings made of Vanadium steel; all teeth are accurately planed and hardened.

Bodies and Capacity—Ford Model T cars are furnished with five styles of bodies—Fore-door Touring Car, capable of carrying five (5) passengers; Torpedo Runabout for two (2) passengers; Commercial Roadster, with rumble seat, three (3) passengers; Town Car, six (6) passengers; Delivery Car, two (2) passengers, 750 pounds merchandise capacity.

Prices—Fore-door Touring Car, f. o. b. Detroit $690
    Torpedo Runabout " " 590
    Commercial Roadster " " 590
    Town Car " " 900
    Delivery Car " " 700

Equipment—All Ford Model T's are sold completely equipped—no Ford cars will be sold unequipped. Standard equipment includes Top, Windshield, Gas Lamps, Generator, Speedometer, Three Oil Lamps, Horn and Kit of Tools.

Weight—Touring Car, 1200 pounds. Others in proportion.

Wheel Base—100 inches; Standard tread 56 inches; 60 inches for Southern roads where ordered. All Ford Model T cars will turn in a twenty-eight (28) foot circle.

Fig. 16

placed with leatherette and this was protected from wear by little pressed-steel caps.

RUNNING GEAR

The 60-inch tread, which required larger fenders, longer fender brackets, longer axles, housings, tie rods, etc., was discontinued after July 31 and Dixieland was compelled at last to superimpose the standard 56-inch-tread Fords on their 60-inch ruts.

Hubcaps were still fabricated of thin, polished brass.

1917

In September, 1916, Model T developed a "new look" for 1917; streamlining came—almost.

TYPES AND PRICES (AUGUST)

Touring	Runabout	Town	Coupélet	Sedan
$360	$345	$595	$505	$645

WEIGHTS

1,500	1,385	——	1,580	1,745

PROFITS: $38,500,000. (Profits were smaller because of the tremendous building program at the new River Rouge Plant, subject of the famous Dodge Brothers' stockholders suit.)

SALIENT FEATURES: High steel radiator shell; larger engine hood matching the cowl contour; crowned, curved, fenders; low-compression engine; nickel-plated hub- and radiator caps.

ENGINE

By increasing the height of the cylinder head, engine compression was lowered to 45-pounds-per-square-inch with a 3.98 to 1 ratio. The cast-iron nozzle for the water hose on top of the cylinder head was increased in length because of the higher radiator. The fan was made larger and had a peripheral reinforcing ring, which was later omitted.

The transmission cover was cast of iron instead of aluminum, and the pedals were smooth-surfaced. Rubber pedal pads were available and could be slipped onto the pedals.

The muffler still had cast-iron heads, but the tail pipe was eliminated.

BODIES

A major step was taken this year toward modernizing Model T. Most striking of all changes was the high, pressed-steel radiator shell with the well-proportioned hood clashed down to pressed-steel sills and fairing gently back to the cowl contour. Crowned fenders were the completing touch. For the first time nickel plating appeared on the hubcaps and radiator cap. The front bracket holding the body to the frame was then made of a steel stamping rather than the steel casting previously used.

STEERING GEAR

The front-wheel hubs and the spindles were made about 1/8 inch longer, the better to accommodate tapered roller bearings introduced as standard this year. These roller bearings could, however, replace the ball bearings in any of the earlier Fords.

LAMPS AND ACCESSORIES

An electric horn powered by the magneto was included as regular equipment this year.

1918

There was no change from the 1917 to the 1918 style, but starting this year many cars were fitted with squared-end spring leaves, as well as the regular tapered-end spring leaves. For the last time, the Coupélet and Town Cars were offered; following this year the Coupé type was revived, having doors hinged at the front.

TYPES AND PRICES (AUGUST)

Touring	Runabout	Coupélet	Sedan
$525	$500	$650	$775

1919

While styling remained identical to 1917, many engineering advances were incorporated in the new Ford for 1919.

TYPES AND PRICES (AUGUST)

Touring	Runabout	Coupé	Sedan
$525	$500	$650	$775

WEIGHTS

1,500	1,390	1,580	1,750

SALIENT FEATURES: First with electric starter and demountable rims as limited optional equipment.
PROFITS: $70,000,000.
Motor Company capitalized at $100,000,000.

ENGINE

For the open-type cars no engine changes *at first* appeared; but for all the closed types the engine was modified in order to accept the starting equipment as optional equipment; later, all engines were so modified. The flywheel was altered to take a ring gear; the engine block

Windshield wiper won't get out of whack.

Fig. 17. 1917 Ford Model T Roadster

and (for the fifth time) the timing-gear cover were changed to support and drive the 6-volt generator from the camshaft gear, and the transmission cover was redesigned to receive the starting motor.

Because of the generator load on the timing gears these were changed from spur to helical; this also reduced backlash and gear noise. The helical gears were interchangeable with the earlier spur type and were recommended by Ford for replacements.

BODIES

Body styles were not changed from those introduced for 1917, except for reviving the Coupé, which had doors hinged at front.

RUNNING GEAR

Demountable clincher rims for 30 x 3½ tires were optional equipment for the closed-type Fords only. Tire size in front remained 30 x 4 otherwise.

The front radius rods were relocated to a position below the front axle on extensions of the spring perches; this better braced the axle against torque.

LAMPS AND ACCESSORIES

All cars fitted with the optional electric starter, generator, and storage battery were also supplied with an electric tail lamp; and the 6-volt lighting system, wired in parallel, was powered by the battery. Later, and until the passing of the hand crank and the oil tail lamp in 1925, the electric tail lamp became a popular accessory for those Fords still lighted by the magneto.

1920

Styling remained unchanged.

TYPES:	Touring	Runabout	Coupé	Sedan
PRICES:				
(March)	$575	$550	$850	$975
(Sept.)	$440	$395	$745	$795
WEIGHTS:	1,485	1,380	1,685	1,875

SALIENT FEATURES: Steering wheel was increased to 16-inch diameter.

ENGINE

Lightweight connecting rods were introduced having a bore of $1\frac{3}{8}$ inches with $\frac{1}{16}$ inch of babbitt thickness.

At this time electric starting equipment became optional on all types at an extra cost of $75, adding 90 pounds extra weight.

The Ford carburetor Model NH was introduced on many cars and the Model F carburetor was continued until 1923. Kingston carburetor Model L-2 was discontinued after this year.

BODIES

Bodies remained unchanged from the 1917 style, except that only the Sedan was fitted with a dashboard.

In anticipation of lowered bodies, the original style round fuel tank was abandoned early in 1920 in favor of the oval shape for all type bodies except the Sedan, which still required the square tank (Fig. 12), as used on many of the earlier Coupés. Figure 19 is a gauge table of gallonage for the three regular sizes of Ford fuel tanks.

STEERING GEAR

The familiar cast-steel spider was replaced by a pressed-steel unit and the wheel, now made of "composition" similar to hard rubber, was increased to 16-inch diameter.

RUNNING GEAR

The malleable-iron spool at rear of drive-shaft housing was replaced by a cheaper, pressed-steel, flanged sleeve having exposed bolts.

At last optional equipment for *all*-type Fords, the demountable rims, including spare, cost $21 extra and added about 70 pounds to the car weight.

LAMPS AND ACCESSORIES

The dashboard (Sedan only) sported an ammeter and a combination light and ignition switch mounted in an escutcheon plate. Stewart speedometers, when added, appeared on the lower right edge of the dashboard.

Fig. 18. Commutators (1912 catalogue). Rarest of the many forms of Model T "timers" was the early 1912 having the oil fill pipe made integrally with the timer case. Item 3200 above shows the conventional form.

1921

The style was the same as the 1920 except for minor changes.

TYPES:	Touring	Runabout	Coupé	Sedan
PRICES:				
(June)	$415	$370	$695	$760
(Sept.)	$355	$325	$595	$660
WEIGHTS:	1,485	1,380	1,685	1,875

PROFITS: Ford *owed* $50,000,000 in the postwar depression.

ENGINE

Front engine support and front spring clamp were forged in one single unit; the pair of U bolts formerly holding spring to frame were abandoned.

A Kingston carburetor, Model L-4, was furnished on many cars in 1921–1922.

The cast-iron muffler heads were no longer used, being replaced by pressed-steel units.

1922

This style was identical to the 1921.

TYPES:	Touring	Runabout	Coupé	Sedan
PRICES:	$348	$319	$580	$645
WEIGHTS:	1,485	1,380	1,685	1,875

PROFITS: $119,000,000.

Fuel Tank Measurements for Most Model T Ford Cars			
Gallons	Square Tank	Round Tank	Oval Tank
1	$\frac{3}{4}$"	$1\frac{17}{32}$"	$1\frac{7}{16}$"
2	$1\frac{1}{2}$"	$2\frac{9}{16}$"	$2\frac{3}{16}$"
3	$2\frac{1}{4}$"	$3\frac{1}{2}$"	$2\frac{15}{16}$"
4	3"	$4\frac{11}{32}$"	$3\frac{5}{8}$"
5	$3\frac{3}{4}$"	$5\frac{1}{8}$"	$4\frac{5}{16}$"
6	$4\frac{1}{2}$"	$5\frac{29}{32}$"	5"
7	$5\frac{1}{4}$"	$6\frac{3}{4}$"	$5\frac{11}{16}$"
8	6"	$7\frac{11}{16}$"	$6\frac{7}{16}$"
9	$6\frac{3}{4}$"	$8\frac{23}{32}$"	$7\frac{3}{16}$"

Fig. 19

BODIES

The Sedan with the two centrally located doors and with the oval rear window appeared for the last time this year.

1923

Distinctive, new styling for 1923 appeared in August, 1922.

TYPES AND PRICES				
Touring	Runabout	Coupé	Sedan 2-door	Sedan 4-door
$393	$364	$530	$595	$725

WEIGHTS				
1,650	——	——	——	——

PROFITS: $82,000,000.

SALIENT FEATURES: Lowered, more "streamlined" bodies; one-man top.

BODIES

The lowered bodies, planned since early 1920 when the oval tanks (and the postwar depression) appeared, marked the first real styling advancement since 1917. On all types the radiator was heightened and sported an apron at the bottom of the shell.

Two sedans were offered for the first time, the two-door and the four-door; these and the Coupé featured a large, rectangular rear window and, for the first time, rotary window regulators, a cowl ventilator, and of course, the square fuel tanks.

The Coupé this year had the rear compartment formed integrally with the body (see Fig. 14); the Runabout still retained the detachable compartment, until the 1926 style, so that it could be readily converted for commercial use.

The open-body types had the oval fuel tank, the new, one-man top, and windshields set at a rakish angle with the upper section pivoted at the top of the frame. Characteristic of the one-man top was the extension of back curtain around the side of the bow sockets (see Fig. 15).

The running-board brackets were one-piece flared channel section and were without the familiar tie rod.

1924

There was no change in style for 1924.

TYPES AND PRICES (AUGUST)

Touring	Runabout	Coupé	Sedan 2-door	Sedan 4-door
$295	$265	$525	$590	$685

PROFITS: $100,000,000 (averaging $50 per car). Ford started his first nationwide paid advertising program.
SALIENT FEATURES: Last year in which the open cars were available with the 30 x 3 clincher front tires.

1925

Still in the pattern of 1923, the Ford for 1925 had minor improvements.

TYPES AND PRICES

Touring	Runabout	Coupé	Tudor Sedan	Fordor Sedan
$290	$260	$520	$580	$660

PROFITS: $80,000,000.
SALIENT FEATURES: First with "balloon" tires and hand-operated windshield wiper.

BODIES

The names "Tudor" and "Fordor" were coined to designate the two forms of the Sedan; these names are still used by Ford.

The large, black escutcheon plate for the ammeter and the ignition and light switches appeared for the last time on the dashboard. New, as factory equipment, was the hand-operated windshield wiper.

RUNNING GEAR

Demountable rims for 30 x 3½ clincher tires were supplied on all body types; the spare was carried at rear on a triangular mounting. Balloon tires, size 4.40 x 21, were optional equipment for all Fords at $25 extra (see Fig. 15).

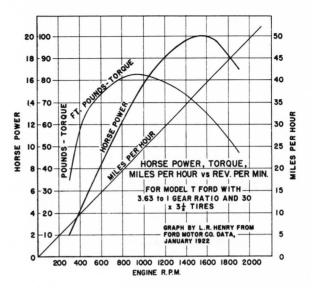

Fig. 20

This was the last year for the small brake drums and the cast-iron brake shoes on the rear wheels.

LAMPS AND ACCESSORIES

This was the last year in which the open cars were *available* with no starter, with magneto-powered head lamps, and with the same round oil tail lamp introduced in 1915—Ford *did* resist change! Customers still willing to crank preferred, however, to have their Ford fitted with the magneto-powered electric tail lamp instead of the oil lamp.

1926

In an heroic rejuvenation, Ford brought forth a glamorized Model T for 1926 starting with No. 12,225,528 in November, 1925. By July 21, 14,000,000 Model T cars had been built.

TYPES AND PRICES (AUGUST)

Touring	Runabout	Coupé	Tudor	Fordor
$380	$360	$485	$495	$545

PROFITS: $75,000,000.
SALIENT FEATURES: Lowered chassis; nickeled radiator shell; choice of colors; lightweight pistons.

ENGINE

To help compensate for the heavier bodies, an effort was made to pep up the engine by installing lightweight cast-iron pistons having the oil ring below the wrist pin, and by redesigning the intake manifold for more efficient vaporization of fuel.

The engine-block casting was altered to provide bosses to which a pair of ears on the new transmission cover could be bolted.

The transmission brake band was increased in width from 1⅛ to 1¾ inches, and all bands were factory-fitted with the removable ears to permit relining of bands without removal of the transmission cover.

The water nozzle on engine head had a projection for mounting the fan.

BODIES

After a decade of nothing but black Fords, colors for the closed cars only became optional; blue, gray, and brown were offered. This year the cowl ventilator (introduced in 1923) was included in all cars and was made to serve a double duty in that the fuel tank was now located in the cowl and filled through the opened ventilator. Of course there was an exception; the Fordor had the usual square fuel tank under the seat.

At last the left front door of the open cars was given hinges and allowed to open, and the

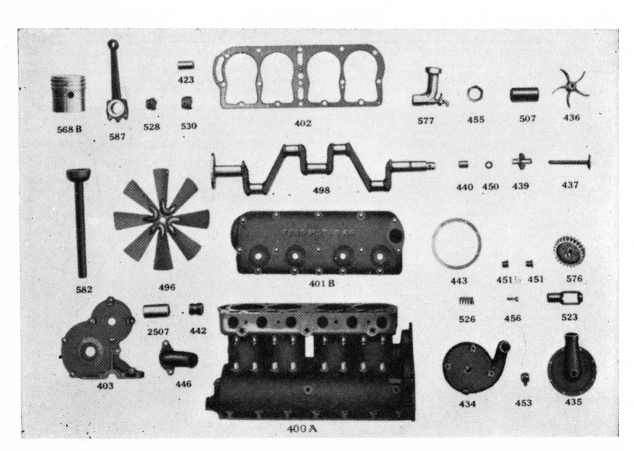

Fig. 21. Early engine parts (1913 catalogue). These parts were peculiar to the first 2,500 of the 1909 Fords. Note the eight-bladed fan, the water pump, and the flat cylinder head. Head gasket, part 402, clearly shows absence of front water jacket in these engines; compare with parts shown in Fig. 23.

No special gasoline necessary. (High-octane may be dangerous.)

Runabout was finally constructed with an integral rear compartment as the Coupé had been in 1923. Running boards were made 1½ inches wider.

Since bodies had already been lowered to the practical limit in 1923, these remained essentially unchanged and the height of Model T was reduced 1½ inches by lowering the chassis. This was accomplished by lowering the crown of the rear spring 1½ inches, and by lowering the crown of the front spring 1 inch, then gaining the extra ½ inch in front by raising the wheel spindle on the steering-knuckle body. Again there was an exception; the Tudor body was lowered another 2½ inches for a total of 4 inches.

Now proudly displaying a nickel-plated shell, the radiator was ⅝ inch higher. The engine hood was longer, had more louvers, and sloped smoothly into the cowl which appeared to be but a continuation of the hood. In all, the bodies had thus been lengthened 3½ inches, and a better sense of proportion was gained by enlarging the crowned fenders and by eliminating the bead on them.

The Coupé and Tudor type only were fitted with a new one-piece windshield, but on all types the dashboard was furnished with a small, nickel-plated escutcheon plate for the ammeter and switches.

STEERING GEAR

The steering-wheel diameter was increased to 17 inches and the planetary-steering-gear ratio was changed to 5 to 1 reduction to compensate for the extra resistance of balloon tires.

RUNNING GEAR

Balloon tires, size 4.40 x 21, were standard equipment on all cars, as were the wooden artillery wheels. This year wire wheels of the drop-center type were available as optional equipment. The spare was mounted at the rear on a tubular post with a flange for the wire wheel or with a three-legged spider for the demountable rim, as required.

The rear-wheel brake drums were increased in diameter from 8 to 11 inches and in width from 1⁵⁄₃₂ to 1½ inches, and the brake shoes were of the asbestos-lined, self-energizing type.

IGNITION

The metal spark-coil box was relocated from

Full, unobstructed vision

the dashboard to a bracket on the left side of the engine head.

LAMPS

Because of the tubular post, the taillight was relocated from the center of the spare-tire bracket to the left rear fender.

Head lamps had nickel-plated rims and were at first mounted as usual on flanged posts. Starting January, 1926, the head lamps were mounted on a tie bar connecting the front fenders and passing in front of the radiator shell.

1927

After nineteen years, production of Model T ended with car No. 15,007,033 in June, 1927.

TYPES AND PRICES (JUNE)

Touring	Runabout	Coupé	Tudor	Fordor
$380	$360	$485	$495	$545

PROFITS: Ford ended the year with a loss of $30,-280,000.

SALIENT FEATURES: The 1927 style was identical to 1926, except that only the wire wheels were available. All cars were offered in colors, with maroon and green added.

BIBLIOGRAPHY

Here presented are but a few of the more interesting books dealing with the most forceful and dominant personality of motordom, Henry Ford, and/or his omnipresent Model T car:

Ford, Henry, in collaboration with Samuel Crowther, *My Life and Work*. Doubleday, Doran & Company, Inc., New York, 1922.

Marquis, Samuel S., *Henry Ford: An Interpretation*. Little, Brown & Company, Boston, 1923.

Mertz, Charles, *And Then Came Ford*. Doubleday, Doran & Company, Inc., New York, 1929.

Ford, Henry, in collaboration with Samuel Crowther, *Moving Forward*. Doubleday, Doran & Company, Inc., New York, 1931.

White, Lee Strout, *Farewell to Model T*. G. P. Putnam's Sons, New York, 1936.

Glasscock, C. B., *Motor History of America*. The Bobbs-Merrill Company, Inc., Indianapolis, 1937.

Simonds, William A., *Henry Ford: His Life, His Work, His Genius*. The Bobbs-Merrill Company, Inc., Indianapolis, 1943.

Richards, William C., *The Last Billionaire*. Charles Scribner's Sons, New York, 1948.

Bennett, Harry, in collaboration with Paul Marcus, *We Never Called Him Henry*. Gold Medal Books, Fawcett Publications, Inc., New York, 1951.

Page, Victor W., *Model T Ford Car*. The Norman W. Henley Publishing Company, 254 West 54th Street, New York. (Some still available, $3, from the publisher.)

Nevins, Allan, *Ford: The Times, the Man, the Company*. Charles Scribner's Sons, New York, 1954.

A BRIEF DIRECTORY FOR PARTS AND SERVICES FOR MODEL T FORDS

To aid members in the restoration and maintenance of their Model T Fords, the following are suggested as a few sources of supply:

PARTS

B. S. Wisniewski, Inc., 2133 South Kinnichinnic Avenue, Milwaukee 7, Wisconsin. (Manufacturer of new parts.) Joseph J. Murchio, Antique Auto Museum, Greenwood Lake, New York. Magee & Amato, 51 Schaefer Road, Middletown, Connecticut. Harry Pulfer, 2700 Mary Street, LaCrescenta, California. (Specializes in racing parts.) William Scharff, 1322 Myrtle Avenue, Brooklyn, New York. (Bought out Ford factory stock.) Frank Hankins, Route 25, R.D., Riverside, New Jersey. Montgomery Ward and Company. (See catalog for parts, including tires.) Sears, Roebuck and Company. (See catalog for parts.)

SERVICE

Engine reboring, line boring, main bearings, rebuilding—Thul Machine Works, 325 East Third Street, Plainfield, New Jersey. Frank Hankins, Route 25, R.D., Riverside, New Jersey.

MODEL T TIPS AND SUGGESTIONS

TOWING

Never tow a Model T Ford except in an emergency! Because of the unit power-plant design which depends on the rapid rotation of the engine flywheel for lubrication of all parts, including clutch and throw-out bearing, towing the Model T in "neutral" position results in damage to clutch parts and transmission bands for want of lubrication.

If the car must be towed, then do so with the clutch engaged in high-speed position and with the spark plugs removed so the engine may turn over freely. Keep towing speed below 25 miles per hour. In such dire cases where a tow truck must be engaged, then lift the rear wheels, lock the steering, and tow the Model T backward on the front wheels.

An alternative method, requiring considerable effort, is to remove the universal joint before towing.

STORING

When storing a Model T, even if only overnight, the high-speed clutch should be engaged. This forces the hot oil from between the plates of the multiple-disk clutch, thereby reducing transmission drag on the engine when cranking for starting (in neutral, of course) later. This is particularly true in cold weather.

STARTING

Always unpredictable, Model T sometimes fails to *respond* to the usual methods of starting even when interspersed with the usually effective invectives, maledictions, imprecations, and profanations. In such case, when even the de-oiled clutch fails to help, there is yet a way to coax life into old Model T. Jack up one rear wheel, chock the others fore and aft, engage the high-speed clutch, set the spark and gas, then spin the crank. This by-passes the metaphysical transmission and allows the rear wheel to act as a flywheel connected directly to the engine. This method rarely fails.

Sometimes it does, though. Then, if there is any glimmer of spark at all, a shot of ether (sulfuric, not petroleum) from a medicine dropper into the intake manifold or the carburetor of Model T will bring forth a tumultuous roar of explosions from the engine. After a little of this, even the most recalcitrant of Model T Fords will catch on and run without further hypodermics.

Never "race" a cold Model T engine—pistons will break!

OVERHEATING

The "antique" Fords will tend to overheat if driven too fast for any distance because the little brass radiators were somewhat undersized.

Planned to sell for $10 to $1,000—depending on supply-if-demand

Model T can actually run so hot that shutting off the ignition will not stop the engine—it continues to run after the fashion of a diesel! This is disastrous because if the bearings do not burn out, the magneto magnets will surely become demagnetized and an engine overhaul will be necessary.

LUBRICATION

Straight mineral oils (without additives) of SAE 10 for winter and SAE 20 grade for summer in well-adjusted engines are recommended if this oil is drained and changed frequently. But because of the somewhat limited usage given most antique cars, the "heavy-duty" or detergent oils will prove valuable in preventing sludging, valve and ring sticking, and rusting of internal surfaces because of condensed water and corrosive products of combustion.

Do not use any product in the crankcase which contains graphite, for this substance will short out the magneto. It is best to use the highest-quality oil offered by any of the *major* oil refineries; these companies are highly competitive and each offers quality oils having the best of time-proven additives in them; don't experiment with additives yourself. The detergent oils do not have any deleterious effect on the insulation of the Model T magneto coils, but will keep the engine clean and rust-free.

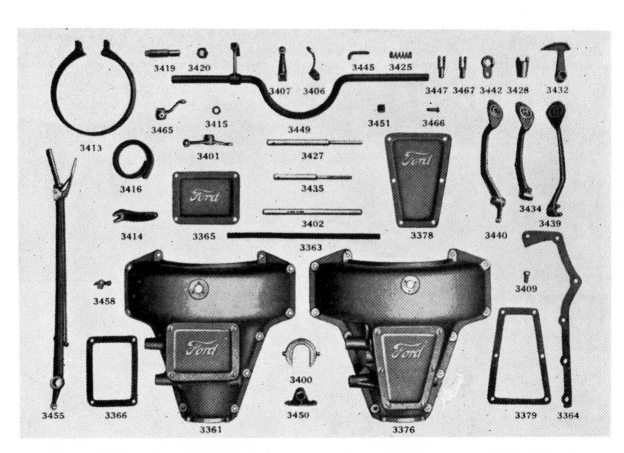

Fig. 22. Transmission parts (1913 catalogue). Part 3361 was the 1909–1910 transmission cover with small door for adjusting bands (part 3413); part 3376 was the cover for 1911–1918. All were aluminum until 1917, when changed to cast iron. In 1919 a part was added to accept a starting motor. Note the letters on pedals, prevalent until 1915. Ford script did not appear on all transmission doors (part 3378).

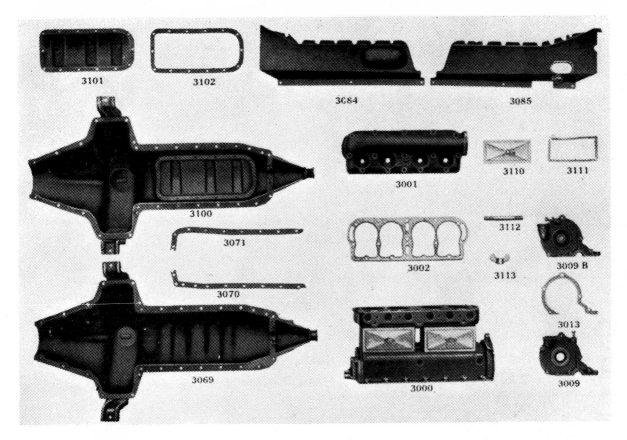

Fig. 23. (1913 catalogue). The engine block, part 3000, was altered in 1911 to provide enclosed valve chambers; compare with part 400A, Fig. 21. The one-piece oil pan, part 3069, was abandoned in 1911 in favor of one (part 3100) with a door for adjusting the connecting rods without removing the entire engine from car. Compare 1909–1911 timing-gear cover (3009) with the late 1912–1919 cover (3009B), and with those shown in Figs. 18 and 21.

HILL CLIMBING

Most Model T Fords develop highest engine torque at about 23 miles per hour (as shown in Fig. 22); consequently, when approaching a long hill, it is best to gain some momentum first, then allow the car to settle down to this speed for a good, steady pull up the hill. Trying to force the car faster will only cause overheating and a tendency to "choke" the engine.

While capable of attaining speeds up to 55 miles per hour on the level, Model T will perform best and last longer at a cruising speed of about 35 miles per hour. This speed represents approximately the maximum horsepower while retaining a good degree of torque and maintaining a conservative engine speed of about 1,400 revolutions per minute (see Fig. 20). Higher speeds only strain the engine.

We know that Model T is well-nigh indestructible; but there *are* limits.

APPENDIX

PRODUCTION DATA

While the Ford Motor Company was organized June 16, 1903, the following production figures refer to the Ford *fiscal* year, commencing August 1:

1903	1708
1905	1695
1906	1599
1907	8423
1908	6398
1909	10607
1910	18664
1911	34528
1912	78440
1913	168220
1914	248307
1915	308213
1916	533921
1917	751287
1918	642750
1919	521600
1920	945850
1921	989785
1922	1216792
1923	2055309
1924	1991518
1925	1966099
1927	1629184
1927	380741

CASTING DATES

Dates appearing on cylinder-block castings (as for example 7–15–15) only indicate when the block was cast; this date will usually be several months earlier than the engine number because the castings were allowed to "age" to relieve internal stresses before machining.

ENGINE NUMBERS

Early Model T cars had a body-number plate to which the Ford Motor Company attached no significance; the engine number was always considered to be the car serial number also. On some Ford engine numbers a letter was prefixed; the letter "C" indicated Canadian manufacture and the letter "B" indicated manufacture at the factory in Detroit (rather than at Highland Park). Fords numbered from B 1 to B 12247 were built between October 1, 1912 and September 30, 1913.

Reference to the appended list of motor-serial numbers can establish the exact month and year of manufacture for any Model T Ford of known engine number, but will not necessarily indicate the correct "style year" of the car. For example, it is possible for a 1915 Sedan to have the number 590000 (November, 1914) while a 1914 Touring could have the number 680000 (March, 1915)! Even without such overlapping, the style year rarely coincided with the calendar year, or even with the Ford fiscal year.

MODEL T SERIAL NUMBERS

Date	Motor numbers		Cars built
1908			
Oct. 1–31	1 to	11	11
Nov. 1–30	12 to	101	89
Dec. 1–31	102 to	309	207
1909			
Jan. 1–31	310 to	646	336
Feb. 1–28	647 to	1052	405
Mar. 1–31	1053 to	2025	972
Apr. 1–30	2026 to	2691	665
May 1–31	2692 to	4036	1344
June 1–30	4037 to	5980	1943
July 1–31	5981 to	8107	2126
Aug. 1–31	8108 to	9840	1732
Sept. 1–30	9841 to	11148	1307
Oct. 1–31	11149 to	12405	1256
Nov. 1–30	12406 to	13132	726
Dec. 1–31	13133 to	14161	1028
1910			
Jan. 1–31	14162 to	15500	1338
Feb. 1–28	15501 to	16600	1099
Mar. 1–31	16601 to	19700	3099
Apr. 1–30	19701 to	23100	3399
May 1–31	23101 to	26500	3399
June 1–30	26501 to	29500	2999
July 1–31	29501 to	30200	699
Aug. 1–31	30201 to	31000	799
Sept. 1–30	31001 to	31900	899
Oct. 1–31	31901 to	32500	599
Nov. 1–30	32501 to	33700	1199

Date	Motor numbers		Cars built
Dec. 1–31	33701 to	34900	1199
1911			
Jan. 1–31	34901 to	37000	2099
Feb. 1–28	37001 to	40000	2999
Mar. 1–31	40001 to	45000	4999
Apr. 1–30	45001 to	50800	5799
May 1–31	50801 to	57200	6399
June 1–30	57201 to	60500	3299
July 1–31	60501 to	62100	1599
Aug. 1–31	62101 to	66700	4099
Sept. 1–30	66701 to	70500	3799
Oct. 1–31	70501 to	83100	12599
Nov. 1–30	83101 to	86300	3199
Dec. 1–31	86301 to	88900	2599
1912			
Jan. 1–31	88901 to	92000	3099
Feb. 1–29	92001 to	95900	3899
Mar. 1–31	95901 to	103800	7899
Apr. 1–30	103801 to	112900	9099
May 1–31	112901 to	123800	10899
June 1–30	123801 to	132000	8199
July 1–31	132001 to	139700	7699
Aug. 1–31	139701 to	144500	4799
Sept. 1–30	144501 to	147300	2799
Oct. 1–31	147301 to	156300	8999
Nov. 1–30	156301 to	161200	4899
Dec. 1–31	161201 to	171300	10099
1913			
Jan. 1–31	171301 to	186900	15599
Feb. 1–28	186901 to	203300	16399
Mar. 1–31	203301 to	218900	15599
Apr. 1–30	218901 to	242300	23399
May 1–31	242301 to	260000	17699
June 1–30	260001 to	282700	22699
July 1–31	282701 to	298200	5499
Aug. 1–31	298201 to	306800	8599
Sept. 1–30	306801 to	314800	7999
Oct. 1–31	314801 to	324900	10099
Nov. 1–30	324901 to	344900	19999
Dec. 1–31	344901 to	370400	25499
1914			
Jan. 1–31	370401 to	395500	25099
Feb. 1–28	395501 to	419500	23999
Mar. 1–31	419501 to	447600	28099
Apr. 1–30	447601 to	473200	25599
May 1–31	473201 to	490920	17719
June 1–30	490921 to	507102	16181
July 1–31	507103 to	517800	10697
Aug. 1–31	517801 to	538200	20399
Sept. 1–30	538201 to	558300	20099
Oct. 1–31	558301 to	583400	25099
Nov. 1–30	583401 to	599100	15699
Dec. 1–31	599101 to	611100	2099
1915			
Jan. 1–31	611101 to	614200	3099
Feb. 1–28	614201 to	630500	16299
Mar. 1–31	630501 to	682400	51899
Apr. 1–30	682401 to	723500	41099
May 1–31	723501 to	805500	81999
June 1–30	805501 to	839700	34199
July 1–31	839701 to	855500	15799
Aug. 1–31	855501 to	881000	2599
Sept. 1–30	881001 to	913000	31999
Oct. 1–31	913001 to	949000	35999
Nov. 1–30	949001 to	985400	35999
Dec. 1–31	985401 to	1029200	43799
1916			
Jan. 1–31	1029201 to	1071800	42599
Feb. 1–29	1071801 to	1119000	47199
Mar. 1–31	1119001 to	1167900	48899
Apr. 1–30	1167901 to	1219400	51499
May 1–31	1219401 to	1272000	52599
June 1–30	1272001 to	1326900	54899
July 1–31	1326901 to	1362213	35312
Aug. 1–31	1362214 to	1400900	38686
Sept. 1–30	1400901 to	1452200	51299
Oct. 1–31	1452201 to	1510500	58299
Nov. 1–30	1510501 to	1570700	60199
Dec. 1–31	1570701 to	1614600	43899
1917			
Jan. 1–31	1614601 to	1680000	65399
Feb. 1–28	1680001 to	1739900	49899
Mar. 1–31	1739901 to	1812000	72099
Apr. 1–30	1812001 to	1888000	75999
May 1–31	1888001 to	1968629	80628
June 1–30	1968630 to	2044100	75470
July 1–31	2044101 to	2113500	69399
Aug. 1–31	2113501 to	2162800	49299
Sept. 1–30	2162801 to	2231000	68199
Oct. 1–31	2231001 to	2310400	79399
Nov. 1–30	2310401 to	2383900	73499
Dec. 1–31	2383901 to	2449100	65199
1918			
Jan. 1–31	2449101 to	2503200	54099
Feb. 1–28	2503201 to	2558200	54999
Mar. 1–31	2558201 to	2611400	53199

Date	Motor numbers		Cars built	Date	Motor numbers		Cars built
Apr. 1–30	2611401 to	2657500	46099	**1922**			
May 1–31	2657501 to	2700800	43299	Jan. 1–31	5638072 to	5683808	45736
June 1–30	2700801 to	2735700	34899	Feb. 1–28	5683809 to	5737278	52469
July 1–31	2735701 to	2756251	55450	Mar. 1–31	5737279 to	5812608	75309
Aug. 1–31	2756252 to	2774600	18348	Apr. 1–30	5812609 to	5922968	110359
Sept. 1–30	2774601 to	2787800	13199	May 1–31	5922969 to	6058671	135702
Oct. 1–31	2787801 to	2792300	4499	June 1–30	6058672 to	6199796	141124
Nov. 1–30	2792301 to	2805100	12799	July 1–31	6199797 to	6334196	134399
Dec. 1–31	2805101 to	2831400	26299	Aug. 1–31	6334197 to	6473196	138999
				Sept. 1–30	6473197 to	6582724	109527
1919				Oct. 1–31	6582725 to	6713881	131156
				Nov. 1–30	6713882 to	6953071	239189
Jan. 1–31	2831401 to	2880170	48769				
Feb. 1–28	2880171 to	2933000	52829	**1923**			
Mar. 1–31	2933001 to	2997100	64099				
Apr. 1–30	2997101 to	3067700	70599	Jan. 1–31	6953072 to	7084225	131153
May 1–31	3067701 to	3140000	72299	Feb. 1–28	7084226 to	7217971	133745
June 1–30	3140001 to	3210800	70799	Mar. 1–31	7217972 to	7386112	168140
July 1–31	3210801 to	3277850	67049	Apr. 1–30	7386113 to	7564111	177998
Aug. 1–31	3277851 to	3346900	69049	May 1–31	7564112 to	7738372	174260
Sept. 1–30	3346901 to	3429400	82499	June 1–30	7738373 to	7927374	189001
Oct. 1–31	3429401 to	3515430	86029	July 1–31	7927375 to	8122674	195299
Nov. 1–30	3515431 to	3588000	72569	Aug. 1–31	8122675 to	8311581	188906
Dec. 1–31	3588001 to	3659970	71969	Sept. 1–30	8311582 to	8477681	166099
				Oct. 1–31	8477682 to	8664281	186599
1920				Nov. 1–30	8664282 to	8843065	178783
				Dec. 1–31	8843066 to	9008381	165315
Jan. 1–31	3659971 to	3743075	83104				
Feb. 1–29	3743076 to	3817430	74354	**1924**			
Mar. 1–31	3817431 to	3910000	92569				
Apr. 1–30	3910001 to	3969150	59149	Jan. 1–31	9008382 to	9232671	224289
May 1–31	3969151 to	4055280	86129	Feb. 1–29	9232672 to	9427721	195049
June 1–30	4055281 to	4141450	86169	Mar. 1–31	9427722 to	9622521	194799
July 1–31	4141451 to	4233350	91899	Apr. 1–30	9622522 to	9814521	191999
Aug. 1–31	4233351 to	4329900	96549	May 1–31	9814522 to	9984771	170249
Sept. 1–30	4329901 to	4426385	96484	June 1–30	9984772 to	10126471	141699
Oct. 1–31	4426386 to	4526540	100154	July 1–31	10126472 to	10266471	139999
Nov. 1–30	4526541 to	4617925	91384	Aug. 1–31	10266472 to	10404821	138349
Dec. 1–31	4617926 to	4698420	80584	Sept. 1–30	10404822 to	10560821	155999
				Oct. 1–31	10560822 to	10734504	172683
1921				Nov. 1–30	10734505 to	10886259	151754
				Dec. 1–31	10886260 to	10999901	113641
Jan. 1–31	None						
Feb. 1–28	4698421 to	4736431	38010	**1925**			
Mar. 1–31	4736432 to	4810010	73578				
Apr. 1–30	4810011 to	4907500	97489	Jan. 1–31	10999902 to	11135308	135406
May 1–31	4907501 to	5008000	100499	Feb. 1–28	11135309 to	11302019	166710
June 1–30	5008001 to	5114530	106529	Mar. 1–31	11302020 to	11477655	175635
July 1–31	5114531 to	5223135	108604	Apr. 1–30	11477656 to	11688647	210991
Aug. 1–31	5223136 to	5337545	114409	May 1–31	11688648 to	11869207	180559
Sept. 1–30	5337546 to	5447816	110270	June 1–30	11869208 to	12052486	183278
Oct. 1–31	5447817 to	5529519	81702	July 1–31	12052487 to	12222528	160041
Nov. 1–30	5529520 to	5602301	72781	Aug. 1–31	12222529 to	12290760	68231
Dec. 1–31	5602302 to	5638071	35769	Sept. 1–30	12290761 to	12399496	108735

Date	Motor numbers	Cars built	Date	Motor numbers	Cars built
Oct. 1–31	12399497 to 12621501	222004	Oct. 1–31	14331153 to 14472253	141100
Nov. 1–30	12621502 to 12823126	201624	Nov. 1–30	14472254 to 14577135	104881
Dec. 1–31	12823127 to 12990055	166928	Dec. 1–31	14577136 to 14619254	42118
1926			**1927**		
Jan. 1–31	12990056 to 13138675	148619	Jan. 1–31	14619255 to 14623502	4247
Feb. 1–28	13138676 to 13286289	147613	Feb. 1–28	14623503 to 14762945	139442
Mar. 1–31	13286290 to 13454890	168600	Mar. 1–31	14762946 to 14851445	88499
Apr. 1–30	13454891 to 13619705	164814	Apr. 1–30	14851446 to 14927495	76049
May 1–31	13619706 to 13769814	150108	May 1–31	14927496 to 15007033	72504
June 1–30	13769815 to 13912754	142939			
July 1–31	13912755 to 14049029	136274			
Aug. 1–31	14049030 to 14194489	145459			
Sept. 1–30	14194490 to 14331152	136662			

Here ended the production of Model T.

Fig. 24. 1926 Sport Runabout. The T Sport Runabout of 1926 with split windshield and folding top, rear tire, and no bumpers. Twenty horses stood under the hood, awaiting your slightest command.

4. The Model T in Diagram

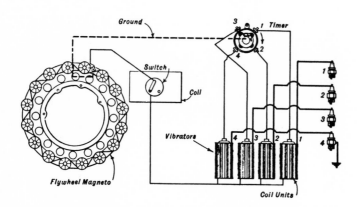

Many a car owner today isn't sure just what is under his hood. Though regrettable, this is partly understandable, as our modern automobile has become a very complicated mechanism. But in the years between 1908 and 1927, many Model T owners knew what made their flivvers tick. They knew the various critical points for lubrication; they could check the oil supply; they could remove a connecting rod (and understood what it connected—piston and crankshaft); they could clean the carbon deposit from a valve and distinguish between the different kinds of knocks.

Model T advertisements and manuals claimed that this was "the simplest of all cars." Most of the ordinary adjustments an owner could soon learn to make for himself. On this and the following ten pages are twenty-eight simple diagrams from which thousands of Model T owners learned what went on under the hood and elsewhere.

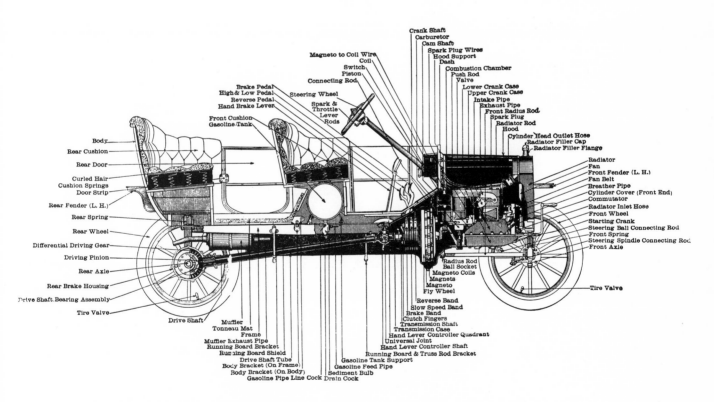

Sectional view of Ford Model T Touring Car showing construction of chassis and body parts

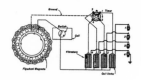

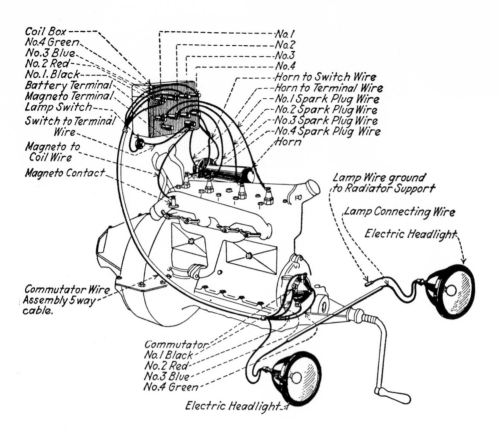

Coil Box
No.4 Green
No.3 Blue
No.2 Red
No.1 Black
Battery Terminal
Magneto Terminal
Lamp Switch
Switch to Terminal Wire
Magneto to Coil Wire
Magneto Contact

No.1
No.2
No.3
No.4
Horn to Switch Wire
Horn to Terminal Wire
No.1 Spark Plug Wire
No.2 Spark Plug Wire
No.3 Spark Plug Wire
No.4 Spark Plug Wire
Horn

Lamp Wire ground to Radiator Support
Lamp Connecting Wire
Electric Headlight

Commutator Wire Assembly 5 way cable.

Commutator
No.1 Black
No.2 Red
No.3 Blue
No.4 Green

Electric Headlight

How lamps are wired when current from ignition magneto is taken for bulbs

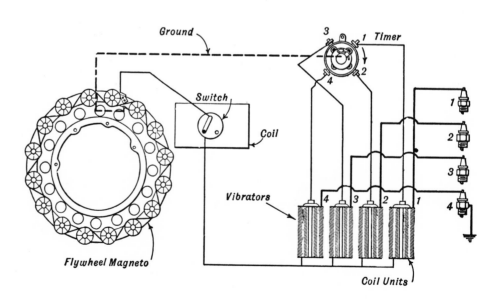

Ground
Switch
Coil
3 1 Timer
4 2
1
2
3
4
Vibrators
Flywheel Magneto
4 3 2 1
Coil Units

Wiring diagram showing method of connecting parts of the Ford ignition system

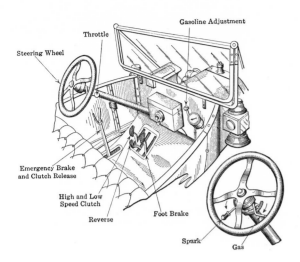

The control system of the Ford Model T Car

Top view of the Ford steering gear at A showing steering wheel and spark and throttle levers. Planetary reduction gearing is depicted at B, which shows gear compartment with cover removed.

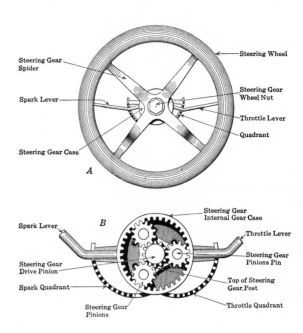

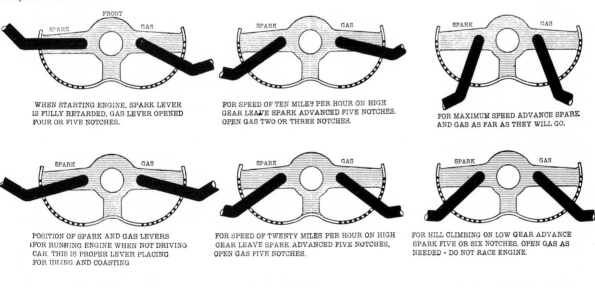

WHEN STARTING ENGINE, SPARK LEVER IS FULLY RETARDED, GAS LEVER OPENED FOUR OR FIVE NOTCHES.

FOR SPEED OF TEN MILES PER HOUR ON HIGH GEAR LEAVE SPARK ADVANCED FIVE NOTCHES. OPEN GAS TWO OR THREE NOTCHES.

FOR MAXIMUM SPEED ADVANCE SPARK AND GAS AS FAR AS THEY WILL GO.

POSITION OF SPARK AND GAS LEVERS FOR RUNNING ENGINE WHEN NOT DRIVING CAR. THIS IS PROPER LEVER PLACING FOR IDLING AND COASTING

FOR SPEED OF TWENTY MILES PER HOUR ON HIGH GEAR LEAVE SPARK ADVANCED FIVE NOTCHES. OPEN GAS FIVE NOTCHES.

FOR HILL CLIMBING ON LOW GEAR ADVANCE SPARK FIVE OR SIX NOTCHES. OPEN GAS AS NEEDED - DO NOT RACE ENGINE.

FOR STARTING CAR ON LOW SPEED ADVANCE SPARK FIVE NOTCHES. OPEN GAS LEVER FOUR OR FIVE NOTCHES.

FOR SPEED OF THIRTY MILES PER HOUR ADVANCE SPARK SEVEN NOTCHES. OPEN GAS SEVEN OR EIGHT NOTCHES.

FOR HILL CLIMBING ON HIGH GEAR RETARD SPARK SO IT WILL BE ADVANCED ONLY TWO OR THREE NOTCHES. OPEN GAS TO EXTREME. AS SOON AS ENGINE BEGINS TO LABOR -PUT IN LOW SPEED AND SET LEVERS AS ABOVE.

Chart showing positions of spark and throttle levers on steering-post quadrants for various conditions of car operation. These are the average positions and may vary slightly on different Ford cars.

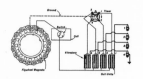

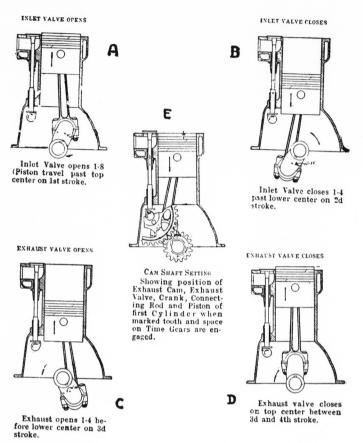

INLET VALVE OPENS

A

Inlet Valve opens 1-8 (Piston travel past top center on 1st stroke.

INLET VALVE CLOSES

B

Inlet Valve closes 1-4 past lower center on 2d stroke.

E

CAM SHAFT SETTING
Showing position of Exhaust Cam, Exhaust Valve, Crank, Connecting Rod and Piston of first Cylinder when marked tooth and space on Time Gears are engaged.

EXHAUST VALVE OPENS

C

Exhaust opens 1-4 before lower center on 3d stroke.

EXHAUST VALVE CLOSES

D

Exhaust valve closes on top center between 3d and 4th stroke.

Diagram showing method of timing Ford valves

Henry's Model T engine was simple in design, economical to operate, and easy to work on, although special tools were required for some operations. Partly sectional view of the Ford four-cylinder unit power plant showing important parts of the power generating and transmission system.

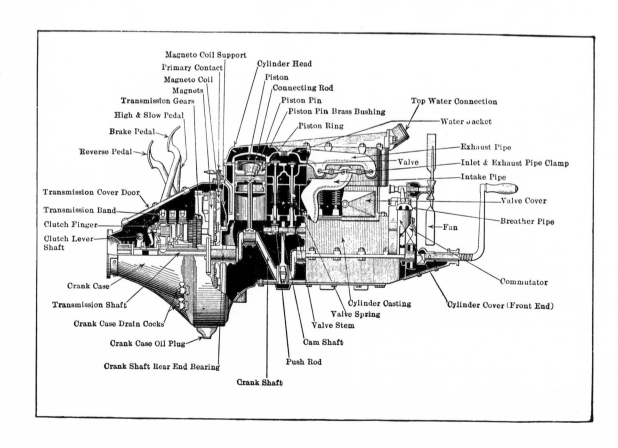

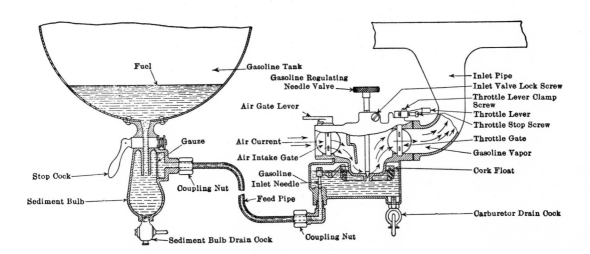

Fuel

Gasoline Tank

Gasoline Regulating Needle Valve

Air Gate Lever

Gauze

Stop Cock

Sediment Bulb

Coupling Nut

Air Current

Air Intake Gate

Gasoline Inlet Needle

Feed Pipe

Sediment Bulb Drain Cock

Coupling Nut

Inlet Pipe

Inlet Valve Lock Screw

Throttle Lever Clamp Screw

Throttle Lever

Throttle Stop Screw

Throttle Gate

Gasoline Vapor

Cork Float

Carburetor Drain Cock

The Model T required no fuel pump or vacuum tank. The gasoline tank was mounted under the seat and gas flowed easily to the carburetor, which was located below the level of the tank. Sometimes this arrangement caused difficulty in climbing steep hills, as the carburetor would run out of gasoline before the top of the hill was reached. Above, a diagram of the Ford Model T fuel-supply and gas-making system.

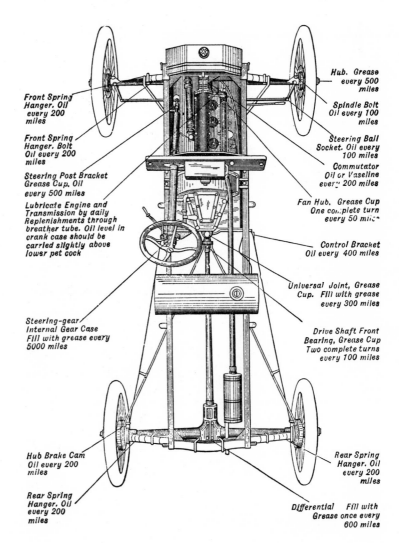

Front Spring Hanger. Oil every 200 miles

Front Spring Hanger. Bolt Oil every 200 miles

Steering Post Bracket Grease Cup. Oil every 500 miles

Lubricate Engine and Transmission by daily Replenishments through breather tube. Oil level in crank case should be carried slightly above lower pet cock

Steering-gear Internal Gear Case Fill with grease every 5000 miles

Hub Brake Cam Oil every 200 miles

Rear Spring Hanger. Oil every 200 miles

Hub. Grease every 500 miles

Spindle Bolt Oil every 100 miles

Steering Ball Socket. Oil every 100 miles

Commutator Oil or Vaseline every 200 miles

Fan Hub. Grease Cup One complete turn every 50 miles

Control Bracket Oil every 400 miles

Universal Joint, Grease Cup. Fill with grease every 300 miles

Drive Shaft Front Bearing, Grease Cup Two complete turns every 100 miles

Rear Spring Hanger. Oil every 200 miles

Differential Fill with Grease once every 600 miles

Plan view of Ford Model T chassis showing important points requiring lubrication and showing when this attention is needed

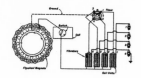

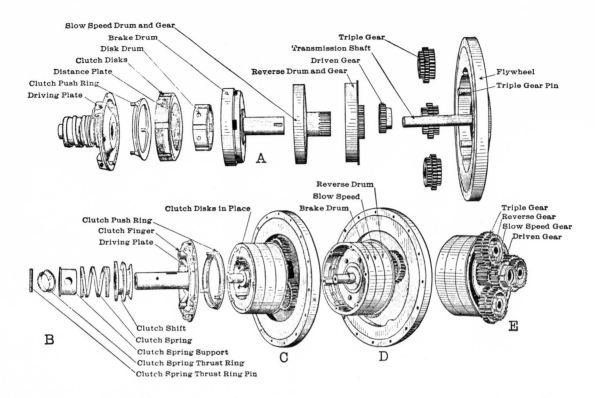

Labels on figure A: Slow Speed Drum and Gear · Brake Drum · Disk Drum · Clutch Disks · Distance Plate · Clutch Push Ring · Driving Plate · Triple Gear · Transmission Shaft · Driven Gear · Reverse Drum and Gear · Flywheel · Triple Gear Pin

Labels on figure B: Clutch Disks in Place · Clutch Push Ring · Clutch Finger · Driving Plate · Clutch Shift · Clutch Spring · Clutch Spring Support · Clutch Spring Thrust Ring · Clutch Spring Thrust Ring Pin

Labels on figures C, D, E: Reverse Drum · Slow Speed · Brake Drum · Triple Gear · Reverse Gear · Slow Speed Gear · Driven Gear

Exploded view showing parts comprising the Ford transmission when disassembled at A, and when joined together to form various groups to facilitate assembly at C, D, and E

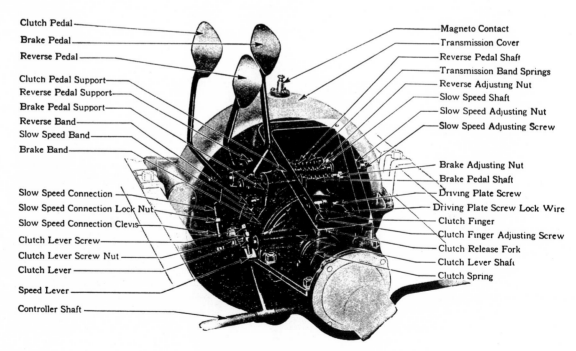

Labels: Clutch Pedal · Brake Pedal · Reverse Pedal · Clutch Pedal Support · Reverse Pedal Support · Brake Pedal Support · Reverse Band · Slow Speed Band · Brake Band · Slow Speed Connection · Slow Speed Connection Lock Nut · Slow Speed Connection Clevis · Clutch Lever Screw · Clutch Lever Screw Nut · Clutch Lever · Speed Lever · Controller Shaft · Magneto Contact · Transmission Cover · Reverse Pedal Shaft · Transmission Band Springs · Reverse Adjusting Nut · Slow Speed Shaft · Slow Speed Adjusting Nut · Slow Speed Adjusting Screw · Brake Adjusting Nut · Brake Pedal Shaft · Driving Plate Screw · Driving Plate Screw Lock Wire · Clutch Finger · Clutch Finger Adjusting Screw · Clutch Release Fork · Clutch Lever Shaft · Clutch Spring

The above drawing of transmission shows clearly the operation of clutch, reverse, and brake pedals.

View of Ford power plant showing main parts of the Ford ignition system. Note location of timer and induction-coil box.

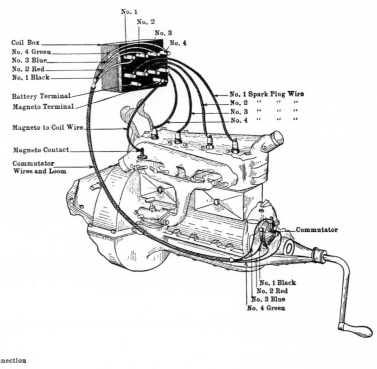

No. 1
No. 2
No. 3
No. 4

Coil Box
No. 4 Green
No. 3 Blue
No. 2 Red
No. 1 Black

Battery Terminal
Magneto Terminal

Magneto to Coil Wire

Magneto Contact

Commutator Wires and Loom

No. 1 Spark Plug Wire
No. 2 "   "   "
No. 3 "   "   "
No. 4 "   "   "

Commutator

No. 1 Black
No. 2 Red
No. 3 Blue
No. 4 Green

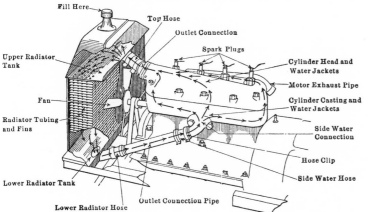

Fill Here
Top Hose
Outlet Connection

Spark Plugs

Cylinder Head and Water Jackets

Motor Exhaust Pipe

Cylinder Casting and Water Jackets

Side Water Connection

Hose Clip

Side Water Hose

Upper Radiator Tank

Fan

Radiator Tubing and Fins

Lower Radiator Tank

Lower Radiator Hose

Outlet Connection Pipe

The Ford thermo-syphon water-cooling system

Diagram showing the relation of the pistons and crankshaft throws of the Ford four-cylinder motor when piston No. 1 is about to receive the force of gas exploded in the combustion chamber.

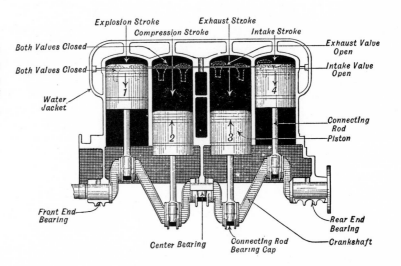

Explosion Stroke
Exhaust Stroke
Compression Stroke
Intake Stroke

Both Valves Closed

Both Valves Closed

Exhaust Valve Open

Intake Valve Open

Water Jacket

Connecting Rod
Piston

Front End Bearing

Center Bearing

Connecting Rod Bearing Cap

Rear End Bearing

Crankshaft

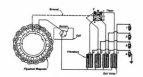

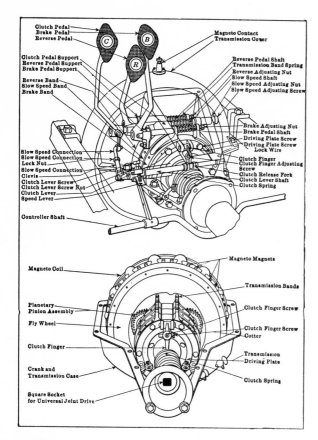

Phantom view of the Ford planetary gearset showing the control-pedal assembly at top. View of gearing partially disassembled showing brake bands and other parts at the bottom.

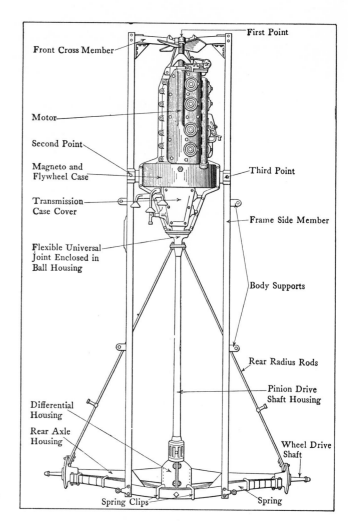

Plan view of Ford frame with power plant and rear axle in place, showing three-point-suspension principle ultilized in this design

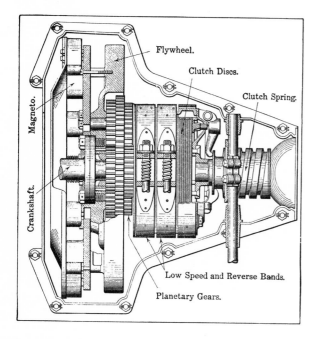

Plan view of the Ford planetary gearing showing method of carrying triple planetary spur pinion assemblies and actuating the high-speed disk clutch assembly (left)

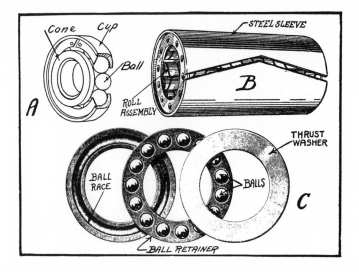

Types of antifriction bearings used in the Ford car. A. Cup-and-cone-type angular contact ball bearings similar to those used in the front wheels. B. Hyatt flexible roller bearing. C. Special ball bearings for resisting end thrust only.

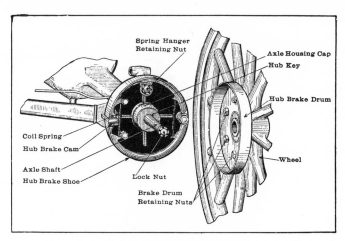

End view of Ford rear axle with wheel removed to show emergency-brake construction

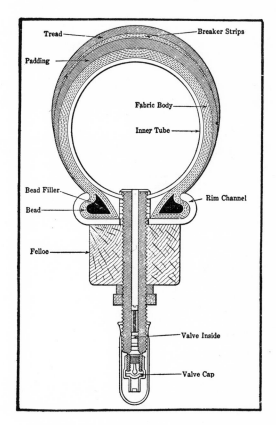

Sectional view of standard clincher double-tube pneumatic tire such as was used on Ford cars

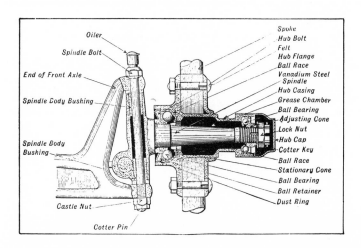

Sectional view of Ford front-wheel hub showing method of installing cup-and-cone-type ball bearings

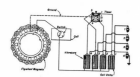

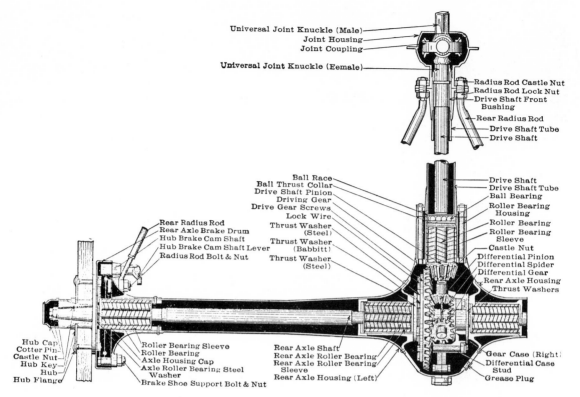

Universal Joint Knuckle (Male)
Joint Housing
Joint Coupling
Universal Joint Knuckle (Eemale)

Radius Rod Castle Nut
Radius Rod Lock Nut
Drive Shaft Front Bushing
Rear Radius Rod
Drive Shaft Tube
Drive Shaft

Ball Race
Ball Thrust Collar
Drive Shaft Pinion
Driving Gear
Drive Gear Screws
Lock Wire
Thrust Washer (Steel)
Thrust Washer (Babbitt)
Thrust Washer (Steel)

Drive Shaft
Drive Shaft Tube
Ball Bearing
Roller Bearing Housing
Roller Bearing
Roller Bearing Sleeve
Castle Nut
Differential Pinion
Differential Spider
Differential Gear
Rear Axle Housing
Thrust Washers

Rear Radius Rod
Rear Axle Brake Drum
Hub Brake Cam Shaft
Hub Brake Cam Shaft Lever
Radius Rod Bolt & Nut

Hub Cap
Cotter Pin
Castle Nut
Hub Key
Hub
Hub Flange

Roller Bearing Sleeve
Roller Bearing
Axle Housing Cap
Axle Roller Bearing Steel Washer
Brake Shoe Support Bolt & Nut

Rear Axle Shaft
Rear Axle Roller Bearing
Rear Axle Roller Bearing Sleeve
Rear Axle Housing (Left)

Gear Case (Right)
Differential Case Stud
Grease Plug

Sectional view of Ford Model T rear axle showing driving gears, differential, power-transmission shafts and supporting bearings. This simplicity of construction is still the envy of the auto world.

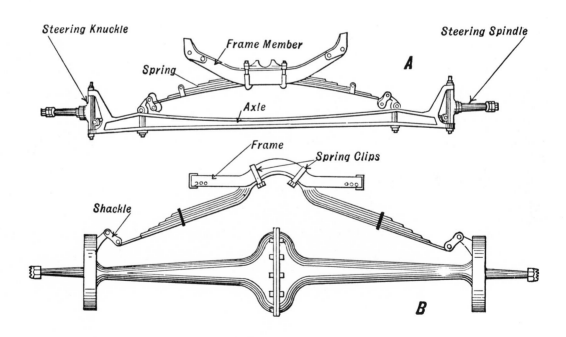

Steering Knuckle
Frame Member
Steering Spindle
Spring
Axle
A

Frame
Spring Clips
Shackle
B

Outline of method of Ford front- and rear-spring retention

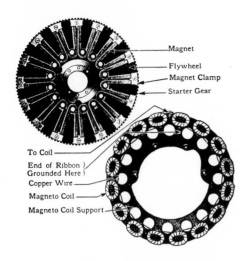

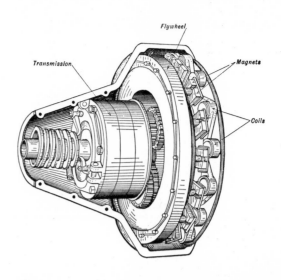

The Ford magneto. The flywheel with magnets revolves while magneto coils remain stationary.

Showing coils and magnet that comprise the Ford magneto and their relation to the flywheel and transmission gear

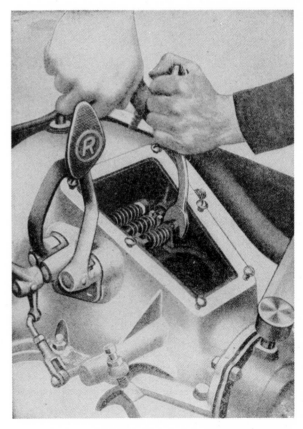

The first step in removing the Ford engine from the chassis is to take the radiator from the front of the frame.

Method of adjusting transmission brake band

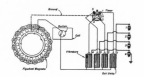

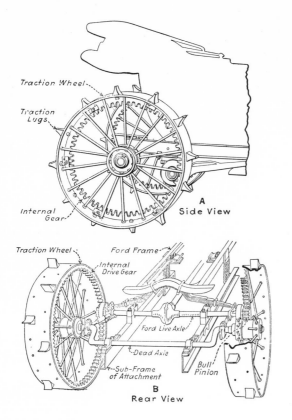

Traction Wheel

Traction Lugs

Internal Gear

A
Side View

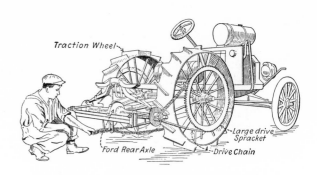

Traction Wheel

Ford Rear Axle

Large drive Sprocket

Drive Chain

The Acason chain-drive tractor attachment

Traction Wheel

Ford Frame

Internal Drive Gear

Ford Live Axle

Dead Axle

Sub-Frame of Attachment

Bull Pinion

B
Rear View

The Make-a-Tractor attachment for Ford cars

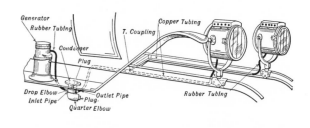

Generator

Rubber Tubing

Condenser

Plug

Copper Tubing

T. Coupling

Drop Elbow
Inlet Pipe

Plug
Quarter Elbow

Outlet Pipe

Rubber Tubing

Acetylene-gas lighting system similar to that used for Ford lights on 1910 to 1914 models

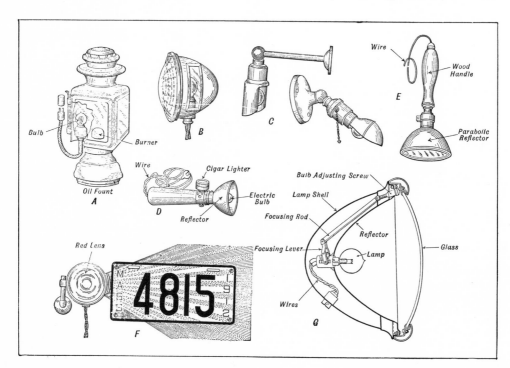

Bulb

Burner

Oil Fount

A

Wire

Cigar Lighter

Electric Bulb

Reflector

D

B

C

Wire

Wood Handle

E

Parabolic Reflector

Red Lens

4815

F

Bulb Adjusting Screw

Lamp Shell

Focusing Rod

Focusing Lever

Reflector

Glass

Lamp

Wires

G

In 1915, the year of the big changeover, owners of the older Model T cars were offered units to convert the kerosene dash lamps and gas head lamps to electricity. Above are some electric lamps and fixtures.

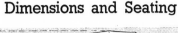 Christmas Road Test No. 19/51

Makers: Ford Motor Co. (England) Ltd., Trafford Park, Manchester.
(Test car submitted by Dagenham Motors, Ltd., 56, Park Lane, London, W.I)
Make: Ford.   **Type:** Model T (1912) 2-seater Runabout.

Dimensions and Seating

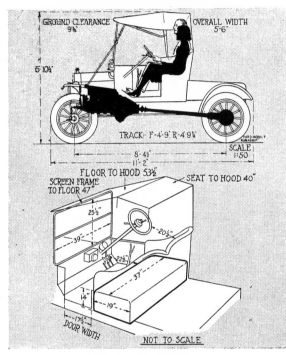

In Brief

Price, in 1912, £135 (inclusive of hood and windscreen).

Capacity	.. ..	2,890 c.c.
Unladen kerb weight	..	13¾ cwt.
Fuel consumption	..	28.5 m.p.g.
Maximum speed	..	42 m.p.h.
Maximum speed on 1 in 20 gradient	.. ..	35 m.p.h.
Maximum top gear gradient		1 in 11.1

Acceleration
10-30 m.p.h. in top .. 12.8 secs.
0-40 m.p.h. through gears 35.8 secs.

Gearing 24.5 m.p.h. in top at 1,000 r.p.m.
92 m.p.h. at 2,500 ft. per min. piston speed.

Specification

Engine

Cylinders		4
Bore	..	95 mm.
Stroke	..	101.5 mm.
Cubic capacity	..	2,890 c.c.
Piston area	..	44 sq. in.
Valves	..	Side
Max. power	..	approx. 20 b.h.p.
at		approx. 1,800 r.p.m.
Piston speed at max. b.h.p.		approx. 1,200 ft. per min.
Carburetter	..	Holley (updraught choke)
Ignition	..	Flywheel magneto (trembler coils for starting)
Fuel feed	..	By gravity from tank under seat
Oil circulation	..	By splash from flywheel

Transmission

Clutch	..	Multiple steel disc
High gear (direct)	..	3.64
Low gear (epicyclic)	..	10.0
Reverse gear (epicyclic)	..	14.5
Propeller shaft	..	Enclosed in torque tube
Final drive	..	Bevel

Chassis

Brakes		Foot, enclosed band brake on transmission; hand, internal expanding brakes on rear wheels
Suspension front	..	Transverse leaf
rear	..	Transverse leaf
Shock absorbers	..	Nil
Tyres	..	B.T.R., 765×105

Steering

Steering gear	..	Epicyclic
Turning circle	..	37 ft.
Turns of steering wheel, lock to lock	..	1¼

Performance factors (at laden weight as tested)

Piston area, sq. in. per ton	..	52.5
Specific displacement, litres per ton mile		4,230

Described in "The Motor," November 9, 1911.

Test Conditions

Cold, damp weather, stiff breeze, smooth tarmac surface, Pool petrol.
Windscreen fully erect during tests.

Test Data

ACCELERATION TIMES on Two Ratios

	High	Low
10-30 m.p.h.	12.8 secs.	—
20-40 m.p.h.	31.5 secs.	—

ACCELERATION TIMES Through Gears

0-20 m.p.h.	8.5 secs.
0-30 m.p.h.	15.3 secs.
0-40 m.p.h.	35.8 secs.
Standing Quarter Mile	32.9 secs.

MAXIMUM SPEEDS

Mean maximum speed in high gear approx. 42 m.p.h.
Max. speed in low gear .. 16 m.p.h.

WEIGHT

Unladen kerb weight	13¾ cwt.
Front/rear weight distribution ..	49/51
Weight laden as tested	16¾ cwt.

FUEL CONSUMPTION

35.0 m.p.g. at constant 20 m.p.h.	
32.0 m.p.g. at constant 30 m.p.h.	
Overall consumption	28.5 m.p.g.

INSTRUMENTS

Speedometer at 30 m.p.h. ..	16% fast
Distance recorder	3% slow

HILL CLIMBING (at steady speeds)

Max. high gear speed on 1 in 20	35 m.p.h.
Max. high gear speed on 1 in 15	32 m.p.h.
Max. gradient on high gear	1 in 11.1 (Tapley 200 lb./ton)

BRAKES at 30 m.p.h.

0.41g retardation (=73 ft. stopping distance) with 50 lb. pedal pressure

Maintenance

Fuel tank : 8 gallons. **Sump (engine and gearbox) :** 6-8 pints, approx. S.A.E. 20 (NOT graphited, to avoid shorting flywheel magneto). **Rear axle :** Fill every 500 miles with grease (in extremely cold weather, use heavy oil). **Steering Gear :** Grease every 5,000 miles. **Radiator :** 3 gallons (drain tap). **Chassis Lubrication :** Apply oilcan to 12 oilers, and screw down 6 grease cups one turn, every 200 miles. **Front hubs :** Re-grease every 500 miles. **Ignition :** Clean and re-oil commutator every 500 miles. **Spark plug gap :** 1/32 in. **Tappet clearances (cold) :** Inlet and exhaust 1/32 in. **Front wheel toe-in :** Nil. **Tyre pressures :** Front and rear, 55 lb.

Ref. U.S-B/29/12-51.

Motor Magazine *in England tested a 1912 English-built T in 1951 against a background of modern road conditions and arrived at the information above. One* *of their conclusions: "The T is in some respects still modern."*

5. Model T Ads

Some extraordinary inventions and contributions to civilization are not recognized as such until years after their birth. Such was not the case with Henry's Model T. It is reliably reported that in March of 1908, when the first circulars announcing the Model T went out to Ford dealers, many of them reacted as if they knew full well that they were participating in a great event. One dealer complained that it was a mistake to send out circulars so far in advance of the delivery of the cars because customers would certainly become dangerously impatient. Another wrote back that the circular alone "will flood the factory with orders," and a third carefully locked his circulars in a drawer in order not to be besieged by buyers.

For nineteen years after this auspicious launching, Model T advertisement writers continued to reach an ever growing market with news of their improving product. On the following pages are reproduced some of the more memorable ads for the T, from the initial 1908 advertisement for the $850 four-cylinder Touring Car to the 1926 Runabout which sold for the astonishingly low price of $260.

FORD Four Cylinder Touring Car $850.00

WHEN you can couple the Ford guarantee — the guarantee of the best known automobile manufacturer in the world, whose imprint is already on more good cars than any other concern has made or promised with the Lowest price ever announced for a Touring Car, it's a mighty safe buy.

1908

MODEL T TOURING CAR. $850.00
High Priced Quality in a Low Priced Car

Here is the first and only chance ever offered to secure a touring car at a reasonable price, a price any man can afford to pay. It is a big, roomy, powerful car of handsome appearance and finish, at a price lower than you are asked to pay for any 4 cylinder runabout excepting the "FAMOUS FORD." This car sounds the death knell of high prices and big profits.

When this now famous FORD runabout was announced, other manufacturers, despairing of being able to compete, knocked—"A good car could not be built at the price, much less sold." Every knock was a boost. With twenty thousand cars Ford proved the car was right. Ford's financial standing to-day proves the price was right. And the knocking that will be done on this new car will be silenced in the same fashion.

Henry Ford promised three years ago to build a high grade touring car and sell it at a heretofore unheard-of price and now, just as surely as every claim made for the small car was made good, just so surely has Ford made good this promise.

The Model T is that car, the car that was promised, a four cylinder, twenty horse-power touring car—a roomy, commodious, comfortable family car, that looks good and is as good as it looks.

This is no imitation car. Henry Ford has never found the need to copy, and the fact that he has never designed a failure is your security that in the Model T touring car Ford continues to be two years ahead of any car manufactured to-day.

We have no high-sounding names with which to charm sales. It's the same old name, "plain as any name could be;" it's just "FORD" but it has the advantage of being already on twenty thousand cars (real automobiles) that have "Delivered the Goods."

You know that Henry Ford can build a better car for less money than any other manufacturer on the face of the earth. You know it because he has always done it, and that is your guarantee of his ability and your security in dealing with him.

Our organization is made up of that same force of men that you have learned to know as being connected with the manufacture and sale of an honest product. It's the same old Company that has been doing business right along; the same old successful organization and plant.

Not having anything new but the car; and, because it is unnecessary for us to spend money to solicit confidences in our Company (that being already secured by past performances), we can devote all our time and money to taking care of the orders for the car that people have actually been waiting for—a family car at an honest price

The Model T is a four cylinder, twenty horse-power car of graceful design, powerful in appearance and reality and of sturdy construction. It is not a new car in the sense that it has been conceived, designed and built all in a few weeks. Mr. Ford started on the car three years ago. Two years were spent in designing, experimenting and research. A year ago the first cars were shown and for twelve months have been in constant service.

These experimental cars have been run under every conceivable condition. All last winter they were tried on the snow and slush covered country roads—all summer they have worked on the hills, on the sand and mud roads, in good and bad weather.

It is a new car, however, in the sense that it is not an old chassis with a new body or an old engine in a new chassis, but it is a new car built throughout to meet the requirements of a family car. The engine is new (twenty horse-power), cylinders, pistons, valves, etc., are get-at-able. The chassis is new, a hundred inch wheel base and thirty inch wheels. The transmission is of new design (planetary, of course) and altogether silent. $150,000.00 worth of new machinery and tools were added before we could start to build.

Vanadium steel, the strongest, toughest and most enduring steel ever manufactured, is used throughout the entire car. The only reason every automobile manufacturer is not using Vanadium steel is either that they cannot afford to or do not know how. To use it in Fords required two years of experimenting and an expenditure of two hundred thousand dollars, plus the increased price of steel.

FORD—THE CAR THAT LASTS LONGEST

Ford Motor Company

254 Piquette Ave., DETROIT, U. S. A.   "Standard Manufacturers, A. M. C. M. A."

NEW YORK CITY   BOSTON   PHILADELPHIA   BUFFALO   CLEVELAND   CHICAGO
ST. LOUIS   KANSAS CITY   DENVER   SEATTLE   PARIS   LONDON
CANADIAN TRADE SUPPLIED BY FORD MOTOR CO., LTD., WALKERVILLE BRANCH AT TORONTO

HIGH PRICED QUALITY
IN A LOW PRICED CAR

Buying a "Ford" is Automobile

If prestige, if reputation, if experience, if past performance counts for anything, can serve in any way as an aid to a selection in automobile buying, then the purchaser of a Ford Car can feel amply protected, and have the assurance that no matter how much of a risk the buying of some cars involves, every element of chance is removed when Ford secures the decision.

The same old Ford Motor Company has been manufacturing Ford Cars designed by Henry Ford, since the very earliest days of the industry. The first automobile ever seen in Detroit was a Ford; one of the first half dozen built in America was designed and built by Ford; 40,000 Ford Cars have since been built, and all have made good. There never was a Ford failure—there never was an unfilled Ford promise, and the years have built up a reputation for Ford that it would be folly to risk at this late date.

Did you ever stop to think how short lived has always been the success of an inferior product? Enormous advertising expenditures could not keep it going Why, the very fact that the output of the Ford factory has doubled each year of the seven of its existence is the strongest proof of the superiority of the product. Price never built up a successful anything. Quality and merit is back of every venture that ever made good.

And Ford has made good. There isn't a town in America, there is hardly a town, and certainly not a country in Europe, Asia Africa or Australia where Ford Cars are not in use, and bringing credit upon the maker. In 1909 the Ford Motor Company sold $11,000,000.00 worth of cars, and already for 1910 $16,000,-000.00 worth have been contracted for by dealers There's the proof that the car has made good.

Ford does not want sales that are made only because of price. Ford wants the sales to be gotten in a competition of quality. Buy a Ford Car because it is a better car, not because it is cheaper. Buy it because the name, Ford, means merit, and has meant merit more years than ninety-nine per cent of the manufacturers of automobiles have been in business. Ford owners are praising their cars, because of their high quality, not their low price.

254 PIQUETTE AVENUE, DETROIT, U. S. A.

Send for Catalog E
Now Ready

Ford Motor Company

By 1910, the Model T was well established in the minds of American automobilists. The tone of

HIGH PRICED QUALITY
IN A LOW PRICED CAR

Buying with the Risk Cut Out

Buy a Ford Car, because when you do, you are in the forefront of automobile advancement. A Ford Car is years ahead of every other car offered at this time   1906 saw the $500 Ford four cylinder runabout — 1910 finds a score of imitators; 1903 saw Ford insisting on light weight — 1910 sees the majority in line; 1910 sees a number of Ford features that will be widely copied by 1912. And it is just so with almost every advance of the last decade in automobile design. The Ford owner has had it first.

If the price is not the result of inferiority, what is it ? It is the result of a combination of many items. Here are a few of them — immense volume and smaller profits, the division of profits into fewer parts, the absence of entangling alliances, the one profit per sale in place of several, the development of inextravagant manufacturing methods, efficient sales, organization and conservative advertising campaigns. These are the things that make the Ford price low, for the Ford Motor Company makes a very satisfactory profit on every car it builds.

The Ford price has, however, made it possible for thousands to buy who never could have bought an automobile otherwise. Not only has it made Ford sales, but it has forced the prices of other cars down to a figure where one hundred men could buy in place of one, had there never been a Ford. But the Ford price has ever been subordinated to quality, a fact that has built up sales, and so made possible a still lower price.

Summary of Specifications for 1910

Brakes—Two sets.
Clutch—Multiple steel discs, operating in oil.
Control—All speeds forward and reverse by foot pedals. Spark and throttle under steering wheel.
Cooling—Thermo syphon and fan.
Final Drive—By carbon shaft with single universal joint to bevel drive gears in live rear axle.
Ignition—Ford magneto generator.
Interchangeable Bodies.
Lubrication—Combination splash and gravity system.
Motor — 4-cylinder, 4-cycle, 20 h. p., 3¾-inch bore, 4-inch stroke.   Cylinders cast in one block with water jackets and upper half of crank case integral, water jacketed cylinder head detachable, fine grain gray iron castings.
Prices— Touring car, $950; roadster, $900; tourabout, $950, with full equipment; coupe, $1050; town car, $1200, f. o. b. Detroit.
Transmission—New design Ford spur planetary, bathed in oil — all gears from heat-treated Vanadium steel, silent and easy in action.
Wheel Base—100 inches; tread 56 inches; 60 inches for southern roads, where ordered.
Equipment—The touring car, tourabout and roadster include at the prices shown, an extension top; an automatic brass windshield; a speedometer; two 6-inch gas lamps and generator; three oil lamps and a tubular horn.   The coupe and town car include three oil lamps and horn.

254 PIQUETTE AVENUE, DETROIT, U. S. A.

See our exhibit at the Palace Show, New York, Dec. 31 Jan. 7

Ford Motor Company

this advertisement, pointing to $11,000,000 worth of Fords sold in 1909, is nothing if not confident.

In the Ford Times of September, 1913, some clever adman compared the weight and power of the Model T to that of poor old Dobbin, a comparison favorable to the flivver, of course.

OLD Dobbin, the family coach horse, weighs more than a Ford car.

But—

He has only one-twentieth the strength of a Ford car—cannot go as fast nor as far—costs more to maintain—and almost as much to acquire.

In 1911, Ford put out five models—the Torpedo Runabout for $590, the Commercial Roadster for $590, the Touring Car for $690, the Delivery Car for $700, and the Town Car for $900.

Demand for Ford Cars Doubles Annually

1911

100,000 Ford Cars Are in Service Now

Model T Delivery Car

$700

Fully Equipped with Automobile Brass Windshield

Speedometer

Three Oil Lamps

Two Gas Lamps

Generator

Horn

Tools

$590   1911 FORD Model T Torpedo

4 Cylinders, 2 Passengers
Completely equipped as follows:
Extension Top. Speedometer
Automatic Brass Windshield

Two 6-inch Gas Lamps. Generator
Three Oil Lamps
Horn and Tools
Ford Magneto built into the motor
This car thus fully equipped for $590, F. O. B. Detroit

Ford Coupelet $750
(Fully Equipped, f. o. b. Detroit)

This car is the most practical two-passenger model we have ever built. When the top is folded, the Coupelet becomes an open Runabout of unusual smartness and style.

The change from closed to open car can be made in two minutes, so that the Coupelet is quickly adaptable to all conditions of weather and driving.

It is especially popular with women who drive their own cars. As convenient and exclusive as an electric.

For physicians, architects, contractors, and all business and professional men who have to cover a great deal of territory it is admirably suited.

The Ford Coupelet may be driven twelve months in the year, in the city or over country roads, without personal discomfort, no matter what the weather.

Its distinctive style and attractiveness give it an exclusive appearance not found in any open runabout.

Buyers of this car will share in profits if we sell at retail 300,000 new Ford cars between August, 1914, and August, 1915.

Ford
THE UNIVERSAL CAR

In 1914, Ford offered the Ford Coupélet for $750, a stylish convertible which he hoped was "clean enough for women to drive." With this car, Henry also announced his famous profit-sharing stunt. (See copy in ad on left.)

At the bottom is Ford's 1914 New Year Greeting to the world, as printed in the Ford Times and entitled "The New Chauffeur." In that year the company netted over $25,000,000, as compared to a little over $246,000 ten years before, in 1904, before the birth of the Model T.

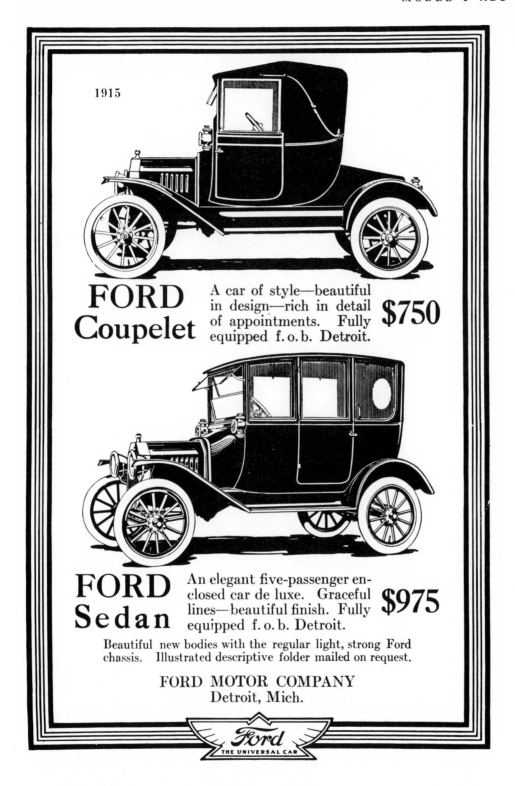

1915

FORD Coupelet A car of style—beautiful in design—rich in detail of appointments. Fully equipped f. o. b. Detroit. **$750**

FORD Sedan An elegant five-passenger enclosed car de luxe. Graceful lines—beautiful finish. Fully equipped f. o. b. Detroit. **$975**

Beautiful new bodies with the regular light, strong Ford chassis. Illustrated descriptive folder mailed on request.

FORD MOTOR COMPANY
Detroit, Mich.

Ford
THE UNIVERSAL CAR

By 1915 there were almost 19,000 employees working at Ford's home plant. The company's net income for the 1915–1916 fiscal year was over $57,000,000.

In the advertisement above, the Coupélet and Sedan for 1915 are shown.

In 1923, Ford ran this classy low-pressure ad. No mention of special features or specific claims for performance. Simply a few well-penned lines about the universal faith in Ford being the natural result of its reliability.

Dependable as the doctor himself

THE dependability of the Ford car—like that of the family physician who uses it so extensively—has become almost traditional.

Instinctively you place a trust in this car rarely, if ever, felt even for a larger, higher-powered automobile. And it is not uncommon to expect from it a far more difficult service.

Such universal *faith* is the result of Ford reliability proved over a long period of years —years in which quality has grown consistently better, while price has been steadily reduced.

RUNABOUT, $260;   TOURING, $290;   COUPE, $520;
TUDOR SEDAN, $580;   FORDOR SEDAN $660;
All prices F. O. B. Detroit
On Open Cars Starter and Demountable Rims $85 Extra
Full-Size Balloon Tires Optional—Closed Cars $25; Open Cars $45

FORD MOTOR COMPANY, DETROIT, MICHIGAN

THE UNIVERSAL CAR

MAKE   SAFETY   YOUR   RESPONSIBILITY

The NEW FORD "TUDOR" SEDAN

HE Five-Passenger Ford "Tudor" Sedan is suitable for all occasions. It is a car in which one would feel proud to conduct one's friends to social functions or to take one's family on a tour.   Comfort and style are the predominant characteristics of this all-season enclosed car.   The Ford "Tudor" Sedan is a dignified car, justly appreciated for the perfect finish of its paint work and general refinement. The large plate-glass windows, with mechanical lifts, ensure delightful airiness.

On New Lowered Chassis
Fully equipped with Starter and Lighting Set.   Ask your Authorised Dealer for a demonstration run.

McKenna Duties
Ford Passenger Cars will be reduced in price when these Duties are discontinued.   Refund of the whole difference will be made through the Authorised Dealer supplying.

By 1924, the Model T had earned wide acceptance in England. The ad above is from the July, 1924, edition of London Motor Magazine. *Notice the right-hand steering for English usage.*

In 1926, the year before the last T appeared on the market, Henry's four-door Model T Touring Car sold for the amazing price of $290 and boasted a "one-man top."

B E A U T Y ~ C O M F O R T

Today's High Peak *in* Motor Car Value

DISPLAY rooms of all Authorized Ford Dealers are thronged with those eager to see the latest Ford body types. Admiration for these attractive cars is expressed everywhere. The low stream-line bodies, the increased roominess, the greater riding comfort and the many convenient new features are advantages which are widely welcomed and appreciated.

The fact that all this has been accomplished without raise in price is even more impressive. Ford value, for years holding unchallenged leadership in the motor car market, now reaches a new high peak, through Ford production—its volume and economy of manufacturing methods.

Demand for Ford cars has exceeded all previous records during summer months. Now it is sure to outstrip even the huge production Ford facilities permit.

F O R D   M O T O R   C O M P A N Y   D E T R O I T

**All-steel bodies
Closed cars in
color**

THE TOURING
Black. All-steel body. One-man top. Weather proof side curtains opening with all four doors. Four cord tires, nickeled head lamp rims, wind shield wiper. Starter and demountable rims $85 extra. Balloon tires $25 extra. *Price f. o. b. Detroit.* **$290**

CONVENIENCE - UTILITY

for BEAUTY

Chassis has been lowered; bodies have also been lowered and lengthened. This stream-line effect is further emphasized by the raising of radiator and head lamps.

Closed bodies in color are unusually pleasing; the Fordor Sedan comes in a rich Windsor Maroon, while the Coupe and Tudor Sedan are finished in deep Channel Green; new and finer upholstery gives an artistic harmony to the whole car.

Bright nickeled radiator and head lamp rims feature closed cars. On open cars, head lamp rims are also nickeled.

Fenders are larger, longer and more attractive, conforming to stream-line treatment. The hood also is longer; louvres on sides are redesigned and increased in number.

Rear deck of both the Coupe and Runabout has a full sweep of line which greatly improves these cars' appearance.

for COMFORT

Seats are set further back, lowered and redesigned to permit easy relaxation.

Lowering of the car's center of gravity tends to give greater sense of security and to increase roadability.

Improvement in both the transmission and rear wheel brakes, with wider drums and bands, makes breaking smoother and more positive.

One-piece ventilating windshields in the Tudor Sedan and Coupe give greater visibility.

Running boards are wider and nearer the ground; doors are designed for easier entrance and exit.

for CONVENIENCE

In the Tudor Sedan, Coupe and open cars, gasoline tank is under the cowl and may be filled from the outside.

Brake and clutch pedals are wider and more conveniently spaced. Steering wheel is larger and lower.

Coil box and gasoline sediment bulb are placed under hood, where they may be more conveniently reached. Improved fan bracket simplifies adjustment of fan belt.

for UTILITY

Bodies of all-steel construction mean longer wear and lower upkeep.

The Touring Car and Runabout have removable storm-curtains opening with all doors. Compartment space under the rear deck of the Coupe and Runabout has been greatly increased.

There is added capacity in the gasoline tank of the Tudor Sedan, Coupe and open cars.

No increase in prices

THE RUNABOUT

Black. All-steel body. Large compartment under rear deck. Weatherproof side curtains opening with both doors. Four cord tires, nickeled head lamp rims, windshield wiper. Starter and demountable rims $85 extra. Balloon tires $25 extra. *Price f.o.b. Detroit.* **$260**

THE COUPE

Channel Green. All-steel body. Nickeled radiator and head lamp rims. Large compartment under rear deck. Starter, four cord tires, demountable rims, windshield wiper, rear view mirror and dash lamp. Balloon tires $25 extra. *Price f. o. b. Detroit.* **$520**

THE TUDOR SEDAN
Channel Green. All-steel body. Nickeled radiator and head lamp rims. Starter, demountable rims, four cord tires, windshield wiper, rear view mirror and dash lamp. Balloon tires $25 extra. *Price f. o. b. Detroit.* **$580**

Three of the best Model T's ever to appear, the 1926 Runabout, Coupé, and Tudor Sedan. The Coupé and the Sedan came in "channel green," and the gas tank on both these models could be filled from the outside.

A Ford for family use on Sundays and a tractor for farm work on weekdays. No wonder the T was called

"The Universal Car." Many farmer Ford owners used this Geneva Adapto.

WRITE FOR THIS

FREE BOOKLET→

and a description of our Dealers' Co-operative Plan included in our Exclusive Territory Contract

The Adapto is easily demonstrated. It does not require all day to make a demonstration. Simply mount our wheels on stub axle and drive your Ford roadster at 20 miles per hour to demonstrating field. Remove Ford wheels—attach ours and demonstrate. Return home in two to four hours.

DISTRIBUTORS

The Geneva Tractor Sales Co., 232 Bryson Bldg., Los Angeles, Cal.

The Mutual Motor Car Co., Syracuse, N. Y.

The Ridgely - Shepard Motor Truck Co., Baltimore, Md.

Ward B. Martin, Fairhope, Alabama

Geneva Tractor Co.
Geneva, Ohio.

6. Model T Humor

Henry Ford's Model T, working its way into the center of American life, came to be known familiarly and affectionately as the "Tin Lizzie." The contraption gave rise to literally thousands of jokes. A few examples appear below, some more valuable for their historical interest than for their humor. The voluminous jokes about his Model T always amused Henry Ford. He once said, "The jokes about my car sure helped to popularize it. I hope they never end."

Though affectionate in tone, the jokes and songs and poems invariably emphasized the negative. The Model T's parts were always dropping out on the road. She wouldn't start on cold mornings. An unhappy dealer lost his Ford agency to the five-and-ten-cent store. The Model T was rumored to be constructed of housewives' discarded tin cans. A rattling T made more noise than a herd of cows with bells around their necks.

Every Model T owner, it seemed, was a disgruntled grouch with a thousand complaints. But they were the good-natured complaints of a proud owner, of an adoring parent. Certainly he intended to trade in his Model T next year— on another Model T.

Stan Laurel and Oliver Hardy, famous M-G-M–Hal Roach comedy team, are shown in a freak Model T Ford in the picture County Hospital. *The T was Hollywood's favorite get-a-laugh car.*

FILLING STATION

DIALOGUE

A Cadillac pulls up, and the driver says, "How far is it from here to Kansas City?"

"One hundred and forty miles," replies the man at the pump.

"Gimme twenty gallons of gas and a gallon of oil," says the driver.

. . . And he drives on.

A Buick draws up, and the driver says, "How far is it from here to Kansas City?"

"A hundred and forty miles," replies the man at the pump.

"Gimme ten gallons of gas and a half gallon of oil," says the driver.

. . . And he drives on.

Along comes a flivver. It rattles up, the driver unwinds himself, gets out and stretches, and asks, "How far is it from here to Kansas City?"

"Oh, about a hundred and forty miles."

"Is that all? Gimme two quarts of water and a bottle of 3-in-1, and hold this son of a gun until I get in."

WHEN TALK IS EXPENSIVE

"Hey, Bill, your doctor's out here. His flivver has a flat tire, and he wants to know what it's going to cost him," announced the garage owner's assistant.

"Diagnose the case as flatulency of the perimeter, and charge him five dollars," Bill answered.

OUT OF A HOLE

A gentleman, who was visiting his lawyer for the purpose of making his will, insisted that a final request be attached to the document. The request was that the family Ford be buried with him after he died. His lawyer tried to make him see how absurd this was, but failed, so he asked the man's wife to use her influence with him.

She did the best she could, but also failed.

"Well, John," she said finally, "tell me *why* you want your Ford car buried with you."

"Because I never have got in a hole yet but what my Ford couldn't pull me out," was the reply.

*   *   *

The guy who owns a secondhand flivver may not have a quarrelsome disposition, but he's always trying to start something.

THE SISTER WAS HAPPY

In one of the small churches in a country town the pastor took for the subject of his sermon "Better Church Attendance."

The parson held forth on the theme that the automobile has taken more people away from church than any other single invention. He concluded with this exclamation:

"The Ford car has taken more people to hell than any other thing I can mention."

Whereupon an old lady in the congregation began to clap her hands and moan:

"Glory to God! Praise the Lord!"

"What's the matter, sister?" asked the parson.

"A Ford never went any place that it couldn't come back from, so I reckon all them folks in hell will be comin' back someday. So praise the Lord!"

*   *   *

Two horns will make more noise of course,
Than one will make, 'tis true;
But a Model T makes more with one
Than a cow can make with two.

*   *   *

"As a matter of fact," said the defendant's attorney, trying to be facetious, "you were scared half to death and you didn't see whether it was a Ford or something resembling a Ford that hit you."

"It resembled one, all right," the complaining

witness made answer. "I was forcibly struck by the resemblance."

* * *

BACON: He named his Ford after his wife.
EGBERT: How funny!
BACON: Not at all! After he got it he found he couldn't control it.

* * *

PERKINS: Did you see Smith's new Ford?
JERKINS: Not in time.

* * *

"Did you get the number of that Ford?" asked the policeman of the prostrate pedestrian.

"No, but it got mine," gasped the man who was given to slang.

* * *

JONES: Do you think the horse will survive the Ford?
BROWN: Not if it gets in its way.

* * *

A Ford plowing along a country road met a large limousine hub-deep in mud. The Ford was hitched to the large car and pulled it to solid ground.

"I'm much obliged for the lift," said the driver of the large car; "that's a powerful little machine—what is it called?"

"This is a Ford."

"Guess I'll have to get one for my toolbox."

* * *

"I thought you had the agency for the Ford automobile?"

"I did, but they took it away from me."

"Who took it away?"

"The five-and-ten-cent store."

* * *

A dealer in Indiana wrote to the home office asking if they would paint his Fords yellow. He wanted to hang them in bunches and sell them like bananas.

* * *

After all, the Ford is the best family car. It has a tank for Father, a hood for Mother, and a rattle for Baby.

* * *

"I understand you have just bought a Ford."

"Yes, I saw seven of them chasing one pedestrian the other day, and I decided that I was on the wrong end of the sport."

* * *

"The Ford rode right over your face, you say? Do you feel any effects from it?"

"Yes, I've had a taste of india rubber in my mouth ever since!"

* * *

"Why is it called a runabout?"

"Because it will run about a mile without stopping."

* * *

Mr. Jones was prowling through the house in the middle of the night and stubbed his toe against a baby carriage in the hall. "Damn Fords," he muttered; "they get in everywhere."

* * *

A lady was telling her husband about the fine new automobile their neighbor was going to get.

"What is the name of the car?"

"I can't remember, but it starts with T."

"That must be a Ford. All the others start with gasoline."

* * *

The telephone rang in the office of the famous manufacturer of popular-priced cars, Henry Ford. The great man's secretary answered the ring.

"Well?" he said.

MR. McCOY WAS THE LOCAL DEALER FOR HARD RUBBER TIRES...
HE WAS ON THE ROAD CONSTANTLY LOOKING FOR CUSTOMERS

"MUST WE HAVE 'BANDS'... JUST TO GO ON A PICNIC?"

MR. MAHONEY COULD START HIS FORD ON 'MAG' AND
SAVE HIS BATTERY

DON'T TURN IT OFF!...
LET IT GET WARMED UP FIRST...

....AND FOR THE MILLIONTH TIME I'M SAYING —
I KNOW YOU SMELL SMOKE....THERE IS SMOKE!

"This," answered the voice, "is Mr. J. Henry Begins. I wish to speak with Mr. Ford."

"Mr. Ford is very busy," explained the functionary. "This is his secretary speaking. Can I take the message?"

"You cannot," was the firm reply. "I must speak directly with your chief. I am a customer of your company and what I have to communicate is something which Mr. Ford should in person hear from me."

"Well, in that case, kindly hold the wire a moment," said the secretary. He summoned Henry to the instrument.

"What is it?" inquired the latter gentleman.

"Mr. Ford," stated the unknown patron, "you advertised lately that your concern had turned out a complete car in six minutes."

"Yes, we did. What of it?"

"Well, I'm the guy that bought it!" He hung up with a bang.

*　　*　　*

A farmer stopped at the roadside until a large limousine had passed, and then stepped in front of a Ford. After he had been picked up and dusted he was asked:

"Why didn't you look to see if another car was following the big one?"

"Gosh!" he said, "how was I to know it had a colt running after it?"

*　　*　　*

"I hear they are going to magnetize the rear axle of the Ford."

"What's the idea?"

"So it will pick up the parts that drop off."

*　　*　　*

Two brothers inherited money. Each received $3,500. Both purchased automobiles. One brother sunk his all in a Hotfoot Six. The other one bought a Ford.

In races the Ford refused to be beaten. They held endurance tests, and the Ford was always there at the finish.

"But," said the plunger, "what causes all that rattling I hear?"

"Oh," replied the cautious one, "That's the jingle of my three thousand dollars."

*　　*　　*

A thrifty housewife saved all her empty cans and, after a quantity had accumulated, shipped them to Detroit. After a few weeks she was delighted to receive the following letter:

"Dear Madam: In accordance with your instructions we have made up and are shipping you today one Ford. We are also returning eight cans which were left over."

*　　*　　*

On a cold morning recently a small boy stood intently watching a man drawing a blanket over the hood of his machine. When the operation was completed, the boy said, "It's no use, mister, you can't fool anybody; anyone can tell it's a Ford."

*　　*　　*

A man advertised that he would give away his Ford on a certain corner at a certain hour. When he drove up to the corner he found ten driverless Fords standing around.

*　　*　　*

A new city ordinance in one city provides that Fords be allowed to run on the sidewalks so automobiles won't hit them.

*　　*　　*

A man rushed into a farmyard and requested the use of a ladder.

"What do you want the ladder for?" asked the farmer.

"Why my Ford is up in a tree, down the road."

"Up in a tree? Are you crazy? How in the world did your Ford get up in a tree?"

"Well, you see, I was cranking it and the darned thing slipped out of my hands."

*　　*　　*

In a large garage a man wagered with the owner that he could name any machine merely by the sound of the engine. An attendant was instructed to crank the different machines, the boastful one was blindfolded, and the test began.

"Overland," he called for the first one.

"Correct," said the owner; "try the next one."

"Studebaker."

"Right-o! Crank another."

Just then a load of coal was shot into the alley from a wagon.

"Ford," said the guesser.

*　　*　　*

A little boy watching a man cranking his Ford asked, "Why don't she play, mister?"

*　　*　　*

"Can I sell you a speedometer?"

"I don't use one. When my Ford is running five miles an hour, the fender rattles; twelve miles an hour my teeth rattle; and fifteen miles an hour the transmission drops out."

*　　*　　*

Smith had his new Ford standing in front of his house and saw Jones inspecting it carefully.

"How do you like it?" he asked.

"Fine," answered Jones, "but where do you take out the ashes?"

*　　*　　*

Three neighbors with new cars held a christening. The first man had a Pierce-Arrow.

"I name thee George Washington," he said. "First in war, first in peace, and first in the hearts of his countrymen."

"I name thee Abraham Lincoln," said the owner of a Cadillac. "Of the people, by the people, and for the people."

The last man owned a Ford.

"I name thee Theodore Roosevelt," he exclaimed, "you rough-riding son of a gun!"

*　　*　　*

"What business are you in, Jack?"

"I'll tell you, but I wish you would keep it quiet. I am selling Fords—but Mother thinks I am a burglar."

*　　*　　*

"What is your name, little girl?"

"You won't laugh if I tell you?"

"No."

"Iona Ford."

*　　*　　*

"Have you heard the last Ford story?"

"I hope so."

*　　*　　*

"It looks nice. But does it run?"

NOBODY IN TOWN LIKED OLD MAN HERRICKS... INCLUDING HIS VERY OWN LIZZIE.

"SHE'S RUNNING KIND OF PUNY OUT OF THE BOTTOM SPIGOT— SHOULD TAKE TWO QUARTS!"

"HOW MANY THOUSAND TIMES HAVE I ASKED YOU CHILDREN— NOT TO STEP ON THE SIDE CURTAINS.?!!"

"I'M TELLING YOU IF THE ENGINE GETS WET, WE'LL BE OUT HERE FOR DAYS!"

MR. CURRAN WAS ALWAYS PLEADING WITH HIS WIFE TO 'TRIM SHIP'

RATTLING GOOD
FORD VERSE

Model T versifiers were tireless when it came to ribbing Henry Ford, his "Tin Lizzie," and the Ford owner. Almost every magazine printed sentimental or humorous verse about the marvel of Ford's inventiveness. The three verses below, though they rattle some, will take you back to that era when the Ford owner mixed three parts fuel to one part humor for best running.

LOOK AND LISTEN

It has been said that money talks,
   And as I look abroad
Cash says with unanimity,
   "You'd better buy a *Ford*."
Thus popularity proclaims
   A nation's happy choice,
There's no disguising auto names—
   "A *Ford!*" shouts money's voice.

THE BIG CAR'S LAMENT

I wish I wuz a little Ford
   A-runnin' right along;
I wouldn't need to wheeze and sigh,
   I'd sing a different song.

To me the fact of bein'
   A big car is a fright;
I don't care if I do look fine,
   I never feel quite right.

An' when a Ford goes whizzin' by,
   Great tears most always drop;
For where the Ford can go right on,
   I'm almost sure to stop.

I stick in mud, I don't like rain,
   I can't pull up the hills;
Oh! I could sit here all day long
   An' tell you all my ills.

An' so I wish I wuz a Ford,
   Then I need never worry,
For they go back and forth each day,
   Without such needless flurry.

So just remember when you wish,
   To be so big and grand,
It's not the looks that count so much,
   As do the pluck and sand.

THE UNIVERSAL FORD

You scarce can find a country road,
Where charming birds sing nature's
   ode;
Where wild flowers with them seem
   to vie—
Rich charms for ear, and charms for
   eye!
A lonely spot, where works of man
Scarce interfere with nature's plan;
A little valley, hard beset
By nature's hills; but climbing yet,
A little Ford will make the goal
And o'er your charming valley roll.

THE VILLAGE BLACKSMITH

Under the spreading chestnut tree
The village smithy stands;
The smith a lonely man is he,
For his shop is in other hands;
And before the door a puffing Ford
Now oil and gas demands.

LINES FROM OMAR THE FORD

. . . Come, fill the tank and fix the broken spring,
Your worn-out clutch into the garbage fling:
This car of thine hast but a little way to roll
And then you'll ask what price 'twill bring . . .

We'll make the most of what we have to spend
Before we, too, to the bankrupt's court descend

Dust to the dusty, but no dust we'll take.
Sans hat, sans coat, sans driver—what an end!

Into this old Ford, and why not knowing;
Gullible and fresh as any greenhorn, blowing
All about it. My money gone to waste
I know not whither—and the debt growing.

What, I am asking, made me do this thing;
And, yet I am asking, why keep this thing?
Oh many an hour of bursting brain
Must pay for this wild, wide wandering . . .

Each worn a thousand curses brings my way;
Oh yes, for where's the gas of yesterday?
And this first trial spin that tests the car
Will surely take my home and purse away . . .

With me along the road where wrecks are strown
And parts, and battered corpses thrown;
Where undertakers and their hopes are met
There, pieces of this car will soon be known.

Some for Cadillacs and cars of price, and some
Sigh for the bright-hued models yet to come;
Oh take my Ford and let the others go;
I'll sell my interest for a tiny sum.

Think on this antique battered thing of junk,
In which our petty fortune we have sunk,
How owner after owner in his wrath
Rode his destined hour, then sold for junk.

A brawny son of toil beneath the car,
A wrench, a kit of tools, a sturdy bar
Beside him, sunken in the muddy ground;
Oh Ford, what a bally elephant you are.

Hot perspiration froze upon my brow,
My right arm ached with woe,
For the traffic was stalled behind me
And my flivver refused to go.

H. L. Austin

"He says kerosene will do. Doesn't want to spoil her."

OUR NEW FORD FIRE TRUCK HIT THE 26th STREET BUMP TOO FAST AND LOST THE HOSE

"SAY, GEORGE!..."

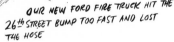

"A NEW FANCY RADIATOR DOESN'T MAKE IT AN OUNCE BETTER THAN OURS!"

The Model T played an important part in the movies. Here the Keystone Cops are shown in many precarious situations with their Ford, a collapsible Model T.

In the early days of movie comedy films almost invariably there was a unique scene in which Model T cars in some form or another were used.

I DIDN'T RAISE MY FORD TO BE A JITNEY

Hiram Lord from Wellsboro,
He bought a Ford a week ago,
And he paid for it in reg'lar dough,
Then took a trip to town;
While goin' up the big main street
A man whose nerve could not be beat
Jumped right up into Hi's back seat,
But Hi he slowed right down.
The man said as he held five cents,
"The jitney bus is sure immense."
But Hi his anger was intense
As he turned to him and said,
"Get out! get out! I know you hate to walk.
No doubt! no doubt! But 'tain't no use to talk."

Chorus:

I didn't raise my Ford to be a jitney bus,
So don't humiliate my poor machine;
Henry Ford made walking a pleasure,
But don't take my little treasure
Or I'll run you out of gasoline.
You'd better take the streetcar right away, sir,
You're the meanest man I've ever seen;
You're in an awful pickle,
Take back your gol-darned nickel.
I didn't raise my Ford to be a jitney.

ON THE OLD BACK SEAT OF THE HENRY FORD

Hiram Brown went to town,
Bought himself a Ford the other day.
Now the charm of the farm,
Loses out whenever he is on his merry way.
Susie Green has been seen
Riding when the moon was shining clear,
Chauffeur didn't tell,
But we know very well,
That Hiram too, was sitting in the rear.

Chorus:

On the old back seat of the Henry Ford,
They didn't mind the rumble of the old buckboard,
The winds were blowing,
And her hands grew cold.
Hiram said, "I'll be a little bit bold!"
He placed his arm right around her waist,
Then the chauffeur loudly roared,
"The motor's getting warmer,
So brighten up the corner,"
On the old back seat of the Henry Ford.

LET'S TAKE A RIDE ON THE JITNEY BUS

Billy Bender was a spender, threw away his dough,
He worked a mill for twelve a week, but easy come
   and easy go,
To a movie he would take his girl each Wedn'sday
   night,
But Sunday was the one day he'd spend money left
   and right,
He'd get his weekly pay, to his girlie he would say:

Chorus:

Let's take a ride on the jitney bus, the jitney bus,
   the jitney bus,
We'll let the neighbors see what a good sport I
   can be;
We'll make love, dear, back in the rear,
Where the chauffeur can't see us—
I'm not fickle,
Zip! goes the nickel, on the jitney bus.

IT'S A RAMBLING FLIVVER

Now listen to me patiently; I'm going to deliver,
A story 'bout a crazy, good-for-nothing little "fliv-
ver";
I bought it for a dollar and an old tobacco sack,
And now I wish to goodness that I had my dollar
back.
Doggoned thing is noisy as the deuce,
They made it out of rattles, every one of them is
loose;
But even so it always seems to go
And when it starts to movin' I will have you know—

Chorus:

It is a rambling "flivver," a rambling "flivver,"
Step on her tail and then stay with her,
She will go, go, when the tank is dry
Do you think it wonderful? I think it is a lie.
It is a rambling "flivver," a rambling "flivver,"
At racing she was fine;
When I timed her for a block, both the hands flew
off the clock,
Oh that rambling "flivver" of mine.

THE PACKARD AND THE FORD

By a lonesome little curb in a lonesome little town,
On a lonesome little Ford a lonesome Packard
looked down,
And the great big car heaved a great big sigh
For the little Ford so modest and shy,
"You shouldn't travel 'round alone, you should have
a chaperon,"
Said the Packard, in a language all its own,
"In my garage, you know, if you will only go,
I've a cozy, cozy cunning little home—

Chorus:

"Honk! honk!" said the great big Packard.
"Aaa! Aaa!" said the little car.
Said the Packard: "Won't you come and cuddle
closer?"
But the Ford said: "I can't go far,"
"But you see how much I need you,
And I love you there's no doubt,
Come and marry and we'll have a little Buick,
You can't afford to run about!"

THE LITTLE FORD RAMBLED RIGHT ALONG

Now Henry Jones and a pretty little queen
Took a ride one day in his big limousine,
The car kicked up and the engine wouldn't crank,
There wasn't any gas in the gasoline tank.
Just about that time along came Nord.
And he rambled right along in his little old Ford;
And he stole that queen as his engine sang a song,
And his little old Ford just rambled right along.

Chorus:

And his little Ford it rambled right along,
And his little old Ford it rambled right along,
The gas burned out in the big machine,
But the darned little Ford don't need gasoline.
The big limousine had to back downhill,
But the blamed little Ford is going up still,
When she blows out a tire just wrap it up with wire,
And the little Ford will ramble right along.

FLIVVER KING

Henry Ford was a machinist,
He worked both night and day
To give this world a flivver
That has made her shivver,
And speeded her on her way.
Now he is a billionaire,
But his record is fair,
He is humanity's friend.

Chorus:

Of all the cars beneath the stars,
The flivver is the car for me.
He makes them nifty,
And they'll do fifty,
And he don't give a rap,
For he makes them out of scrap;
And when you buy a Ford
You are only working for
Tweedle-Dum Doodle-Doo
For John D.
And the flivver king.

In race car No. 24, left, is one of the finest race drivers who ever competed on the dirt tracks of the Midwest, the late Noel Bullock, of Ord, Nebraska. In this hopped-up Model T with overhead valves, Bullock was the scourge of the dirt tracks. He also astounded the racing world when he ran away from the field in the Pikes Peak Hill Climb in 1922, driving a home-made Ford against special factory-built cars.

In the photo below, the unidentified driver of a Model T spared no effort in making it a classy dirt-track-competition car.

The twin racing cars above are 1919 Fords and carry "Roof sixteen overhead-valve equipment" which allowed speeds of up to 100 miles per hour.

During the long life of the Model T, hundreds of special bodies of all types and designs were offered Ford owners. Some of these were racing bodies, others were de luxe custom-built jobs. Some came complete and ready to attach to the chassis, some were offered in kit or "knockdown" form.

Pictured on this page are five such special bodies for the T owner who wanted his flivver to look different from that of his neighbor. The side three are merely representative of literally hundreds of all-purpose bodies made by independent manufacturers for use on the T. At bottom are two racing bodies. The open model is a "cut-down" 1919 Ford (Model 21 body). Note that the driver's seat is 7 inches forward of the passenger's, thus "giving the driver more elbow-room." The racing body with top and windshield is an Arrow, which sold for $69.

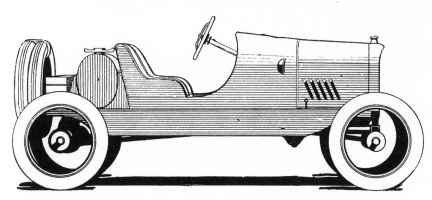

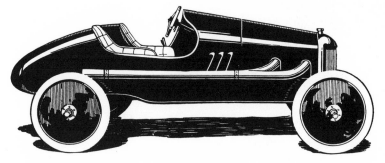

During the 1953 Horseless Carriage Club Caravan, this excellent restored 1915 Model T was driven by Lois and Louis Cook (striped jacket) of Pasadena, California. Roger Mahey of General Petroleum Corporation (center) checks fuel used by the Cooks en route to Yosemite National Park from Los Angeles.

In 1953 many Model T Fords restored to original condition participated in numerous tours promoted by antique-car enthusiasts. Shown here is one of the contestants at the foot of Yosemite National Park Valley's famed El Capitan and Half Dome peaks. Even modern-day expert restoration has failed to eliminate the need of often refilling the Model T with water.

During the reenactment of the Glidden Tour held in 1946 between Albany, New York, and Detroit, many restored Model T's were used. Shown here is a 1909 Model. Left to right, Jerry Duryea of the famous automotive family, William Ford, son of Edsel Ford, now Vice-president of the Ford Motor Company, Harvey Firestone, Jr., and Al Brown of the American Automobile Association.

In the 1946 reenactment of the Glidden Tour a Model T Ford led this part of the procession through Detroit streets (Golden Anniversary Celebration of the automobile).

7. 5,000 Accessories

One might suppose from the innumerable gadgets and accessories developed for use on the Model T that owners of the flivver were constantly dissatisfied with their cars. Such was not the case. But the enterprising T owner yearned to improve his car, make it special in some way, add to the quality of its performance and appearance. Nothing was sacred. Lights, cylinder heads, radiators, bodies, bumpers, tops, fenders, windshields—each or all might be replaced by supposedly superior items manufactured especially for the Model T by independent firms. The accessory makers did not confine themselves to superficial contributions to the Model T. They made new and different parts for the engine, brake and clutch systems, wheels and axles.

Like millions of other Model T customers, I had my eye peeled for the latest inventions listed and illustrated in the fascinating "Auto Accessories" sections of the mail-order catalogues. No Ford owner's home was complete without one of these tomes, printed especially for rainy days or winter afternoons when the driver dared not risk his T on the slippery roads. Maybe he ought to buy a set of chains for the old jitney, or some

cold-weather starting equipment. If his T was an earlier model, he wanted to bring it up to snuff; if he had just purchased the car, he wanted to make a few creative additions.

And so began the hunt for the right gadget. Ultimately some 5,000 accessories for the Model T Ford appeared on the market. These devices were made by outsiders, not by the Ford Motor Company.

Racing bodies for a man's T were much in vogue in the early days of the speed mania around 1913. Remo put out a Raceabout Body, "made as a body should be made," positively the classiest ever built for Ford. Arrow advertised that their racing body for $69 "is primarily for a red-blooded man who wants style and distinctive dash and snap, yet with no sacrifice of comfort."

Dozens of accessory firms proclaimed in their advertisements that the Model T drove like a truck and rode like a wagon, and that for a small amount the motorist could acquire Pullman comfort with so-and-so's vital-life shock absorbers. Snubbers sold for around $15 for four and were guaranteed "to keep you on the seat." There were cowl ventilators, a "gaso-

phone" gas gauge with a warning bell, and a special gas "filler" which allowed the tank to be filled without lifting the seat cushion. All kinds of quick-change transmission bands and new types of braking systems appeared on the market. The T used internal expanding brake shoes, but some accessory makers invented a rig that added external contracting brake bands for extra braking power.

Most Ford owners knew that on a cold morning they could start the car more readily by pouring hot water on the manifold, or by applying a blowtorch to heat it. The "Simon Primer" was guaranteed to heat up the entire manifold by an electric current in 10 seconds. The "Hot Spot" primer in 1922 consisted of a shallow bowl attached under one wing of the manifold. The driver dipped a metal-covered wick in gasoline or alcohol and, placing it in the pan, allowed it to burn for a minute or so, thus heating up the manifold for "easy starting in any temperature." One of the most interesting of those devices was a firetrap built into an extraordinary manifold. It provided a little stove into which the driver could stuff rags or paper, touch a match to them, and then close the door and let the burning flotsam heat up the manifold with safety.

If the ignition system of the early Ford went dead, or at least left something to be desired, the accessory manufacturers filled in the gaps with supposed nonfouling spark plugs and different designs of timers and high-tension magnetos. One of the most popular ignition systems before the 1920's was the Atwater Kent system, which made its inventor and namesake a fortune.

Most roads before 1920 were of dirt or sharp rocks or merely trails with high centers, and the Model T crankcase was especially vulnerable to rough roads. A broken crankcase and the smell of dry, burning metal often distressed the driver when he was nowhere close to a garage. Gemco of Milwaukee sold a special crankcase support for $2.50, on which the

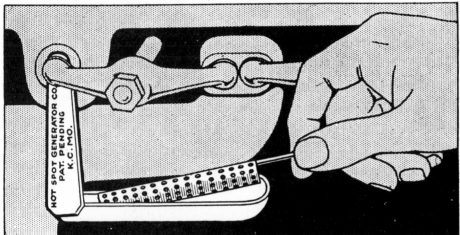
driver "could save himself $20." This saving was figured at $22.50 for a new crankcase ($15 for the case and $7.50 for labor). Gemco's ads insisted that every venturesome tourist needed their crankcase support, and for a time it was a proper assumption.

To serve the happy vagabond who left town in his flivver, the accessory makers built tire carriers and luggage racks that attached to the running boards, to the rear or top of the car, or between the front fender and the hood. Parking lights and rear-wheel grease retainers were also offered to the driver of the Model T, along with bumpers, for country or city driving.

With some mechanical ingenuity or the services of the local mechanic, the T owner might build into his stock model features that gave it an amazing added performance. The T was

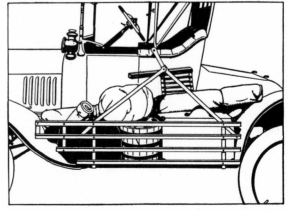

adaptable to many kinds of motoring tastes; it was this appeal to the tinker instinct, as much as economy and performance, that established Ford's T as *The Car* on the American country road up until the late 1920's. And if Henry Ford offered few accessories in the initial years of the T, he did furnish a complete set of tools—far more than the modern owner gets—and the driver knew how to use them.

One of the unusual accessories for the Ford was a front-wheel-axle-and-differential assembly to make a four-wheel-drive Model T. For the park gardener or road repairman or the sand and gravel dealer, there were special dump truck bodies for half-ton or larger truck frames. Iron

4 Wheel Drive Attachment for Ford Cars.
1923

Drives and brakes on all four wheels. More power, more traction with less fuel; less tire expense and less repair bills. Will go through mud, sand and snow without the use of tire chains on any of the tires easier than a two wheel drive with chains. Think what this means. It is much safer to drive, easier to control, does not skid when you apply the brakes and can be attached to any Ford chassis in 3 to 4 hours time.

Prices on request.

J. F. LIVINGOOD   New Virginia, Iowa

shops offered to convert your T frame into the right kind of truck chassis and body for your particular needs. They welded extensions onto the frame to lengthen the wheelbase and added extra-heavy springs to carry the load. Thus emerged side by side with the stock car a type of vehicle called the "truck," a development to which the Model T made an important contribution.

The village of Highland Park, Michigan, a Detroit suburb of 30,000, purchased a Model T Runabout and in 1916 converted the car into an excellent piece of fire-fighting equipment, carrying a chemical tank, a 3-gallon fire extinguisher and 150 feet of ¾-inch hose. Other small cities throughout the country rigged up similar contrivances on the theory that horses were impractical when 20 seconds at the beginning of a fire were—and still are—worth 20 minutes later on.

The Model T owner occasionally had trouble with car thieves and "borrowers" who just wanted to see how the thing drove. Dozens of different kinds of locks were marketed that could be mounted on the steering wheel; others locked the front wheel to the axle or radius rod; and one type set the front spindle so that the front wheel could not be turned. There were ignition locks, and one odd sort made of hinged iron that encircled the rim and tire. A sharp spike protruded. If a thief tried to drive away, the spike would lift the wheel off the ground as it revolved.

For cold winter weather there appeared a variety of hood and radiator covers to keep "Lizzie" warm. These were used by so many drivers that by 1927 they were practically standard equipment. Usually made of leather or heavy canvas, these covers sold at $1.95 to $3.50 and were supposed to be indispensable to the driver who wanted heat control for his engine.

Heaters also for driver and passengers appeared on the market in large numbers. Some were simply pieces of sheet metal that bolted over the exhaust manifold so that the heat from the manifold filtered into the body. Some of the best car heaters I have ever enjoyed were used

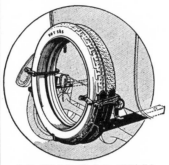
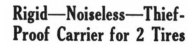

Highland Park, Michigan, Fire Department converted Model T 1916 Runabout

on the Model T, and they sold for as low as $1.75, installed. There was not much control— only a sliding metal door—but lots of heat.

"Standardized equipment" has become almost a byword in mass automobile design and production. Though approximately 5,000 gadgets and devices were invented over the nineteen-year course of the T's life, relatively few survived. Yet inventors, home garage mechanics, tinkerers, and bright young factory men had put their ingenuity to good use. The automobile companies and the American public shared in the real profits when, years later, these or similar accessories became standard equipment.

I was one of those accessory builders, and had the good fortune to see the Clymer spotlight become a fairly standard piece of equipment. It was factory-installed on the Sport Model of the Buick, the Dort, and the Rickenbacker, among others. Thousands of Clymer Spotlights, mounted through the windshield glass on a ball-and-socket joint, were sold during the days of the Model T. More than half of them went onto the Ford jalopies, and most of these sold through Ford dealers.

As season followed season, Ford developed more of his own accessories. By the time the Model T was nearing the end of the trail, Ford dealers were selling quality lines of accessories, made either by independent manufacturers and Ford-approved, or by the Ford Motor Company itself.

The following pages, packed with accessory ads that will awaken nostalgic memories in every ex-Model T owner, are from the pages of an early catalogue of Model T accessories.

SPECIALS for *Fords*

To Owners of Ford Cars:

When it is considered that there are over 1,082,820 Ford cars in service today—one-half of all the cars used in this country—it is plain to be seen what a prominent position the Ford occupies.

The following pages show accessories designed especially for Ford cars. Each article has been selected after an investigation into its qualities and its usefulness. Many of the articles are intended to take the place of regular parts which may have become lost or damaged. Others are for increasing the pleasure of driving and the comfort of the riders.

Practically everything needed to keep your car in good shape can be found here.

Some articles suitable for Fords as well as other makes of cars are shown in the other sections of this book. By referring to the index in the back you will quickly find them.

Our direct way of selling combined with immense sales to thousands of car owners everywhere, permits the low prices, which speak strongly for themselves.

When ordering, kindly give year and model of your car, as it will help us to serve you better.

All Riverside Ford-Size Tires are Guaranteed for 5000 Miles
Read All About Riversides—Pages 4 to 11

New Black and White Universal Riverside Inner Tube
For Either Front or Rear Wheel

New in color and new in construction. Fits either the front, 30x3, or rear, 30x3½ tire. This make is for economy, as it is necessary to carry only one size for emergencies. Made of extra fine quality, new, live, black rubber stock, laminated, with an extra layer of black rubber, in addition to a white rubber strip running completely around the tube on the rim side. These two extra layers make the tube thicker at this point, reinforces at the rim and next to the head of the tire. This extra thickness also tends to prevent rim pinches which are so common with the ordinary tube. Next to a first-class casing, the inner tube is the most important part of your tire equipment. Be fortified by using the Universal Black and White Riverside Tube.
61R3100—Weight, 2 pounds.............................**$2.15**

Plain Tread

Regular Clincher Style	Price	Size	Average Weight, Pounds
61R3002	$ 7.70	30x3	10
61R3006	10.08	30x3½	14

See Tire Descriptions on Pages 4 to 11.

Steering Column Brace

A contrivance needed by every Ford owner. Strengthens the steering wheel for extremely rough roads. Steering wheel is used a great deal as handle for getting in and out of car and is very often broken in that way. This brace is the logical remedy. Quickly attached. Finished in black enamel and furnished with screws. For 1914, 1915 or 1916 model Ford cars. Weight, 14 ounces.
61R4552—For 1914 Cars. Each..**75c**
61R4553—For 1915-1916 Cars.
Each **75c**

Ideal Transmission Brake Band

Saves time and money. You can renew your brake lining or forward speed transmission lining in half an hour without taking off the transmission cover. Made of steel band, drop forged lugs. Full instructions included.
61R7962—Weight, 1 pound....**$1.05**

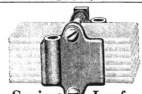

Spring Leaf Lubricator

Oil reservoir plates with felt inserts. Furnishes constant lubrication. Made of semi-steel, black enameled. Set includes two pairs for each spring. Weight, 1¾ pounds.
61R8626—Price, per set **75c**

1916 Non-Skid

Regular Clincher Style	Price	Size	Average Weight, Pounds
61R3055	$ 8.10	30x3	11¼
61R3059	10.55	30x3½	16

See Tire Descriptions on Pages 4 to 11.

Spindle Joint Anti-Rattler

Spindle joints are noise producers and a source of unlimited annoyance. The anti-rattler makes these joints tight, saves the wear and tear and, once in place, is a permanent check to rattling. It also offsets the vibration which affects the steering wheel and therefore lends added pleasure to motoring. Arm made of bronze; bolt of steel. Weight, 1 pound.
61R4933—Per pair **75c**

Compel Your Ford Tires to Give Good Service

Riverside Reliners for Ford Tires

A good reliner tends to prevent blow-outs and punctures, and lengthens life of the tires. After casing runs about 2,000 miles or if it has blown out, strengthen it with a reliner. You can often get good service out of tires that are seemingly useless by using a reliner. Made of fabric vulcanized over a mold. No cement needed if applied as directed. Will not creep or chafe. Full width and extends from bead to bead.

Number	Price	Size	Weight
61R8273	$1.28	30x3	3 pounds
61R8275	1.45	30x3½	3½ pounds
61R8844	1.80	31x4	4½ pounds

Snug Fit Tire Cover

Protect your spare tires from the sun, rain, dust and mud. It will add life to them. A covered tire also gives a much neater appearance when on the holders. Made especially for use to our specifications. Of high quality, black enameled waterproof drill. Fits snug and smooth, and answers every requirement of a cover at a medium price. A highly tempered flat steel spring is inserted along the buttoned edge, which adds to its appearance and seals the cover. Special snap glove buttons are also used to keep the cover closed, and give it a neat appearance. Soft, flexible and will not crack. Weight, 3 pounds.
61R7562—Size, 30x3 ....75c
61R7563—Size, 30x3½ 78c

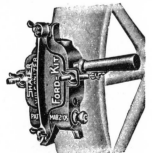

The Ford-Kit Vulcanizer

Mends Ford tube injuries and small casing cuts or sand pockets perfectly. Carried in tool-box. Fill the cut with rubber, clamp on vulcanizer, light generator. No watching required. Can't overcure or undercure. Fuel supply gives just enough heat for perfect work. Furnished with repair rubber and cement. Nickel plated.
61R4676—Weight, 5 pounds...$1.85

Kant-Creep Inside Tire Patch

Made of several plies heavy friction fabric with a good grade of rubber, and thoroughly vulcanized. One flap fits securely over clinch casing. Other flap is made separately and enables you to fit patch accurately to inside of casing under clinch, preventing tube from rubbing against any sharp edge and becoming chafed. Specially made for protecting weak spots and blowouts in casing. Will fit either front 3-inch or rear 3½-inch casing on Ford cars.
61R5135—Weight, 8 ounces.....32c

Gasoline Vulcanizer

For repairing Ford-size inner tubes. Gives a thoroughly unleakable vulcanized patch. Light, compact and handy, requiring no cement or acid—merely repair gum, which comes with each outfit. Economical in fuel consumption. Takes about 1 ounce of gasoline to a job. Packed in substantial box, including roll of gum, gasoline measuring cup, sand paper, pair of scissors, and complete instructions.
61R8945—Weight, 2 pounds...$1.00

Engine-Driven Tire Pump

A mechanically perfect pump made especially for Fords. Tires wear away rapidly unless properly inflated. With this pump you can always keep your tires full of pure oilless air. Simply watch the gauge and throw out clutch when tire is properly inflated. Drive gear attached to crank shaft. No machine work or drilling necessary. Connecting rod of bronze. Other parts cast iron, malleable iron and drop forgings, with cut gears. Can't lose this pump. Always with you when you need it. Tested to 150 pounds pressure before leaving factory. Height, 6 inches; width, 4½ inches.
61R7963—Weight, 3 pounds...$5.25

Genuine Weed Anti-Skid Chains at Reduced Prices

Well known everywhere. Made throughout of enameled steel wire. The cross chains are of case hardened stock. All parts especially treated to prevent rusting. Gives positive traction in mud, sand and snow. A postive anti-skid device and will not injure the tire when used according to directions. Each pair (two chains) put up in a strong cloth bag, convenient to carry when not in use. Weight, per pair, 12 pounds.

61R8374—Size, 30x3.	Pair...	$3.38
61R8380—Size, 30x3½.	Pair...	3.75
61R8386—Size, 31x4.	Pair...	4.50

Ford Tire Savers

A model that has been thoroughly tried out, and one of the lightest, yet strongest and simplest to operate of any tire saver. Lifts wheel with one operation. Every Ford owner should have a set, as they will greatly prolong the life of tires. Made of tough steel, and will last a long time. Shipping weight, set of four, 20 pounds.
161R7545—Set of four.......$1.40

Auto Jack

Light, strong, efficient, simple and reliable. Works smoothly. Has continuous lift, raising on both upward and downward stroke of handle. Built to give an extremely short pinch on the upward stroke, making the lift much easier. This is perfectly natural because one has more power on the down stroke.

The length of stroke is less than one-half as long as other ratchet jacks, which enables one to get under any part of car. Another important feature—the weight of the load rests on two pawls. Handle can be used as a tire tool. Height, collapsed, 10 inches; raised, 17 inches. Capacity, 1,500 pounds. Made of cast iron, aluminum finish.
61R5473—Weight, 4 pounds....56c

Brake Rod Support

Takes the place of present pressed steel support on Ford T cars. Malleable iron. Hardened steel ball is held in tension against brake rod. Ball turns and does not wear rod. Attached without removing rod. Weight, 8 ounces.
61R5480—Set of two...........30c

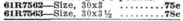

Make a Full-Fledged Speedster of Your Ford

Cyclone Speedster Body

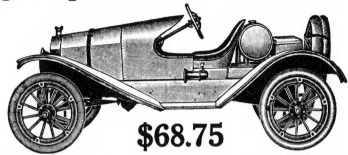

Here is a real nifty, classy, up-to-the-minute speedster body that would do credit to any car. We have correctly named it Cyclone because it glides so easily, noiselessly and swiftly through the air on any Model T Ford chassis. A body of this design lightens the burden on the engine and consequently means more speed and less cost of operation. It is all the craze now to fit out your Ford in speed style—and it is really a good thing on account of the added pleasure of traveling faster, the saving in tires and gasoline and the different appearance it gives your car.

Equipment consists of body with Cowl, 2-bucket seats with removable upholstering. One 18-gallon gasoline tank. One tool box with lock. Sloping hood. One complete set of fenders and splash guards.

Specifications. Width of body, 32 inches. Length of body from dash to rear, 74 inches. Seat, height, 19 inches; width, 16 inches; depth, 16 inches. Tank, Cowlhood,

$68.75

toolbox and fenders are heavy gauge pressed steel. Seats and cushions trimmed in black. Each body is fitted to a Model T Ford chassis before leaving factory and it will therefore fit perfectly. Shipping weight, 250 pounds. Requires about 15 days' time.

Note: Demountable rims, tire carrier, horn, radiator or hood are not included but can be furnished separately. See index for page numbers of each item.

261R4523—Speedster Body finished in lead color priming coat, and equipment as listed. Each...**$68.75**
261R4524—Speedster Body painted in Red, Yellow, Blue or Black, and equipment as listed. Each..**$78.75**

When ordering mention color wanted.
Shipped from factory in Southern Michigan.

$68.00

Greyhound Speedster Body

This body is specially designed to be lighter and stronger than other racing bodies and at the same time to be symmetrical and pleasing to the eye. It will relieve your Ford of a great deal of weight and increase the power and speed of your engine. You will immediately notice the difference. The car will take up speed smoothly and quickly without the usual jerking motion and will fairly sail through the air because of its peculiar non-friction shape.

It can be quickly attached to any Ford chassis. Frame work is the finest selected, kiln-dried hard wood. Cowl dash is correctly designed and the bucket seats are fitted with removable upholstering.

Note the graceful and well balanced placement of the 18-gallon oval gas tank with the 5-gallon round Polarine tank immediately behind it. Tanks have direct con-

nections with the motor. Tool box is built in the body; fenders are long racy design. A speedster body that is unsurpassed.

Width of body, 32 inches; length of body, 83 inches; length over all, 11½ feet. Seats, 16x18 inches. All screw construction. Tanks, tank supports, seats, tool box and cowl are pressed steel with heavy rolled wire edge. Trimming of seats and cushions a clear, lustrous red with black edge binding and diamond quilted backs. Shipping weight, 225 pounds. Requires about 15 days' time.

Note—Radiator, engine hood and lamps not included with outfit.

261R4520—Painted Battleship Gray **$68.00**
261R4521—Light Blue with white stripe **$68.00**
261R4522—Red with black stripe.. ....**$68.00**
Shipped from factory in Southern Michigan.

Differential Gears for Fords

Special ratio differential ring gear and drive pinion for the Ford. More speed with maximum power at a decreased cost in gasoline and oil consumption. They prevent rolling of motor, thus eliminating undue wear and tear on parts. The Ford engine will take care of the higher gear, either the 2-4/7-1 or 3-1 ratio. The 3-1 ratio gears are suitable for country roads, city driving and where conditions permit 55 miles or more per hour. Gears are changeable with present gears. Changed quickly. Made of nickel gear steel properly hardened and sand blasted, giving gears almost a polished appearance. Weight, 5 pounds.

61R5749—2-4/7 to 1.........**$13.50**
61R5750—3 to 1.............13.50

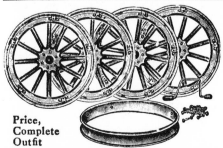

Price, Complete Outfit

161R4910—Black Finish ... **$12.25**
161R4911—Natural Finish.. 12.25

Wheel and Demountable Rim Outfit

Equip your Ford with demountable rims. It brings it up-to-date and greatly adds to the convenience when changing tires. The wheels are made by one of the foremost manufacturers in this country. In their construction nothing is used but well seasoned hickory, primed and painted. They are uniform in size (30x3½), which is a big advantage, as you can use the same tire on all the wheels, enabling you to switch front and rear tires whenever the rear tires show signs of wear. To make a tire change on the road it is only necessary to remove three lugs, loosen two and slip off the rim. You can then put on your spare tire and rim. Takes about five minutes to make the change. Outfit consists of five demountable clutcher rims, four wood wheels, rim wrench and bolts for attaching to your hubs. Furnished in either black or natural wood. Shipping weight, about 135 pounds.

Increased Beauty and Efficiency for Your Ford

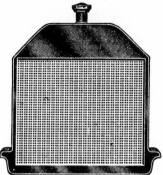

Wind Shields

Quick-Cool Radiators

Including Streamline Hood

Has 25 to 30 per cent greater cooling capacity than most Ford radiators. Will not break when frozen. It is a cellular radiator with copper tubes, three-inch core top and bottom tanks, brass casing and auxiliary water tank which gives total capacity of 2 gallons, 1 quart, 1 pint. Triple japanned, 20-gauge steel hood with six louvres on a side. Extended starting crank and bonnet clamp brackets, and hood edges with models prior to 1915. Mention model and year of car when ordering. Shipping weight, 80 pounds.
261R5752—Nickel finish **$32.50**
261R5773—Brass finish **31.50**
Shipped from factory in Southern Michigan.

Radiators for Fords

We have arranged with one of the largest and most reliable radiator concerns to supply our customers with radiators designed and built especially for Ford Cars. These are built of high-grade radiator materials (brass and copper), and when it comes to efficiency, appearance, strength, lightness and durability, non-leaking and non-freezing qualities, we invite comparison with all other makes. In this cellular type you get full air and water space. The core will not leak. No head sheets are used, and annoying and inevitable sources of leaks common to most radiators are eliminated. Freezing doesn't injure it. Shipping weight, 40 pounds.
261R5658—Price, each **$18.50**
Shipped from factory in Southern Michigan.

For Fords prior to 1915. Strictly high class construction. Frame is best quality steel, black enameled. Adjustable ball bearing hinges. Shield adjusts automatically. Will not rattle or loosen. Heavy imported glass, perfectly clear and set in rubber channels. All attachments included. Top strap loops to fasten top to shield included. Straight type shield for 1911 or 1912 models. Zigzag type for 1913, 1914 and early 1915 models. Shipping weight, 50 pounds.
161R5659—1911-12 Models **$8.25**
161R5660—1913-14-15 Models.. **8.25**

Water Circulator

An entirely successful water cooler. Will actually outlast the life of the car. The Ford should have a water circulator the same as other cars. A great many repair bills are due to overheating. This circulator pays for itself in a short time by eliminating those repair bills and by saving of oil and gasoline. Made of cast iron. Installation made in a few minutes. Keeps water cool in hottest weather. In a test, a Ford equipped with one of these circulators actually ran ten miles on low gear without boiling the water.
61R5722—Weight, 5 pounds... **$3.95**

Streamline Hood and Radiator Shell

Makes the Ford look like a high-priced car. Shell fits over present Ford radiator. Rigidly and quickly attached. Several large ventilators pressed in side of hood facilitate passage of gases and heated air from motor compartment. Allows greater air space around motor. The lower portion of present Ford fasteners may be utilized without alterations. Heat from radiator does not affect finish on shell. Get one and make your car impressive looking. Hood is heavy sheet steel. Hinges concealed waterproof type. Shell and hood finished in two coats of black enamel. Full directions sent. Shipping weight, 50 pounds.
161R4525—For 1913 models.**$11.75**
161R4526—For 1914 models. **11.75**
161R4527—For 1915-1916 models. Each **$11.75**

Adjustable Rain Vision Wind Shield

For the 1915-16 Streamline Ford Touring Car and Roadster. Adjustable at top and bottom for ventilation, or rainy weather. Easily substituted for the one now on car. Complete directions included. Strongly constructed. Will not rattle. Hinges lock automatically. All metal parts, black enameled. Shipping weight, 50 pounds.
161R4912—Price, Each **$8.25**

Rain Vision Ventilating Cowl Shields

Upper half adjustable. Locks automatically. Lower half opens inward. Rubber strip on bottom rail makes lower half wind and rain-proof. Curve-shaped pressed-steel cowl improves 1915 models equipped with the old zig-zag shield. Cowl and metal parts are black enameled and nickel trimmed. Best polished plate glass, held by metal clips. Shipping weight, 65 pounds.

161R4909—For 1914-15 models **10.75**

Water Connections for Ford Cylinders

Made of malleable iron and will not break. A feature is the slots for bolts which permits removal and replacement by simply loosening bolts. Weight, ¾ pound.
61R8685—Top Connection **22c**
61R8686—Side Connection **22c**

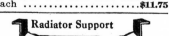

Radiator Support

Saves the side lugs from breaking off. Made of stamped steel, black enameled.
61R4915—Weight, 1 pound..... **35c**

Every Ford Auto Should Have a Starter

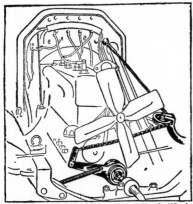

Easily attached. Simply drill hole through the wood dash. The cable, which connects the handle with the starting mechanism, works through this hole. Nothing is shown outside of the hood except starter handle.

$10.00 Challenge Starter for Ford Engines

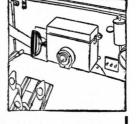

$4.75

Additional pleasure and comfort comes to the Ford owner who has his machine equipped with this engine starter. It is a great convenience in muddy, sloppy weather, when the engine is stalled or stops. It does away with getting out of the car to start it. You remain in the seat, adjust the speed lever and pull the starting handle which turns the engine over and starts the motor.

In case of back firing no damage will result to car or operator. This starter automatically disconnects when the motor back-fires, a feature not to be overlooked, as a great many accidents occur on account of back-firing when the motor is cranked the old way.

Built to stand up under the very hardest usage. Constructed of high-grade steel stock; machined and hardened by best process known. Cable is of sufficient size to give the very best wear and to last as long as the other parts. We have given this starter the most severe tests and have found it to be mechanically perfect. It will do everything claimed for it and we heartily recommend it to you. Usual price, $10.00.
161R5424—Shipping weight, 10 pounds $4.75

Top Prop Nut

To replace nuts lost because of vibration, failure to tighten properly, or other causes. Well made of steel, finely enameled black. Weight, 2 ounces.
61R5055—1¼-inch size 3c
61R5056—1½-inch size 3c

Fender Brace

No. 1. Designed to fasten over rear fender support rod to fender of Runabout. Effectually stops noise, and prevents fenders from being worn by vibration. Made of steel, enameled black. Supplied with screws and nuts.
61R5054—Weight, 2 ounces......3c

Fender Brace

No. 2. For fastening front or rear fender to runningboard shield, making it stiff and rigid. Eliminates the squeak, rattle or noise that is so often caused by these parts when loose. Made of steel, enameled black, and furnished with screws and nuts. Length, 2 inches; width, 1½ inches; height, 1¼ inches.
61R5057—Weight, 3 ounces......5c

Safety Pilot for Fords

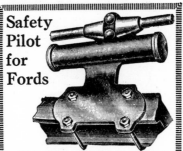

This device eliminates the necessity of constantly gripping the steering wheel. It automatically directs the car straight ahead, and, in case the steering gear breaks, will keep you on the road.

On rough roads it saves the nerves and strength of the driver and saves one-fifth tire wear. It overcomes the one objection to Ford cars—that of a too sensitive steering gear. Think what this means to you in the course of a year's time. An improvement you can't afford to be without. Made of malleable iron. Attachable in ten minutes.
61R8410—Weight, 2 pounds.$1.95

Bow Clamp for Ford Top

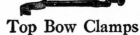

This steel clamp has a powerful level gear pull, holding the bows securely. Has large range of tightening action. Will not slip or mar the bows. Fits all Ford models since 1912. State whether yours is Roadster or Touring Car. Weight, 24 ounces.
61R4546—For Touring Car.....95c
61R4547—For Roadster 95c

Top Bow Clamps

Made especially for clamping together bows of Ford touring cars when top is down. Prevent rattle and noise. Well made of steel, finely enameled black. Top hook is fitted with leather to prevent marring and slipping. For all models of Ford touring cars. Sold in pairs only. Weight, 6 ounces.
61R5317—For Touring Cars....35c
61R5318—For Roadsters 35c

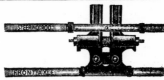

$15.00 Engine Starter for $9.50

A well-known engine starter for Fords that usually sells for $15.00. Primes and starts a Ford from the driver's seat. Large wheel for cable gives powerful leverage.

Backfire arrangement enclosed in large bevel gear. Impossible to feel a back fire at starter handle. Clutch sprocket and fan pulley fitted on main shaft of motor. Sprocket and chain stand idle while engine runs. Made of best malleable iron and steel. All wearing parts case hardened.
61R5461—Weight, 20 pounds.............. $9.50

Bestford Steering Device

Takes strain off driver as well as the wear off tires, knuckles and mechanism of car. Relieves the Ford of the lateral shock and will make it keep the road as well as high-priced cars. Safe, simple, strong and durable. Easily adjusted to suit any driver. Easily attached to steering rod. Full directions sent.

Made of malleable castings, and may be bent and hammered into shape again without injury. Spring and other mechanism cannot clog—strong and durable throughout.
61R7964—Weight, 2 pounds...$2.25

Added Convenience and Safety for Your Ford

Rear End Tire Holder

For Model T Ford Cars. The tires are supported low enough to permit the exhaust pipe to come within the circle of the tire, preventing damage to tires by smoke and soot. The tire bracket is heavy malleable iron. It is supplied with a special supporting bracket for holding license pad and lamp in position. Illustration shows method of fastening. There are no holes to be drilled; simply clamp tire bracket to spring, as illustrated. Straps furnished for holding tires on arms and tire bracket. Finished in black enamel. Suitable for one or two tires. Weight, 16 pounds.

61R5149—With license bracket.....**$2.15**

Running Board Tire Holder

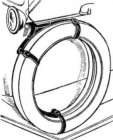

For Ford runabouts and touring cars. Light weight, strong and durable. Cold rolled steel, black enameled. Furnished complete with rivets and screws. No leather straps are used, but a metal hinge strap, with a hole drilled in the end, comes down over the tires. Can be locked with a small padlock, making the tires fast and secure. Will not fit 1915-16 models. Weight, 2½ pounds.

61R7501—For Runabouts..........**75c**
61R7502—For Touring Cars.........**75c**
61R7503—Padlock for use with above. Weight, 4 ounces **25c**

Tire Holder

For 1915 and 1916 Models only. Holds perfectly one or two tires on running board. Suitable for demountable rims or wheels. Attaches to left front lamp bracket. Made of steel.

61R7861— Weight, 3 pounds ..**$1.15**

New Tire Carrier for Model T Fords

Expanding rim for one or two tires, either plain or with demountable rims, 30x3 or 30x3½. Expanding device can be locked with padlock, making it impossible to get tire off. Made of pressed steel, enameled black. No lock furnished.

Weight, about 10 pounds.
61R4544—Single Tire Holder.....**$2.25**
61R4545—Double Tire Holder......**3.50**

Cradle Tire Holder

Forms a snug cradle for each tire which prevents chafing. Thiefproof snap lock on the rear style. A lamp bracket is attached, and provision made for attaching license plate. Cross strap is drilled, and wing nuts furnished, so any sized license can be easily attached. Either tire can be removed in ten seconds without disturbing the other, by merely unlocking. Made throughout of heavy pressed steel, enameled black. Can be attached in a few moments. Holds two tires, 30x3 or 30x3½. Also made in runningboard style, with upright brackets for screwing to board. Weight, 15 pounds.

61R7512—Regular style **$4.45**
61R7513—Running Board style.....**4.05**

Rear Tire Holder
For Demountable Rims

For Model T Fords. Easily accessible. Lamp and license bracket is rigidly clamped around the two vertical supporting arms. By locking two adjusting levers makes tires secure against theft. One or two tires are carried in a vertical position clear of exhaust. Strongly built of malleable iron and steel, finished in baked Ebony enamel. Complete with straps.

61R4543—Weight, 20 pounds......**$2.95**

Rear Demountable Tire Holder

For Model T Ford. One or two tires are held rigidly in position without the use of straps. Locked to prevent theft by simply passing padlock around the two adjusting screws. Rigidly made from malleable iron and steel throughout. Will carry the spare tire in a vertical position below the exhaust. Finished in ebony enamel. Shipping weight, 20 pounds.

161R4541—For One Tire........**$2.80**
161R4542—For Two Tires........**3.65**

Trunk Rack for Ford

Bolts on lower sill of body. Side arms attach around goose neck rod on which auto top rests when down. Folds back against body of car when not in use. Strongly made of cold rolled steel, black enameled.
61R7517—28-in. size **$1.15**
61R7518—30-in. size.........**$1.25**

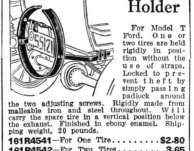

Weight, about 16 pounds

Clamp-On Bumper

Cold rolled steel channel bar style, finished in black or nickel, with black side arms and fittings. The clamps attach to the spring bar and spring, and the supporting braces attach to the lamp brackets with a U bolt. Springs are concealed and rightly tempered to insure proper resiliency. Will not fit 1915 Models. Weight, 25 pounds.

61R7509—Nickel **$4.25**
61R7511—All Black **3.75**

Clamp-On Bumper

Strong and well made. No car is complete without one. Easily attached. Diameter of bar, 1¼ inches. Will not fit 1915 models. Weight, 26 pounds.

61R7506—All black finish........**$2.95**

Lyon Bumper

Practically new but already widely used by the large taxi-cab companies and thousands of individuals. Simple and nothing to break or get out of order. Made of two specially formed oil tempered springs which overlap in front, making it adjustable to all widths of frames. Indestructible. No drilling of frame to attach. Shipping weight, 18 pounds.

161R7783—Black finish **$5.40**
161R7785—Nickel finish **7.20**

New Model Clamp-On Bumper

For Ford Cars. A 2-inch cold-rolled steel channel bar finished in black or nickel. Extending arms enclose a resilient spring which tends to lessen shock in case of accident. Arms attach to frame at side of radiator. Enameled black. Weight, 20 pounds.

61R4677—All black bar, black fittings.**$3.35**
61R4678—All nickel bar, black fittings**3.75**

Exhaust Deflector

Clamps around end of exhaust pipe on any model Ford. Easily turned in any direction. Deflects heat, smoke and oil from tires when carried in rear. Does not interfere with exhaust. Stamped steel, black enameled.
61R5146—Weight, 8 ounces.........**15c**

Safety-First Requisites for Your Ford

Hand Horn for Fords

Gives a loud, clear warning signal simply by pressing down lever. Mechanism is simple, operates easily. Attaches to left side. Made of malleable iron, black enameled. Bell stamped steel, black enamel, nickel tip. Length, over all, 6 inches.

61R4551—Weight, 2½ pounds.**$1.15**

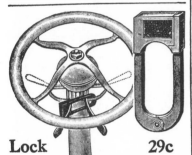

Lock   29c

Protect your car from theft. Why leave it standing on the street or in garage unprotected, when for this small sum you can lock up the control levers, as illustrated above, and make your car safe? A positive, substantial protector. Made of brass, highly polished and buffed. All machine parts are fitted. Phosphor bronze spring, noted for their long life without getting out of order. Self-locking device. Equipped with two flat push keys.

61R5214—Weight, about 5 ounces **29c**

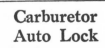

Carburetor Auto Lock

This lock is applied between the flanges of the carburetor and intake pipe. It is a genuine Yale lock and is so made that it cannot be picked. A quarter turn of the key throws a shut-off gate entirely across the gas passage and locks in position. Nothing can move the gate except turning of the key. No chance of partially closing gate as key cannot be withdrawn until gate is fully closed. Easily attached. Not necessary to raise hood to operate. Full instructions with each lock. Size, 6x4½x1 inch.

61R4732—Weight, 14 ounces ...**$3.75**

Stewart Speedometer

At this unusually low price, no one need be without one. The name Stewart on a speedometer means quality. An instrument like this is the motorist's best friend. It checks gasoline consumption and tire wear; furnishes a positive warning against speeding, and helps you in following a guide book when traveling over new routes.

The case is made of steel and enameled jet black; polished brass trim covered with heavy French plate glass, and protected by a heavy bezel. The white figures stand out sharp and clear on the black dial. Has a speed dial of 60-miles capacity. Gears are of hard bronze, locked in place to prevent slipping. Always registers correctly. No lubrication needed. Will register 10,000 miles; trip register up to 100. Made especially for Ford cars. Regular price, $12.00. Diameter, 3¼ inches; depth, 2⅜ inches.

61R5268—Weight, 11 pounds...**$6.50**

Standard Speedometer

The Standard is accurate. The hand is steady. Miles per hour, trip and total mileage easily read. Fifty-mile dial, 100-mile trip and 10,000-mile automatic repeating season register. Attached in ten minutes. Used on over 150,000 Fords. Bearings all steel with hardened and ground ball cups pressed in. Finished in black.

61R7921—Weight, 12 pounds..**$7.25**

Auto Clock

A neat, inexpensive timepiece that will give excellent satisfaction. Movement is well made, and not easily susceptible to jolting or vibration. Stem wind and stem set. Dial, 2 inches; width of clock, 2⅞ inches. Weight, 1 pound.

61R5764—Brass finish **$1.45**
61R7731—Nickel finish 1.45

Radius Rod Support

Will prevent breakage or bending of the radius rod. Many accidents are caused by bending or breaking of the radius rod, causing car to jump the road. It will make the car run more steadily, and preserves the life of it by eliminating the vibration of the front axle, giving that steadiness to the steering wheel found in heavier cars. It reduces wear on ball and socket at rear of radius rod. Easily and quickly put on without partly taking car apart. Does not interfere with shock absorbers. Well made of angle iron, enameled black.

61R5215—Weight, 5½ pounds...**57c**

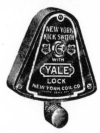

New York Kick Switch with Yale Lock

A switch that is operated by the foot, to start or stop car. By giving the key a turn, a genuine Yale Lock inside the switch locks the connections in the off position. Instantly fits the Ford metal or wood coil box. Two keys and full directions with each switch.

61R7867—Weight, 8 ounces...**$1.95**

Make Your Ford an Easy Rider

The H. & D. attached to the front.

The H. & D. attached to the rear.

Genuine H. & D. Shock Absorbers $3.95

Here is the big shock absorber hit of the season for Ford owners. Moreover, we offer it at a price that seems almost impossible. Ford owners everywhere are intensely interested in this simple but perfect little shock absorber; are trying it out and immediately giving it their hearty endorsement. They can't say enough for it after having ridden in a car equipped with it. It responds instantly to the slightest jar and checks the hardest jolts so effectively that you do not realize you have bumped over anything. Consider what such a shock eliminator means to the mechanism of your car. Then consider the price. Note the simplicity. No complicated parts and nothing to get out of order. Special care has been taken to make all parts that receive any strain extra strong. In fact, we guarantee this absorber to not only please you, but we guarantee it against breakage for the life of your car. Quickly attached. No holes to bore and everything furnished complete. Made of malleable iron. Illustrations show how absorber is attached front and rear. Set consists of four, two for front and two for rear. Shipping weight, 20 pounds.

161R4879—For Touring Model. Price set..................**$3.95**
161R4880—For Roadster Model. Price, set..................

Shock Absorbers

Thousands of high-priced, heavy touring cars have been equipped with shock absorbers, with beneficial results. It is an acknowledged fact that the lighter the car the greater the necessity for a shock-resisting device. Eliminates practically all the shock before it can be transmitted to the body spring. Works directly over the axle, and no matter how light the shock, its action is instantaneous. They make a car surprisingly smooth-riding, even with the lightest load. They prevent the car from going down too hard, when on a rough road or crossing, and greatly reduce the rebound.

The springs are packed in grease, and will lubricate automatically, requiring attention not more than once or twice a year. Steel spring encased in a neat steel housing.

The entire absorber is finished in baked black japan. Can be applied without machining. Full instructions for attaching included with each set. Come in sets of four. Weight, per set, about 20 pounds.

61R5807—Touring Model Set..**$4.45**
61R5808—Roadster Model 4.45

K. W. Road Smoothers

The helical spring takes up the shock, the air cushion chamber with piston checks the rebound, the anti-side motion links prevent side motion, and the chassis from getting out of alignment. This combination will positively smooth out the roughest roads. Save tire bills by keeping the wheels in the road; and add life to the car by stopping vibration. Equipped with phosphor bronze bushings throughout. High-grade, heat-treaded drop forgings and electric smelted vanadium steel springs. Regular price, $15.00 a set. Set of four. Weight, 18 pounds.

61R4923—For Touring Car...**$12.25**
61R4924—For Roadster 12.25

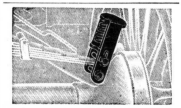

Rebound Check Strap and Springs

Tends to stop that swaying of the car, and holds it to the road. Can be used with or without shock absorbers. No drilling or fitting to attach them. Best tempered steel springs obtainable. Straps are Latigo leather, supposed to be the strongest leather, and tanned by the oldest known formula. The straps are oil and water-proof. Set consists of two rear and one front spring and straps, as illustrated.

61R5152—Weight, 6 pounds.
Set **$2.95**

Challenge Shock Easers

Apply a set of these to your Ford car and it will ride much easier. They tend to reduce wear on tires and lengthen the life of car by absorbing shocks. They also prevent rebound, making it almost impossible to break a spring. Made of malleable iron; springs of steel; finish in black. Can be easily applied without removing rear wheels or taking down front axle. Made only for Ford Touring and Roadster Cars. Sold in sets of four. Weight, 13 pounds.

61R5470—For Touring Car Set.**$1.50**
61R5472—For Roadster Set... 1.45

Rebound Checks

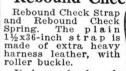

Rebound Check Strap and Rebound Check Spring. The plain 1½x36-inch strap is made of extra heavy harness leather, with roller buckle.

It is a simple, effective recoil attachment, which allows a natural downward motion, yet prevents breakage by absorbing the shocks when springs rise above neutral position. It fits entirely over frame, eliminating the strain that is often placed on the edge in other makes. Springs are made of oil tempered steel, attached to an oak tanned leather strap. Steel clamps furnished, making it unnecessary to drill holes. Easily and quickly placed in position.

61R8866—Plain Rebound Check Strap. Weight, 12 ounces......**65c**

61R5753—Rebound Check Spring and Strap. Weight, 2¼ pounds.**70c**

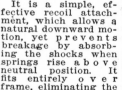

Front.

Rear.

Springs for Fords

Ford front or rear springs, for models N. S. R. and T. Special alloy steel of high quality. The tension and flexibility are perfect. Buying cheap springs to save money is like stopping a watch to save time. Our springs not only combine quality and workmanship, but fit perfectly as well.

161R5757—Front Spring. Shipping weight, 24 pounds...........**$1.95**

161R5758—Rear Spring. Shipping weight, 36 pounds...........**$7.**

Mr. Ford Owner—Fan Belts and Other Needs for You

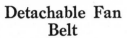

Non-Slip Fan Belt

Somewhat different from other leather belts now sold. It is tanned; also treated by a process which makes it non-slipping, oil and moisture-proof. Treated so there is a clinging surface on the pulley side of the belt that will last until belt is worn out.
61R5213—Weight, 4 ounces....**15c**

Detachable Fan Belt

A high-grade leather belt that can be quickly and easily put on or taken off. The quick-action fastener works easily and satisfactorily. It will not come apart while in use. For Ford cars only.
61R8604—Weight, 6 ounces **19c**

Wheel Puller

Indispensable for removing Ford wheels, which, because of a tapered axle, frequently become firmly fixed or set in place. Easy to disengage them with this puller. Made of best quality gray iron, accurately threaded. Steel set screw, round pointed, which prevents injury to axle.
61R7529—Weight, 1 pound.....**19c**

Breather and Oil Filler

A funnel shaped device, that is permanently fastened into the breather pipe on the Ford car. A fine screen near bottom, through which all oil passes before entering motor. Makes it easy to put in oil without spilling it all over the engine.
61R7525—Weight, 1½ pounds...**34c**

Little Steersman

For Ford cars. An auxiliary steering gear, which gives the driver absolute control over the car on account of the right tension between the front springs and steering rod. Automatically takes up lost motion between steering wheel and road wheels when steering gear is worn, keeping wheels in perfect alignment. A helical spring, length, about 3 feet, made from oil tempered steel wire, attachments drop steel forgings.
R7530—Weight, 3 pounds...**$1.45**

Fabric Fan Belt

For Ford cars. Constructed of six plies, strong, tightly woven special army duck. Well threaded with a special compound, which increases the friction; also makes the belt proof against action of oil, water and heat. All stretch is taken from fabric before treatment. Made endless, the splice being sewed above and below, eliminating all chance of opening. Sewed with especially treated thread.
61R7523—Weight, 6 ounces....**15c**

Radiator Cap

New design. Made of cast brass, highly polished. Has projecting arms, which permit easy removal even when radiator is hot. Accurately threaded to fit Ford radiator.
61R7534—Weight, 12 ounces.....**27c**

Molding Assembly

Consists of a complete set of mahogany finish body moldings, cut to exact length, with all necessary screws and washers for attaching. By placing this molding on the top edge and doors of Ford cars it will greatly add to their appearance. Weight, about 2 pounds.

Number	Price	Model	Year
61R4861	95c	Touring	1912
61R5206	95c	Touring	1913
61R5207	95c	Touring	1914
61R5208	95c	Touring	1915
61R4862	95c	Runabout	1912
61R5209	95c	Runabout	1913
61R5210	95c	Runabout	1914
61R5211	95c	Runabout	1915

Ritesize Muffler

No back pressure—no noise. A duplicate of the Ford muffler, arranged so that it may be attached to any Ford automobile (except 1915 models), by simply removing the old muffler and attaching the Ritesize in its place.

If the muffler on your Ford is worn out, rattles, or has blown to pieces, use this and get the best results at a low price. Furnished complete with tail pipe as shown.
61R5202—Weight, 10 pounds..**$1.70**

Rigid Rear Axle Truss

Braces the Ford rear axles so as to prevent sagging. Keeps the differential pinion and gear in perfect alignment. Consists of two black enameled malleable iron clamps and rod, which fasten to rear axle near hubs. Fits all Ford models. Average weight, 5 pounds.
61R5204—For standard 56-inch tread. Each **45c**

Leather Fan Belt

Made of best quality fan belt leather, endless. Impervious to oil, water or heat. For Ford cars. Cemented laps that will not come apart.
61R7528—Weight, 6 ounces **30c**

Fan Belt Holder

Prevents fan belt from slipping off pulley of car. Every Ford owner should have one, and be always assured that his fan is working. Easily attached. Fastened to fan belt bracket. Length, 2½ inches; width, 2 inches.
61R7532—Weight, 4 ounces....**12c**

Hub Cap

Made of heavy gauge brass, highly polished. Accurately threaded. Made to fit Ford hubs. Occasionally a hub cap is lost or damaged. Have one or more handy in the tool kit.
61R7524—Weight, 3 ounces....**13c**

Timer Lever Anti-Rattling Ball Joint

This ball joint with nut, used regularly on Ford timer levers, on account of natural wear, needs replacing from time to time. Best grade steel, accurately tapped and threaded 7/32x32 inches.
61R7531—Weight, 4 ounces **8c**

Steering Gear Anti-Rattling Ball Socket

For use on steering gear connecting rods, where it takes the place of steel cap. Spring behind pivot takes up the wear, and eliminates all rattle from this source. When once attached no further adjustment needed. Lower in price than other devices of this kind now sold, but fully dependable.
61R7533—Weight, 8 ounces....**20c**

Radius Rod Anti-Rattling Ball Socket

An excellent device, known to most Ford owners. For eliminating the annoying rattle caused by the wear of cap on end of radius rod. Easily adjusted; attached in a few moments.
61R7535—Weight, 1¼ pounds..**30c**

Keep the Valves of Your Ford in Good Trim

K.W. Master Vibrator

Widely advertised and a make that is used on thousands of Ford cars. Offered to you for what it is —a widely advertised and widely used satisfactory instrument. It will give you a hotter spark, which tends to prevent sooty plugs. Makes starting easy, due to the hotter spark. This one, the same as others, is designed to utilize the alternating current of the Ford Magneto. Well made, box of hardwood, finely polished. Brass attaching lugs and snap cover-hinges. Large kick-switch and cut-out plug, as illustrated. Will not fit 1915 Fords with cowl dash.
61R7559—Weight, 4 pounds..**$12.75**

Valve Spring Remover

A practical, simple and efficient tool. Can be placed in position quickly, and will not slip. The indentations in slot will hold the chain firmly in place when pressure is applied. Made of cold rolled steel, dull nickel finish.
61R7547—Weight, 6 ounces 38c

Valve Adjusting Nuts

To screw on valve stems. They silence the noise made by meeting of push rod and valve stem. Lock nut and adjusting nut made of hardened steel.
61R5106—Weight, 2 ounces 8c

Valve Springs

To replace springs, which, through continual use or other causes, break frequently. Made of high-grade crucible steel wire, oil tempered. Give exceptionally good service.
61R7556—Weight, 1 ounce.......3c

Valve Spring Lifter

Compresses two springs at once and holds them securely. The valves may be taken out, ground and replaced without moving the springs, as is necessary with most lifters. So simple to operate that the valves of all cylinders can be taken out without removing manifolds or carburetor. Made of cast iron, finished black. This size made especially for the Ford motor.
61R5061—Weight, 8 ounces.....19c

Marvel Valve Grinder for Fords

Saves half the time of grinding valves. Always laps—does not stop at same spot. Makes a perfect smooth seat. A boy can operate it. Turn the handle in one direction and valve turns back and forth always a little further in one direction than the other.
61R5657—Weight, 3 pounds...**$1.40**

Valve Grinder

The operator pulls the handle which unwinds chain, causing grinder tool to rotate. A strong spring rewinds chain. This means rapidity of operation and a consequent accurate mechanical movement. A better method of valve grinding than most other tools. Malleable iron. Size, 3⅝ x 6¼ x 3⅝.
61R4729—Weight, 30 ounces..**$1.50**

Valve Grinder

Will fit under the dash on the last valve of any Ford Car. Hardwood handle. Rest is steel. The pins are put in to stay.
61R5060—Weight, 1 pound.....14c

Valve Grinding Set

The advantages in keeping the valve ground and the cylinder clean are more power, longer life to the motor and more mileage per gallon of gasoline; also eliminates overheating and knocking when climbing hills, caused by carbon deposit in the cylinders. This set is used for doing the work yourself. Outfit contains one valve spring lifter, one valve turning tool, one cylinder head wrench socket, one tube of course and one tube of fine valve grinding paste; one thickness gauge, and complete instructions.
61R5059—Weight, 2 pounds..39c

Riverside Master Vibrator

Adjustable for all models Ford Cars. A strictly reliable and neat coil. Case is made of hardwood, varnished and polished, with brass fasteners, kick switch, and cut-off plug. It eliminates trouble and annoyance usually experienced in trying to keep four different vibrators adjusted. The contact screws of the oil coil are simply screwed down, and the adjusting is done by the vibrator on the master coil only. This gives one single adjustment for all the cylinders, a hotter spark, cleaner plugs, more engine power, and makes starting easier. Gives as good service as any vibrator on the market regardless of name, make or price. Easily attached in a few minutes. Complete, simple instructions included.
61R8615—Weight, 4 pounds...**$4.95**

Ford Valve Adjusters

Made to take up the wear and lost motion between the ends of valve stems and push rods. They will silence the click and noise caused by these parts meeting, and have a tendency to increase the power of motor by opening the valves to their full capacity. A set consists of 8 bands and 40 hardened discs, all made of finest steel. Will take any degree of temper, will stand great wear and can be bent without showing a fraction.
61R7546—Weight, 4 ounces.....14c

Spring Valve Cover

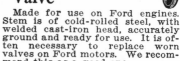

If your engine is not equipped with one, get this. Keeps the oil in and the dirt out. Prolongs the life of your motor. Made of semi-steel and furnished with steel clamps, and thumb nuts for attaching.
61R7557—Weight, 2½ pounds.**$1.35**

Ford Valve

Made for use on Ford engines. Stem is of cold-rolled steel, with welded cast-iron head, accurately ground and ready for use. It is often necessary to replace worn valves on Ford motors. We recommend this as a good one.
61R7552—Weight, 6 ounces.....15c

Valve Lifter

Made especially for Ford Car. Requires no holders while pin is removed. Serves double purpose as spring compressor. Made of malleable iron.
61R4550—Weight, 1 pound......25c

Helpful Accessories for Ford Cars

Foot Accelerator

Permits manipulating throttle with foot. Especially convenient when driving through crowded city streets, because it eliminates the necessity of moving the throttle on the steering column continually, to vary the speed. The throttle lever can be set to a certain speed. If necessary, to increase power for hill climbing, foot pedal is then put into action, and after releasing it, original speed is maintained. Quickly and easily attached. Furnished complete.

61R5201—Weight, 1½ pounds..**50c**

Aluminum Heel Plates

Special tough aluminum. Plain borders with corrugated center. Attached to the rubber mat where heels rest when feet are on pedals. No screws nor rivets necessary. Simply bend corners down, place on mat same position on corner, cut slits in matting, insert corners, and bend to clinch. By using these you will never need a new mat. Length, 5 inches; width, 3¾ inches.

61R5713—Weight, 4 ounces.....**21c**

Lined Brake Shoes

To replace the plain metal brakes regularly supplied with the Ford car. Made of selected casting, carefully drilled and milled to accurate dimensions. Lined with a superior quality asbestos brake lining. To install, simply remove present internal cam brakes and replace with these. Weight, pair, about 4 pounds.

61R5199—Per pair **65c**

Front Wheel Ball Races

Made from best grade steel. Carefully hardened and polished. Large size is the inner ball race—Ford repair No. 2805. Small size is outer ball race—Ford repair No. 2804. Average weight, 2 ounces.

61R5191—Large Ball Race.....**11c**
61R5192—Small Ball Race.....**8c**

Bushings

To take place of Ford repair parts No. 2713-2714. Made of good wearing quality bearing metal, accurately machined to size. Weight, 4 ounces.

61R5194—No. 2713 ....**7c**
61R5195—No. 2714 ....**4c**

Standard Muffler Cut-out

This outfit is well known to Ford owners. As illustrated, it comes complete with a high-grade cut-out valve of the proper size, a lock pedal, and four feet of wire cable with pulley. Can be attached quickly cutting a V-shaped hole in the under side of the exhaust pipe, then clamping over the top and under part of the exhaust pipe, making it unnecessary to remove the exhaust pipe or cut any threads, as is necessary with some cut-out sets now sold. Time tried and tested, and especially assembled for Ford cars. The entire outfit is put up in a neat cardboard box.

61R5717—Weight, 2¼ pounds **38c**

Clutch Release

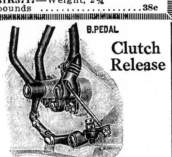

B.PEDAL

A simple device that automatically releases the clutch on the model T Ford when the foot brake is applied. If you wish to coast, you simply push the brake pedal further forward, which releases the clutch; and pushing the brake pedal further forward applies the brake and brings the car to a standstill, without the use of the emergency brake or the clutch pedal. A great help to amateurs, as with it, it is possible to apply the brake without first throwing out the clutch. In reversing, the foot is always on the brake pedal to stop the car instantly without stalling the engine. Applying the brake without first throwing out the clutch wears the brake out quickly and puts a strain on the clutch that will cause it to slip after a few weeks' use.

61R5193—Weight, 2 pounds.....**35c**

Front Wheel Cone

Adjustable cone for front wheel of Ford car. Right and left threads. Made of hardened steel. Weight, 4 ounces.

61R5197—Right thread **10c**
61R5198—Left thread **10c**

Front Wheel

A stationary hardened steel cone for front wheels of all model Fords. Regular Part No. 2704.

61R5196—Weight, 3 ounces....**14c**

Asbestos Transmission Lining

FOR FORD CARS

Every Ford car is equipped with a transmission brake made in three parts, each part lined with a strip of brake lining. Because of nearness to magneto, lining must not contain brass wire, and practically no cotton, or it cannot withstand action of oil and grease to which it is exposed. This lining contains no wire. Composed almost wholly of long fibre asbestos, thoroughly impregnated with a compound, making it impervious to action of oil, grease, water, dirt, gasoline or heat, and causing it to have unusual grip power and durability. Correct size. Neat box contains three pieces, and a sufficient quantity of copper rivets for attaching. Get this—it means safety as far as brake lining is concerned.

61R5715—Weight, 1 pound.....**48c**

Muffler Cut-out

Made of malleable iron that will not break. Furnished complete with lock pedal that will hold cut-out open without holding your foot on the pedal. Easily released when you want to close the cut-out. Positive in action, and will prevent bursting of muffler. Will increase the power of the engine and easily locate skips. Easy to install. Simply cut a 1¼-inch hole in exhaust pipe and clamp cut-out in place. Fasten pedal in floor board, and connect with cut-out by cable furnished with each outfit. Once you install one you would never do without it. Furnished complete, including cable, lock pedal, etc.

61R5716—Weight, 2 pounds....**39c**

Cushion Pedal Pad

Prevents feet from slipping off pedals. Made of rubber with metal bands for attaching for Ford cars. Scientifically designed for comfort and safety. When moderate pressure is applied on pedal by sole of shoe, air is compressed in cells, forming an air cushion which effectively absorbs vibration and jar. Quickly and easily attached to pedal. Weight, set, 1½ pounds.

61R5200—Set of three **38c**

Ball Retainers

Made from special grade of steel, to insure proper action. The larger retainer is Ford repair No. 2807; the small one is No. 2808. Weight, each, 2 ounces.

61R5189—Large Retainer **4c**
61R5190—Small Retainer **4c**

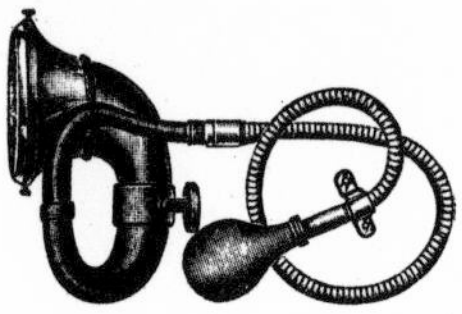

Keep All Parts of Your Ford in Good Condition

Coil Parts, Switch Keys and Plugs

Only the best of materials are used in making our coil parts. Platinum iridium points are used where platinum is necessary. Tungsten contacts of full size where Tungsten in our judgment is equally satisfactory. Springs of spring steel. Switch keys and plugs of brass with hard rubber caps.

Average shipping weight of coil parts or plugs each, 2 ounces.

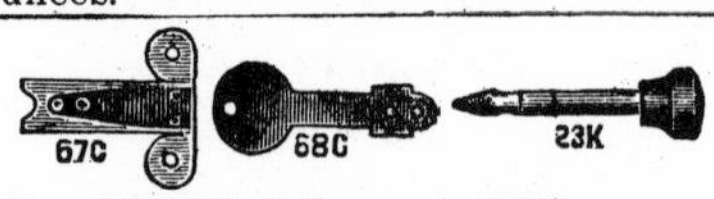

Fit K-W Master Vibrator

Article Number	Number of Part	Name of Part	Price Each
61R5017	67C	Platinum Bridge	$1.15
61R5018	68C	Platinum Spring	1.15
61R5050	23K	Switch Plug	.06

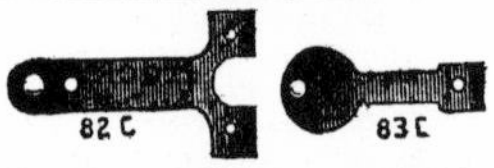

Fit Wells Master Vibrator

Article Number	Number of Part	Name of Part	Price Each
61R5041	82C	Tungsten Bridge	$0.90
61R5042	83C	Tungsten Spring	.75

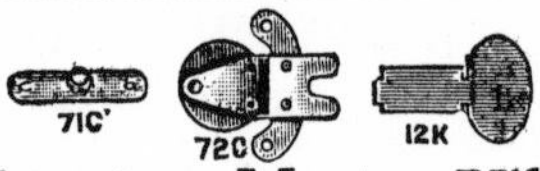

Fit Kingston Master Vibrator

Article Number	Number of Part	Name of Part	Price Each
61R5037	71C	Tungsten Bridge	$0.75
61R5038	72C	Tungsten Spring	.90
61R5048	12K	Switch Key	.04

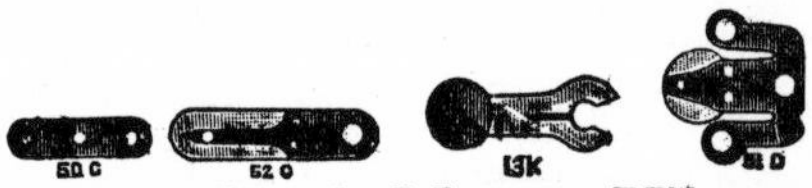

Fit New York Master Vibrator

Article Number	Number of Part	Name of Part	Price Each
61R5021	50C	Platinum Bridge	$1.05
61R5023	52C	Platinum Spring	1.13
61R5022	51C	Platinum Spring	1.13
61R5049	13K	Switch Lever	.07

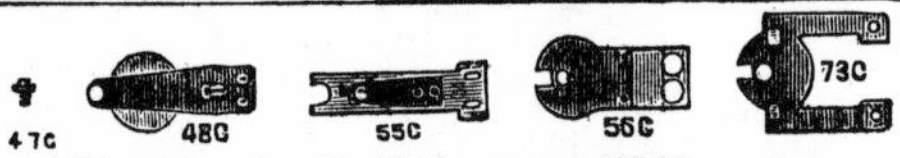

Fit B. & S. Master Vibrator

Article Number	Number of Part	Name of Part	Price Each
61R5026	47C	Platinum Screw	$1.35
61R5027	48C	Platinum Spring	1.35
61R5028	55C	Platinum Bridge	1.05
61R5029	56C	Platinum Spring	1.05
61R5030	73C	Platinum Spring	1.05

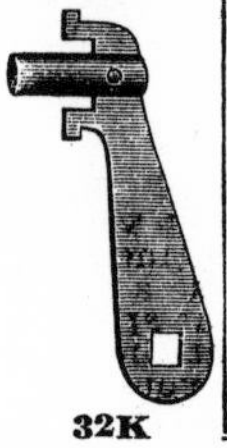

32K

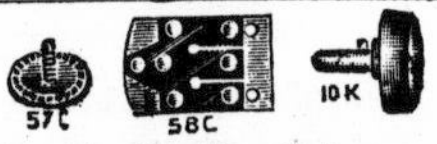

Fit J. & B. Master Vibrator

Article Number	Number of Part	Name of Part	Price Each
61R5024	57C	Tungsten Screw.	$0.60
61R5025	58C	Tungsten Spring.	.75
61R5046	10K	Switch Plug.....	.05

Fits Ford Metal Box

Article Number	Number of Part	Name of Part	Price Each
61R5101	32K	Switch Key	$0.03

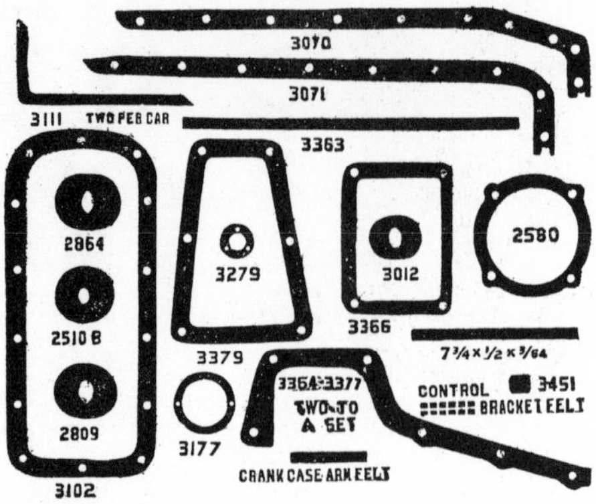

Best Quality Wool Gaskets

Made of best quality wool felt in the correct shapes and dimensions to fit the parts specified.

Number	Style	Location	Each	Dozen
61R5116	2580	Universal ball cap gasket.....	$0.04	$0.40
61R5117	3070	Crank case and cyl. gasket, L. H.	.04	.40
61R5118	3071	Crank case and cyl. gasket, R. H.	.04	.40
61R5119	3102	Crank case lower cover gasket..	.08	.80
61R5120	3111	Cyl. door gasket triangle......	.02	.20
61R5121	3177	Commutator felt ring........	.04	.40
61R5122	3363	Trans. cover front gasket......	.02	.20
61R5123	3364	Trans. cover gasket..........	.08	.70
61R5124	3366	Trans. cover door gasket......	.08	.80
61R5125	3377	Trans. cover gasket..........	.08	.70
61R5126	3379	Trans. sloping door gasket.....	.06	.70
61R5127	3451	Control bracket, felt.........	.02	.18
61R5128	....	Trans. cover strip, 7¾x½x3/64 in.	.02	.18
61R5129	....	Crank case arm strip, 3½x½x3/64 inches	.02	.18
61R5130	2510B	For rear axle, 2 7/16x⅝x5/16 in...	.02	.20
61R5131	2809	For front bulb, diameter, 2½ in.	.02	.20
61R5132	3012	For crank shaft, 2x13/16x⅜ in..	.02	.20
61R5133	3279	For mag. contact, 1½x¾x3/64 in.	.02	.20
61R5134	2864	For use with bulb having 1⅝-in. boss on flange end, 2 7/16x1½x 7/16 in.	.02	.20

Average weight, each, 2 ounces; per dozen, 6 ounces.

Engine Gaskets

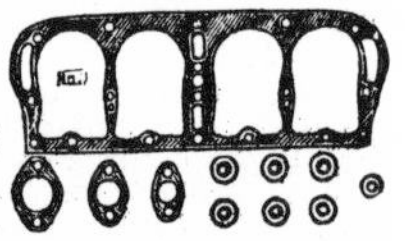

Well made of copper and brass, and lined with asbestos. For Ford cars. Set consists of one cylinder head gasket; one cylinder head outlet gasket; one cylinder water head inlet gasket; one carburetor flange gasket; six inlet and exhaust pipe gaskets. Set furnished complete, or the cylinder head gasket separately.

61R5700—Complete. Weight, 12 ounces. Price, set. **35c**
61R5701—Cylinder Head Gasket only. Weight, 8 ounces. Each **25c**

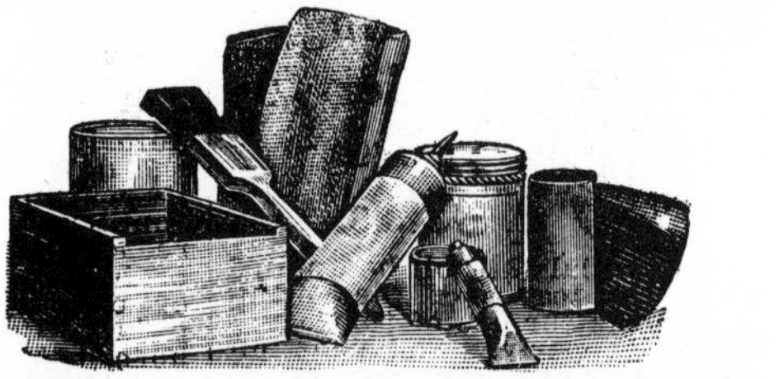

Riverside Ford Tire Repair Outfit

Here is repair for every tire trouble. One 8-ounce tube of Riverside tire cut filler, for filling tears and digouts in the casing, preve ting serious decay, sand blisters and the tread from separating from the fabric; one pint can Riverside tire paint and liquid rubber compound, for preventing premature decay; also make the tires look fresh, clean and new; one brush; one heavy fabric inside blow-out patch, for 3 or 3½-inch casing; one strip of patching rubber, size, 2½x12 inches, for patching purposes; one 4-ounce tube Riverside non-inflammable, triple-strength rubber cement; three cementless patches of great adhesive qualities, requiring no acid or cement when used.

Put up in wooden box. Length, 9 inches. Width, 6 inches. Height, 5 inches.

61R5655—Complete Outfit. Weight, 2 pounds. Price....... **$1.50**

Fit Your Ford with a Horn or Whistle

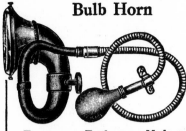

Ford Electric Vibrator Horn

Operates from dry cells, either 4 or 6, or from any storage battery. It must not be attached to the strong current supplied by a Ford magneto as coil inside of horn will not stand it. Consumes little current, and a set of dry batteries will last nearly an entire season. Gives a clear, distinct warning. Operates instantaneously by a slight touch on the push button, which can be installed on the steering wheel or any other convenient place. With each horn we furnish wiring, push button and screws. Bell is of brass, either highly polished or finely nickel-plated finish. Body is of stamped steel, black enamel finish. Takes very little space. If you desire a good efficient electric horn at a low price, get this. Length, over all, 6½ inches. Weight, 4 pounds.
61R5727—Black and Brass...$1.45
61R5728—Black and Nickel.... 1.45

Windshield Reducing Mirror

With this attached to your windshield, you can see what is back of you without turning around or taking your attention off your driving. Convexed reflector diminishes objects and gives a wide range of vision. Adjustable. Diameter, 4 inches; length of arm, 12 inches. Weight, 1¼ pounds.
61R4895—Black finish 60c
61R4896—Nickel finish 60c

Leaf Spring Oiler for Ford Cars

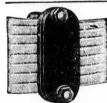

It is essential that oil be applied between the leaves of the spring to enable the surface of the leaves to work properly. Sufficient oil eliminates the rust between the leaves of the spring, making the car ride better and saving every part of the car from wear—both body and engine. On Ford cars this oiler is attached to the end of the shortest leaf. To secure best results a Ford car should have four of these oilers, two on the rear and two on the front springs. Illustration shows method of attaching. Finished in black enamel. Sold in pairs only. Weight, 8 ounces.
61R5114—For 1¼-inch springs.70c
61R5115—For 2-inch springs...70c

New Chime Horn

Owing to the great demand for a reliable, positive chime horn for Ford cars, we have had this outfit made up for us. Has a three-tone chime. Requires very little exhaust pressure to operate. Made of polished brass tubing. Very light and serviceable. Has three distinct tones which blend harmoniously. The volume of tone can be increased or diminished, according to the amount required, by regulating the pressure on the foot pedal. The valve is constructed on a double butterfly principle. It is bored 1½ inches, which is the size required for Ford cars. Valve will not burn out, stick or leak. Is the new bolt-up type, as shown in the illustration, and can be installed without removing the exhaust pipe, by merely cutting a section of pipe between hubs, and bolting on. A big improvement over the old type, which necessitated the removal of the exhaust pipe, and had to be either threaded or brazed. Sets finished complete with chime, valve, foot pedal, and cable. Outside diameter of tubing, 2 inches; length over all, 9¾ inches.
61R5726—Weight, 5 pounds...$2.75

Ford Jericho Horn

Operates from exhaust—costs nothing to operate. Made of aluminum. Effective and efficient. It warns without offense. It helps prevent accidents. Like a bugle note, it rises clear and strong above the noise of city traffic, or sounds its warning far ahead on winding country roads. It never fails to respond to the pedal, never clogs or balks. Simply clamp over tail of exhaust, and attach cable to pedal. Complete outfit contains horn, pedal cable and full instruction for installing.
61R5731—Weight, 3 pounds...$2.65

Horn Reeds for Fords

Made of non-corrosive vibratory composition metal. Not affected by weather. Can be used either in center of tube or at horn connection. A high-grade reed, thoroughly tested. Not a plain end reed.
61R5732—Weight, 2 ounces.....16c

Bulb Horn

For use on Ford cars. Made on pleasing lines. Has oval opening 6¾ inches, which is covered with a removable fine wire screen, which helps to keep out dust, insects and rain. The tube is made of high-grade, flexible brass material, highly polished. Bulb is of the best grade rubber. Will not easily break or crack. Attaching connections furnished with each outfit. Finished in lustrous black enamel, baked on. Ford owners who desire a bulb horn will like this.
61R5730—Weight, 4 pounds...$2.15

Motometer for Fords

Tells when you are obtaining your best gasoline efficiency; when your cylinders or bearings are overheating; when water in radiator is getting too hot, or freezing. It tells you exactly, at all times, "what is going on under the hood." The Ford Special Boyce Motometer shown is already attached to a winged radiator cap, which fits Ford cars, making it easy to attach by simply replacing the radiator cap you now have, with this one. No motorist should be without it. Made of polished brass.
61R7541—Weight, 10 ounces..$4.25

Fogg Horn for Ford Cars

A new model exhaust horn which is located between the engine and the muffler. It delivers a full mellow signal at low engine speeds. Equipped with a cut-out in the body of the horn, giving you both an exhaust horn and a muffler cut-out. Two pedals furnished, one being of the locking type to hold open the cut-out when desired. Full directions for attaching furnished. Length over all, 11¼ inches.
61R4740—Weight, 4 pounds..$3.75

Accessories for Fords—All Genuine Bargains

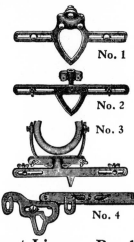

No. 1

No. 2

No. 3

No. 4

Front License Brackets

For Fords. Malleable iron. Black japanned. Weight, each, 1½ pounds.
61R7688—No. 1. Clamps on headlight bracket. All models except 1915-16 ....**25c**
61R7689—No. 2. For 1915-16 models. Clamps on headlight bracket...**25c**
61R7554—No. 3. Clamps on headlight bracket. All models except 1915-16 ....**25c**
61R7902—No. 4. For Fords previous to 1915 ....**18c**

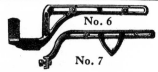

No. 6

No. 7

Rear License Brackets

For Fords. Malleable iron. Black japanned. Weight, each 1½ pounds.
61R7548—No. 6. Clamp to tail lamp bracket. All models except 1915-16 ....**30c**
61R7690—No. 7. Clamp to tail lamp bracket. For 1915-16 models only **30c**

Steering Gear Boots

A necessity on every Ford car. Used to pack the joints of the steering rods with grease, eliminating wear and rattle, and making it easy to steer. Made of good grade water-proof leather. Will fit all models of Ford cars. Set consists of three boots.
61R8873—Weight, 8 ounces.....**58c**

Automatic Windshield Hinge

For 1914-15 Ford Cars or 1915-1916 models with cowl dash. Makes old windshield ventilating and clear vision. Fits old screw holes. Easily attached and easily adjusted. Swings up against top of car, entirely out of way. Tempered steel, enameled black.
61R7956—Weight, 3 pounds...**$1.50**

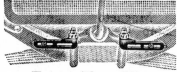

Front Tag Clips

Fasten to spring clip bolts as illustrated. Stamped from heavy gauge steel. Black enameled. Shipping weight, 6 ounces.
61R7880—Per Pair **10c**

Crank Holder License Bracket

Fastens under nuts on front spring clip. Crank holder turns up while using starting crank. Holds crank up out of mud when handle is not in use. Crank lock can be used. Made of stamped steel, enameled black.
61R4539—Weight, 1½ pounds...**25c**

Presto Car-Cool

Keeps out the hot air from the engine in the summer and prevents draft of cold air through the brake and pedal slots in the winter. Automatic in action. Outfit consists of No. 1 and 2 metal and rubber pedal slot covers and No. 3 emergency brake slot cover. All steel parts finished in black japan. Full instructions, and screws for immediate attachment.
61R7527—Weight, 2 pounds...**$1.35**

Perfection Automatic Oiling System

Automatically cares for the uniform flow of lubricating oil. The fresh oil is fed drop by drop (plainly seen through the glass indicator), giving pure oil at all times to the front bearings, where it is most needed, preventing friction, hot bearings, etc. Reduces carbon troubles and improves ignition.

Consists of a cylinder one-gallon oil tank attached by two clamp bands to the side of engine cylinders, as illustrated. A valve adjustment, with a glass feed, is connected to a copper pipe which runs to filler cap, through which oil flows direct to forward bearings. Another copper pipe connects with manifold, causing valve to rise and fall as engine starts and stops. Action is thus automatic, operating only when engine runs. Volume of oil controlled by regulating screw cap. An automatic indicator goes on the dash and shows how much oil is in engine. Quickly installed. Entirely out of way of moving parts.
61R8622—Weight, 10 pounds **$5.35**

Schebler Carburetor

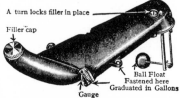

The Schebler Ford Carburetor is more universally known and used than any other. Always dependable. When we placed a Ford type carburetor on the market late last season, it met with instant favor. This carburetor will do everything claimed for it, and once properly installed will end your carburetor troubles. Besides, it will give your engine more power, speed, flexibility; makes starting easier in cold weather. Lower throttling and quicker pick up. Comes complete, as illustrated, with Ford special manifold, priming cup and all attachments together with easy instructions for attaching and operating. Construction is the same as the regular Schebler carburetor, Model L, shown elsewhere in this Book.
61R8670—Weight, 10 pounds.**$16.35**

Fillometer for Fords

A turn locks filler in place

Filler cap

Ball Float Fastened here Graduated in Gallons

Gauge

A gasoline tank filler and gasoline gauge combined. Fastens permanently under cushion of Ford. Sit in your seat while putting gasoline in tank. Gauge easily read from driver's seat and shows correct amount of gasoline in tank while driving or while filling.

Quickly installed with a screw driver by anyone. No need to ever remove it as it is entirely out of way. Air outlet releases air from tank. Impossible to overflow. Great convenience, especially in stormy weather. Made of iron, enameled black.
61R7960—Weight, 7 pounds...**$3.25**

Some Accessories That Your Ford Will Need

Dimit Switch and Regulator for Fords

Can be used both as a switch and headlight regulator. A money-saver for Ford cars, as it protects lamps from burning out. It holds back the light because it is lighted from magneto voltage and doesn't allow excessive current to pass through lamps on starting, stopping and high speeds.

The saving from burned-out lamps will pay for a Dimit in a short time. Adjustable to meet all demands. Mount it on dash or any convenient place. Cut the headlight wires and fasten ends to Dimit posts. It is then ready to use.

Made of steel, nickel plated. Diameter, 3 inches; height, 1⅛ inches.
61R8530—Weight, 1 pound....**$1.85**

Utility Junior Spark Plug Pump

Especially adapted to small cars using tires less than 4 inches diameter. Very simple. Attach the pump to the spark plug hole, set the automatic pneumeter gauge to the pressure desired in the tire, and start your engine—that's all. No danger of over-inflation, as it lets only the correct number of pounds pressure in the tire, then blows off like a safety valve. Gas from engine does not enter tire. Strongly made of pressed steel. Finely finished. Length over all, 7¼ inches; diameter, 2¼ inches; length of hose, 10 feet.
61R5468—Weight, 3 pounds...**$3.95**

Ignition Outfit for Ford Cars

You should rewire your car from time to time, and avoid loss from leakage of current. This outfit consists of high-grade wire, both primary and secondary, cut to correct lengths, and complete with terminals, protected with loom or cable insulation where exposed to grease or oil drippings. Furnished in contrasting colors, for easily replacing in proper position.
61R5720—Weight, 1 pound.....**75c**

Magneto Lamp Regulator

Allows multiple wiring instead of the present objectionable series circuit. Each light operated independently. If one light goes out the others are not affected. Head, side and tail lights may be connected. Steps down voltage generated and increases the amperage. You can also use 6-volt lamps in multiple instead of two 9-volt lamps in series. An excellent feature is the low voltage top for dimming lights for city lighting. Full instructions accompany each regulator. Installed in fifteen minutes. Weight, 2½ pounds.
61R7901—Price, Regulator and Double Throw Switch....**$1.68**

The New York Automatic Head Light Controller

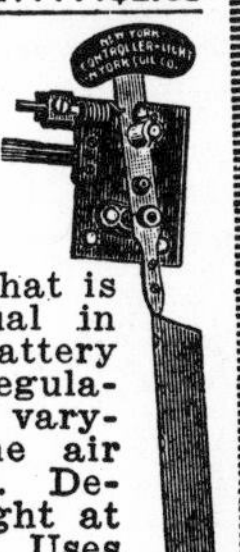

A lighting device that is said to be the equal in power to a $50.00 battery system. Automatic regulation effected by the varying intensity of the air draft created by fan. Delivers a powerful light at lowest engine speed. Uses regular Ford magneto, requiring no batteries or complications. Prevents lamps being burnt out at excessive engine speed. Can be installed in 10 minutes. Weight, 8 pounds.
61R7863—Complete with all connections. Price **$3.95**

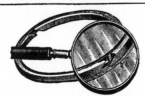

Made of high-grade mixture of gray iron, ground true to size. Strong and tempered and will give satisfaction. Made to fit accurately the bore of the cylinder of all Ford cars. Weight, each, 3 ounces.
61R5702—Price, each...........9c
61R5703—Price, per dozen....**$1.00**

Piston Rings 9c

High Compression Leak-proof Ring

An excellent ring as to either quality or accuracy. Their peculiar construction makes them non-breakable and a perfect compression holder. No matter what the speed of the engine they will lubricate correctly. When installing rings place the upper ring with pin-side up, the lower ring with pin-side down. Diameter, 3¾ in.
61R8677—Weight, 4 ounces.....**68c**

Regulite Lighting Switch

The strength of the magneto on different cars varies and a regulator is therefore necessary to get perfect results. The Regulite is a four-point switch mounted on an enameled case, containing a choke coil. When connected with the headlights and magneto it maintains a constant current regardless of engine speed. This prevents burning out of lamps by sudden rise of voltage, at high speed, or when it races. Has three steps so that it can be adapted to Ford generators of any strength. Can be placed in first position for soft light for city driving. Quickly attached. Full instructions included. Made of steel, hard rubber finish.
61R5719—Weight, 1 pound....**$2.10**

Tool Box

For Ford cars. Constructed of heavy gauge steel, beautifully enameled, baked on. The 18-inch box is fitted with lock and lift, while the 22-inch box has two trunk catches and Yale lock, finished in black. Cover, dust and water-proof. Shipping weight, 10½ pounds.

Number	Each	Length	Width	Height
161R7539	$1.25	18 in.	8 in.	7¼ in.
161R7540	1.30	22 in.	9 in.	7¼ in.

Ford Radiator Hose

A 3-ply fabric and rubber steam hose, with capped ends. Weight, 4 ounces.
61R5724—Inlet Hose, 1¾x2¾...**8c**
61R5725—Outlet Hose, 2x3½....**10c**

Hose Clamps for Fords

Especially adapted for inlet and outlet hose connections between radiator and engine. Made of galvanized steel. Weight, 2 ounces.
61R5143—Inlet Hose Clamp.....**3c**
61R5144—Outlet Hose Clamp....**3c**

Time, Money and Labor-Savers for Your Ford

Carbon Eater

Keeps carbon out of engine and saves from 10 to 30 per cent of gasoline. You have probably noticed that the spark plug in the front cylinder gives you more trouble than any other. This is because

THESE JETS BREAK UP, REMIX AND VAPORIZE ALL OF THE GASOLINE

it gets more fuel than the others. The Carbon Eater remedies this. It is automatic and admits just the right amount of air under all conditions and introduces it through small jets all around the inner wall of manifold. These air jets get under the film of heavy liquid gasoline and blow to atoms. The atomized and vaporized fuel distributes equally to each cylinder, because there is no unvaporized or heavier fuel to disturb equal feeding or cause carbon deposits. The Carbon Eater makes your motor hum steadily and with new life. The saving in gasoline alone pays for it several times a year. Quickly installed by any one. Finished in black and nickel.
61R4537—Weight, 1 pound........**$1.95**

Special Primer

Gives you a quick start in cold weather. Primer may also be utilized for decarbonizing cylinders by feeding some good carbonizer through intake manifold, while motor is in action. Attached quickly and easily by simply tapping manifold for 1/8-inch standard iron pipe, inserting coupling, and then connecting primer. Furnished complete with coupling and compressed coupling, therefore no soldering is required when attaching to car. The gasoline container has a capacity of about 1/2 pint. Made of steel, nickel plated and polished. Dimensions, length, 3 7/8 inches; diameter, 2 inches.
61R7745—Weight, 14 ounces........**45c**

Repair Kit for Fords

Consists of valve grinder of finest steel, triple-end cylinder head and rear axle housing wrench, large socket on the double end gives high powered leverage to tighten cylinder head nuts. Single-end socket "twirls" nuts rapidly after they are loosened. Connecting rod wrench, hub cap wrench, double-end transmission and service wrench. All made of high grade steel. Put up in enameled duck case.
61R4538—Weight, about 5 pounds....**98c**

Combination Wrench

Fits cylinder head bolts, and bolts on rear axle housing on all Ford models. Malleable iron.
61R5107—Weight, 12 ounces........**16c**

Triple Socket Wrench

T end for 5/8 and 3/4-inch hexagon nuts; other end for 5/8 hexagon nuts. The 5/8-inch sockets are designed for cylinder head bolts, but fit any nuts for 5/8-inch bolts on Ford cars. Center socket fits Ford hub caps. Length, 10 inches.
61R5112—Weight, 1 pound......**19c**

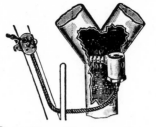

Gasoline Economizer

Will save approximately 20 per cent of your gasoline, and increase the power. The mixer screws into the manifold, as illustrated. A special, durable, flexible shaft runs from the mixer to control lever, which is attached to steering post. This lever, which can be conveniently attached at your finger tips, adjusts the air supply to your cylinder at will, and sprays air into the manifold which breaks up the gasoline and gives your motor a rich mixture. Gives a quicker pick-up and a faster get-away. You will be amazed at the increase of speed from your motor when it is equipped with this. Made of hard brass, nickel plated.
61R5705—Weight, 2 pounds......**$1.45**

Mixolock for Fords

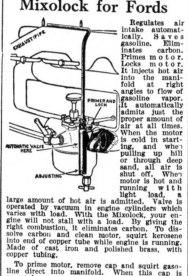

Regulates air intake automatically. Saves gasoline. Eliminates carbon. Primes motor. Locks motor. It injects hot air into the manifold at right angles to flow of gasoline vapor. It automatically admits just the proper amount of air at all times. When the motor is cold in starting, and when pulling up hill or through deep sand, all air is shut off. When motor is hot and running with light load, a large amount of hot air is admitted. Valve is operated by vacuum in engine cylinders which varies with load. With the Mixolock, your engine will not stall with a load. By giving the right combustion, it eliminates carbon. To dissolve carbon and clean motor, squirt kerosene into end of copper tube while engine is running. Made of cast iron and polished brass, with copper tubing.

To prime motor, remove cap and squirt gasoline direct into manifold. When this cap is removed no one can start engine, as only fresh air is drawn into cylinders, which, of course, will not explode. It locks the car, and prevents theft.

To install: Simply remove the two bolts on carburetor flange, slip Mixolock between carburetor and manifold, replace the two bolts, bend copper tube over the exhaust pipe to supply hot air, and the job is done. Not a hole to drill or tap.
61R5137—Weight, 2 pounds......**$1.35**

Hub Cap Wrench

Handy for putting on or taking off Ford hub caps. Made of stamped steel, hardened and machined.
61R5109—Weight, 1 pound..........**8c**

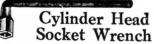

Cylinder Head Socket Wrench

Fits all nuts on all models of Ford cylinder heads. Pressed steel socket and handle.
61R5108—Weight, 8 ounces........**12c**

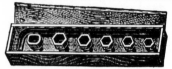

Windshield Ventilator

Made to ventilate fore-door cars. Forces air into body by small clamp arrangement which permits windshield to move in or out. Gives perfect circulation of cool air on the hottest day. Works equally well on other cars. Brackets are of cold-rolled steel, enameled black. Complete with attachments. Length, 3 1/4 inches; width, 3 3/4 inches. Does not fit 1915 Cowl dash.
61R5706—Weight, 12 ounces.......**55c**

Socket Wrench Set

This set consists of five hexagon sockets. Sizes, 1/2, 9/16, 5/8, 11/16 and 3/4 inch, one oval socket which fits main bearing bolt, and one handle. Fits all hexagon head bolts and nuts on Ford cars.
61R5708—Weight, 1 1/2 pounds......**83c**

Mossberg Wrench Set

A product of the famous Mossberg factories, which means quality, dependability, and satisfaction. This Socket Wrench set contains the well known Mossberg 8-inch ratchet handle; one universal joint, one special steel screw driver, one 9 1/4-inch extension tube and one spark plug socket. Provides a wrench to fit every nut and tool on Ford car, including nuts and cap screws on housing and crank shaft bearing, which are practically inaccessible with ordinary ratchet socket wrench sets. Packed in fibre board box.
61R4536—Weight, 6 pounds......**$2.85**

Ratchet Wrench Set

Small, neat, compact outfit that is well made and will meet all ordinary requirements of a Ford owner. Set complete consists of 11 pieces as follows: Ratchet handle, length, 7 inches, and made of drop forged steel; two screw driver bits of tool steel; one 6-inch extension bar; seven sockets steel case hardened for bolts and nuts from 5/16 to 5/8 inch inclusive. Put up in neat, strong enameled cloth carrying case.
61R5099—Weight, 2 pounds......**$1.90**

Heavy-Duty Socket Wrenches

Five sturdy bars with firmly affixed pressed steel sockets on each end. Ten openings: Hexagon, 17/32, 19/32, 21/32, 23/32, 25/32, 29/32, 31/32 inches; squares, 15/32 inch; spark plug socket, 31/32 inch, and an oval socket for main bearing nuts and bolts. Put up in neat canvas case.
61R5110—Weight, 5 pounds......**$1.50**

Classy Electric Lighting Outfits for Your Ford

Electric Headlight Outfit

Those who do not want an electric light converting outfit, c a n replace the gas headlights with up-to-date bullet-shaped or torpedo electric headlights. Strictly up-to-date in design.

Stamped from one piece of extra heavy gauge metal, enameled black. Door is heavy French roll design. The reflectors are true parabola shape, highly silver plated, and have adjustable focusing device. Ediswan connections and sockets used throughout. Genuine Mazda Tungsten bulbs. 6-volt, 12 C. P. Includes two 9-inch headlights, as illustrated. Fits the Ford brackets without altering. Complete wiring assembly for operation from Ford magneto. Weight, 10 pounds.

61R8107—All Black finish.....................**$4.50**
61R8108—Black and Brass finish............. 4.50

Double Bulb Electric Headlights

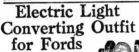

T h e highest priced c a r s are b e i n g equipped with double bulb headlights. The main advantage is the way the current is switched f r o m the magneto to the small lights for city driving and to the large lights for the country. Small lights give no reflection. L a r g e lights very powerful and with strong reflection.

This assembly is made for late 1915 and 1916 Ford models only. Stamped from one-piece extra heavy gauge piece metal. Enameled all black with brass rim door. Silver plated parabolic reflector. Bayonet lock door. No hinges. Easy to clean. Front diameter, 10 inches. Weight, 10 lbs.

61R8034—All Black finish **$6.75**
61R8035—Black and Brass..................... 6.75

New Type Electric Lamp

SIDE VIEW TAILLIGHT   TOP VIEW SIDE LIGHT   BUSHINGS FOR COWL   FRONT VIEW SIDE LIGHT

15 FEET OF DUPLEX CABLE

T h i s set consists of two white lens s i d e lamps and one red lens tail light having white side light for illuminating license p l a t e. Each lamp has 4¾-inch front diameter, and has self-contained s w i t c h. Oufit includes d u p l e x cable for connecting up, two bushings for bringing leads through the dash, and full instructions.

Bulbs are 1½ C. P., 6-volts, and may be operated from storage battery or 4 dry cells. For 1915 Ford Lamp brackets, without change; 1913 and 1914 brackets require drilling hole for bolt. Made of steel, black enamel; brass rim door, semaphore lens.

61R5714—Weight, 3 pounds **$2.95**

Electric Light Converting Outfit for Fords

$3.25

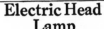

Used with g a s headlights. Place reflectors w i t h bulbs in the gas headlights a n d connect w i r i n g w i t h magneto. Bulbs a r e easily removed as illustrated. Reflectors are s p u n brass, finely silver plated. Ediswan connections. 6-volt, 12 C. P. Tungsten bulbs furnished. New type of flush plate switch to mount right in the dash. Easily attached. Complete instructions furnished. Weight, 4 pounds.

61R5498—With 8-inch reflectors...............**$3.25**
61R5499—With 9-inch reflectors............... 3.25

Electric Lighting Outfit

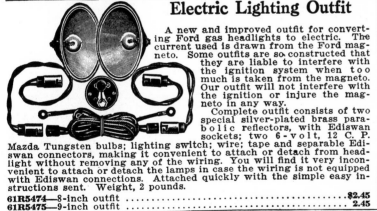

A new and improved outfit for converting Ford gas headlights to electric. The current used is drawn from the Ford magneto. Some outfits are so constructed that they are liable to interfere with the ignition system when too much is taken from the magneto. Our outfit will not interfere with the ignition or injure the magneto in any way.

Complete outfit consists of two special silver-plated brass parabolic reflectors, with Ediswan sockets; two 6-volt, 12 C. P. Mazda Tungsten bulbs; lighting switch; wire; tape and separable Ediswan connectors, making it convenient to attach or detach from headlight without removing any of the wiring. You will find it very inconvenient to attach or detach the lamps in case the wiring is not equipped with Ediswan connections. Attached quickly with the simple easy instructions sent. Weight, 2 pounds.

61R5474—8-inch outfit **$2.45**
61R5475—9-inch outfit 2.45

Electric Head Lamp

A high class head l a m p similar to lamp used in our Electric h e a d light o u t f i t—61R8107. Stamped from o n e piece of extra heavy gauge steel, enameled with several c o a t s of lustrous black, b a k e d on. Heavy French roll door, diameter, 9 inches. Parabola reflectors, highly silver plated with adjustable focusing device. 12 C. P. 9-Volt bulbs. Ediswan connections. Fits late 1915 and the 1916 model. Fords only. Weight, 4 pounds.

61R7995—All Black. Pair.....**$4.50**
61R8032—Black with Brass Rim Door. Pair.............. 4.50

Valve Reseater

Used to ream out Ford valve seat. Makes a clear even surface which cannot be done by grinding. Cutting surface made of carefully machined h a r d e n e d steel. Length, 5 inches.
61R5439—Weight, 6 ounces...**25c**

Valve Refacer

When Ford valves are badly pitted it is hard to get a perfect seat. This refacer tool overcomes this difficulty. It trims valve to exactly the right angle. Well made of hardened steel.
61R7925—Weight, 6 ounces **23c**

Electric Side Lamps for Fords

A neat, classy looking side lamp which adds greatly to the appearance of your car. Replaces oil lights which are inconvenient to fill and difficult to keep clean on account of smoke. Stamped from one piece metal, richly enameled in lustrous black. Semaphore l e n s. Two lamps. F r o n t diameter, 5 inches, complete with Ediswan connections and 4 C. P. bulbs. Fits only late 1915 and the 1916 Ford models. Weight, 3 pounds.

61R8095—All Black finish. Pair.................**$2.48**
61R8106—Black with Brass Door. Pair........... 2.48

Oils and Greases to Make Your Ford Run Smoothly

National Gasometer

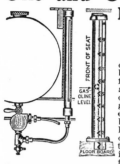

Mounted on riser board in front of seat. It indicates at a glance the exact number of gallons of gasoline in tank, keeping you from getting caught without gasoline on the road. Being in plain view, you know how far you can go with gasoline in tank. Prevents carburetor trouble caused by using a dirty measuring stick. When your tank is filled, you know whether or not you get as much gasoline as you are charged for. The gasometer is easy to install. Takes no drilling or tapping. A boy can do it in fifteen minutes. A ball floats on the surface of gasoline, making it easy to see. It ends your worry and bother. You cannot realize what a convenience it is until you have it on your car. Packed in neat box, with full instructions for installing.

61R5139—Weight, 1 pound.....**90c**

Ford Oil Gauge

By putting one into the crank case you always know how much oil is in it, thus eliminating scoring of cylinders by absence of oil. Glass tube is imported—quite thick, and strong. Quickly attached by removing lower pet cock, and replaced with gauge. Then pet cock is screwed on gauge. This will permit draining out the crank case if necessary. A necessity. Weight, 8 ounces.

61R5737—Plain. Price **15c**
61R8761 — With metal protecting guard around glass **20c**

Universal Cup Grease

A superior compounded cup grease. Made from pure materials. Especially adapted for use on Ford cars. We believe it will give as satisfactory service as any cup grease you can buy.

61R5745—10-pound pail **$0.70**
161R5746—25-pound can **1.60**

Transmission Grease

Recommended for use in transmission. Prevents wear and noisy operation. Where cars have been long in service and the differential gears are somewhat worn, this is a desirable lubricant. Its spongy, fibrous nature causes it to cling close to the moving parts. Changes of temperature do not readily affect it. Its clinging, fibrous characteristics are not lost even at high temperature. This grease is ideal for Ford cars. Give it a trial.

61R7746—10-pound can **$0.85**
161R7748—25-pound can **1.90**

Reserve Gasoline Valve

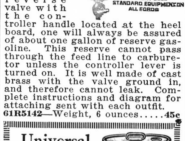

It tells when a gallon only remains in the tank. Easily installed, without cutting or soldering. By closing reverse valve with the controller handle located at the heel board, one will always be assured of about one gallon of reserve gasoline. This reserve cannot pass through the feed line to carburetor unless the controller lever is turned on. It is well made of cast brass with the valve ground in, and therefore cannot leak. Complete instructions and diagram for attaching sent with each outfit.

61R5142—Weight, 6 ounces.....**45c**

Universal Cylinder Oil

Contains no free carbon. A pale straw-color cylinder oil **especially adapted for Ford cars.** Has high fire test and high viscosity. Always uniform in quality. Thoroughly filtered and contains no free carbon. Economical, and a perfect lubricant. No matter how much you pay for cylinder oil it would be hard to improve the quality. Treat your motor right— use Universal. It helps to increase speed, saves worry and expense by keeping your cylinders in perfect working condition. Always lubricates. Heat or cold will not easily affect it. Barrel lots in wood or steel barrels.

61R5741—1-gallon can....**$0.42**
161R5742—5-gallon can ... **1.55**
161R5743—½-barrel (wood) 30 gallons **$8.25**
161R5744 — Barrel (wood) 50 gallons **$11.50**
161R8268—½-barrel (steel) 30 gallons **$8.50**
161R8269—Barrel (steel) 50 gallons **$14.00**

Shipping Weight of Oils

1-Gallon can, 8 pounds.
5-Gallon can, 41 pounds.
Half barrels, about 250 pounds.
Barrels, about 400 pounds.

Spring Hanger Oil Cups

Hanger oil cups are often broken or misplaced. Carry a few in your tool box, and do not leave the holes open to catch dust, dirt, etc. Made of brass, fitted with ⅛-inch standard pipe thread. The sleeve-like cover fits tightly, so they may be used in a horizontal position as well as vertically, without spilling oil. Diameter, 9/16 inch.

61R5734—Weight, 2 ounces **5c**

Dash Board Oil Gauge

Glance at the scale on the dash board. Don't get under car to find out the amount of oil in the Ford crank case. The gauge, operated by the float in the oil chamber, located beneath the floor board and next to the crank case, raises and lowers according to the amount of oil in the crank case. Strongly made of brass pipe with a substantial reservoir chamber. The pipe leading from the crank case to the reservoir chamber is flexible, and can be easily bent to any position. Low in price, substantially made, easily attached.

61R5141—Weight, 2 pounds....**68c**

Challenge Gasoline Filler Cap Gauge

This gauge can be relied upon to register the contents of your gasoline tank. Easily attached. Remove present filler cap on your gasoline tank, insert this gauge, and screw it down tight. Constructed of steel. Contains a float fitted to a spiral upright which turns indicator on dial as the gasoline is raised or lowered in tank. Head containing dial and indicator fits any Ford tank. The extreme simplicity and strong construction means that it will always work perfectly and last as long as the car.

61R5140—Weight, 1½ pounds..**60c**

Safety Pet-Cock Wrench and Gasoline Gauge

With this wrench you can turn the pet cock in your engine crank case to test your oil supply without soiling your hands or clothing. Eliminates back-breaking stooping. Stamped in the handle is an accurate gauge to measure the gasoline in tank. May be carried under seat cushion. Nicely finished in black enamel. Length, 22 inches.

61R8480—Weight, 7 ounces.....**12c**

Grease Retainers

A device that will positively prevent oil and grease from working out of axle housing onto brakes and wheels. Made in spiral form, in rights and lefts, and act as a screw feed, carrying oil and grease back towards differential. Easy to apply. Full directions sent. Thousands in use.

61R7919—Weight, 8 ounces **56c**

Universal Fixtures for the Universal Car

Special Ford Plug

Made especially for us, by one of the largest manufacturers in the United States. An approved design, for use in Ford motors. All parts accurately made. Exceptionally high fire test porcelain. The sparking point is special alloy, designed to give a hot, fat spark. While low in price, this plug will give unexcelled service. Furnished in ½-inch standard pipe thread size only.

61R7561—Weight, 4 ounces 30c

United Terminals

A convenience, and a trouble saver to be used on timer of Ford cars. Brings all the wires on top where they can be easily seen and reached and preventing them from getting oil soaked with consequent short circuiting. Also prevents twisting or straining at their connections. Connecting and disconnecting of wires is easily done without removing timer.

61R8611—Weight, 6 ounces....37c

Kingston Carburetor

This is one of the Carburetors being used at the present time as factory equipment on Ford cars. So constructed that a perfect mixture for all speeds is supplied, automatically governed by motor suction. Both constant and auxiliary air are drawn from a common source. They pass the check throttle or valve, which is so placed that it is possible to cut off the source of air. This produces a strong suction around the spray nozzle, thereby affording a very rich mixture for easy starting in extremely low temperature. Simple and compact, one of the most economical and reliable carburetors for a Ford car. Made of the best hardened brass, finely finished. Needs no extra fittings of any kind. Perfectly fitted for the Ford T manifold hot air pipe, and operating rods.

61R5155—Weight, 5 pounds...$6.85

Champion X Spark Plug

Used as regular equipment on Ford cars. The electrode is of a special design, and affords a larger explosion chamber than the regular Standard Champion Plug. It will also give equally good satisfaction on other makes of cars using a ½-inch standard pipe thread plug. Weight, 4 ounces.

61R7549—½-inch size only.....40c
61R7551—Porcelains only 25c

D-B Carburetor

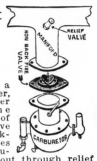

A simple, durable, economical low-priced carburetor for Ford cars. Operates on a new principle. Saves gasoline, gives quick pick-up, and makes a slow, sluggish motor snappy and on edge. Throttles down low without jerking. Easily attached.

61R4548—Weight, 5½ pounds.$7.95

The Direct Route

If you were going to South America—and wanted to get there quickly, and at the least possible expense—you wouldn't go by way of London, Paris, Jerusalem and Johannesburg. You'd go direct and make as few stops as possible—for every stop would mean delay and extra expense. Our merchandise doesn't go through many jobbers and middlemen's hands, **but travels the direct route** when you buy from these pages. We collect it from the producers and send it direct to you in convenient form. And for that real service you pay but one fair profit.

Radiator Covers

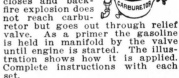

Made to fit Model T Ford cars. For protection against freezing. Not only prevent radiator freezing but protect entire system from cold. High-grade black enameled cloth, lined with heavy kersey. Front curtain lowers and fastens with snaps.

61R5723—Weight, 1 pound....$1.00

Safety-First Non-Backfire Valve

This valve is a wonder. A primer, carbon remover and gasoline saver. In case of back fire the valve closes and backfire explosion does not reach carburetor but goes out through relief valve. As a primer the gasoline is held in manifold by the valve until engine is started. The illustration shows how it is applied. Complete instructions with each set.

61R5656—Weight, 8 ounces...$1.95

Bemus Ball Contact Ford Timer

Has rapid, snappy action in making contacts and yet has durability sufficient for thousands of miles. Made of patented composition, Bakelite. Will not short circuit when wet. No starting trouble because of hardened oil on contact segments. Very little oil used and balls do not retain any to harden. Connections handily made from top. Size, 3⅜ x 3¼ x 2 inches.

61R4730—Weight, 8 ounces...$1.75

Cuno Timer

This is recognized as a high-grade accurate timer and is especially adapted for use on Ford cars. It is very compact. Diameter, 2½ inches. Quite accessible and very easily adjusted. Weight, 8 ounces.

61R5154—For 1913-14-15-16 Ford Cars........95c

Milwaukee Timer

61R5999—For 1910-11-12 Ford Cars........$2.25

Wrench for Champion X Plugs

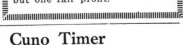

Made of malleable iron, finished with baked ebony enamel. One end fits Champion X plug, Ford Special, Champion, etc.; other end fits Standard ⅞-inch spark plugs.

61R4549—Weight, 6 ounces.....12c

Fixtures for Making Your Ford Better

Slip-On Running Board

Make a big hit with Ford owners as they improve the appearance of the car at a trifling cost. Easily applied—simply slip on. Require no bolt or clamp, fit perfectly, and don't rattle. Stay clean and bright and can't rust. Made of aluminum.

61R5738—Weight, 8 pounds...**$2.85**

Running Board Support

This brace is to prevent running-boards from sagging under the weight of persons entering and leaving car, and from tool boxes, lighting tanks, etc., carried on runningboard. It braces and supports the runningboard step brackets, thus stopping the rattle due to wear at the end of truss rods. Made of steel bar, equipped with all necessary clips, lock-washers, etc., for quick and easy application. Weight, 3½ pounds.

61R4917—Price...............**75c**

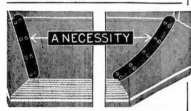

A NECESSITY

Fender Braces

Eliminate the rattle against the mud splashers, strengthen and preserve the fenders by neatly joining both tightly together. Made of heavy pressed steel. Furnished with bolts and nuts, enameled black. Fit all models Ford cars. Length of front, 14½ inches; width, 1¼ inches; length of rear, 11 inches; width, 1¼ inches. Weight, 24 ounces.

61R5145—Set of four...........**35c**

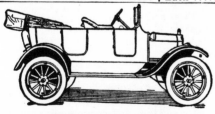

Crown Fenders

Have the graceful, flowing, stylish lines and the rounding arch that you generally see only in high-priced cars. Made of 20-gauge automobile steel, cold drawn and finished in high gloss enamel, thoroughly baked at high temperature. Their design not only insures the utmost beauty but also imparts great strength and rigidity, long life and complete freedom from rattling and drumming. Interchangeable with the regulation Ford Fenders on T-Model Ford roadsters and touring cars. Will not fit the 1915 Ford Sedan or any car having a 60-inch base. Shipping weight, 115 pounds.

161R4931—Per set......................**$12.25**

Spring Crank Holder

For Fords. Extends under crank handle and attaches to headlights. Keeps the crank in an upright position, eliminating rattle, also from conflicting with crank shaft. Keeps crank out of mud. A black enameled spring with a rubber protector where crank handle rests. Stamped steel attaching clips. For all cars except 1915-1916 models.

61R4932—Weight, 6 ounces.....**19c**

Axle Shaft for Ford Car 56-Inch Tread

Duplicate of Ford part 2505D. Made of high carbon steel, tapered, threaded and slotted for keys, exact size and fits all machines. Ready for use.

61R5524—Weight, 8 pounds...**$1.50**

Differential Thrust Plate

Bronze thrust plate. Replaces Ford part 2528. Diameter, 3¾ inches.

61R4530—Weight, 6 ounces. Each........................**22c**

Steel Differential Thrust Plate

Steel. Drilled and punched to fit. Replaces Ford repair part 2529. Diameter, 3¾ inches.

61R4531—Weight, 4 ounces. Each.........................**7c**

Anti-Draft Shield

An inexpensive necessity for comfort. Closes space between windshield and top of car. Fits snugly over front edge of top, and keeps out rain and snow. Made of heavy rubber coated auto cloth. Complete with fastenings.

61R8405—Weight, 1 pound......**50c**

Cam Shaft Bearings

3042   3043

Replace Ford part 3042, front bearing, length, 2 inches, and 3043, center bearing, length, 2⅛ inches. Made of cast iron. Fit all model Fords. Weight, 6 ounces.

61R4528—No. 3042. Each......**16c**

61R4529—No. 3043. Each......**16c**

Rubber Mats

Exceptionally good quality, made of extra heavy fabric foundation which overcomes tearing. Special compound rubber resists wear and gives long service. Weight, 5 lbs.

61R7521—For all but 1915 models........................**90c**

61R7532—For all 1915-1916 models........................**90c**

Slip Roof Outfit

Consists of a black heavy 32-ounce rubber cloth roof, quarters, back curtain and back stays, stitched and ready to slip over the 1912-13-14-15 Ford Model-T touring car top frames. Easily put on. Makes an old top new at about one-third the price of a complete top. Weight, 14 pounds.

Year	1912	1913	1914	1915	Price
Article Number	61R4532	61R4533	61R4534	61R4534	$7.35

One-Man Mohair Top

Easily and quickly raised by one person, without leaving the car. Quick attachable curtains, which can be adjusted without leaving car, furnished with top, giving you complete weather-proof protection at a moment's notice. Top is lined with high-grade water-proofed cloth like that used in first quality slip-covers. A silk mohair dust hood also included. No side bows to get in the way. Convenient rear attachment, patent fasteners. Top strongly reinforced with bows. Will hold its shape permanently under all weather conditions. Rigid steel rods attached to the windshield hold top secure. For Model T. State year of your car when ordering. Shipping weight, about 125 pounds.

261R5802—One-Man Top, Complete...............**$22.50**

Shipped from Factory in Southern Michigan.

Two Perfect Ignition Systems for Your Ford

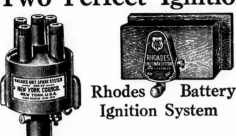

Rhodes Battery Ignition System

This system is entirely new and contains all qualifications for the ideal battery ignition system. Works entirely from six ordinary dry cells. Gives an intense spark regardless of engine speed. Its effect on your Ford will be remarkable; you will at once notice a big increase in power, smoothness and flexibility. Throttles motor down to a walk and picks up speed instantly without that jerky motion. Illustration shows the complete instrument detached from the bracket. This distributor cover is a moulded material which is light, water-proof and not affected by heat of engine. Cover is kept on instrument by two spring clips, allowing instant accessibility to working parts for inspection or oiling. The non-vibrating transformer coil is wound by a peculiar process which guards entirely against break downs. Fine mahogany finish supplied with handsome kick switch, with removable plug. Holes for wires register with those already in the dash. Easy and quick to install.

It undoubtedly increases your Ford's value to you and at our price you can't afford to be without one. Non-vibrating coil, oil type elevating gears, all cables and necessary wire and metal tube for supporting wires furnished.

61R7865—Weight, 20 pounds..............**$17.50**

Unit-Coil Ignition System for Fords

Make the Ford an ideal car by eliminating ignition troubles

Operates either with Ford fly wheel magneto or by storage or dry cell battery, with a single unit of coil. Produces vibrating and not single sparks. A complete, efficient ignition system for Ford cars. Does away with the need for the timer, the source of most ignition trouble and a hard part to reach. Eliminates need for adjusting of vibrator coils.

A combination timer and distributor carried on an elevating gear bracket. Its simple circuit operating mechanism causes one pair of contacts to exactly time the magneto or battery current to a single coil unit, from which it is delivered by means of the high tension distributor direct to the four spark plugs in the same way as a magneto. Throttles give a low, rich fat spark always.

Lubrication system is dustproof. Distributor head and brush holder are of Bakelite, a composition not affected by temperature. Beveled gears of cut steel mesh accurately and are noiseless.

Outfit furnished complete, ready to install—even the wires. Not a hole to drill or a screw to furnish—everything is complete. Easy instructions sent with each outfit.

61R5153—Weight, 8 pounds..................**$9.75**

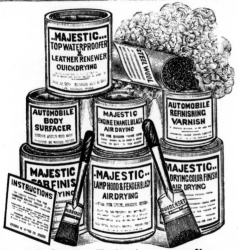

Majestic Painting Outfit

A regular master painters' outfit for all small cars. Put up so that any novice can use it with excellent results. With it you can paint your car in about 4 hours; let it stand over night, and use it next morning.

Compare the price, against what it would cost to have work done for you, and see what a saving we make you. We strongly recommend this outfit because the ingredients are of extremely high quality.

Everything is furnished, except your labor. Outfit contains: 1 can of black gear finish; 1 can of body color finish; 1 can black engine enamel; 1 can lamp, hood and fender black; 1 can top dressing; and waterproofer; 1 can varnish, for dashboard; 1 can surfacer for smoothing up uneven places before putting on body finish; 1 large roll steel wool; 1 roll pure white paste; 2 genuine Rubberset, Fitch brushes; one 1-inch, other 1½-inch. All packed carefully in a substantial box, with complete, easy instructions, telling exactly what to do from start to finish. Weight, about 8 pounds.

61R5667—Body color, Black. Price..............**$3.25**
61R5272—Body color, Dark Gray. Price........ 3.25
61R5271—Body color, Deep Green. Price....... 3.25
61R5270—Body color, Red. Price.............. 3.25

Challenge Paint Outfit for Fords

For those who desire a lower priced outfit than the Majestic. We recommend the other where strictly first-class results are desired; but if you prefer a cheaper outfit, the Challenge will give as good satisfaction as those usually sold for much higher prices.

Outfit contains:
One quart Deep Black Body Paint; one pint Elastic Body Varnish; one pint Leather Renewer and Top Dye; one-half pint can Surfacer; one quart can Cleaner for Gear; one package Waste; one Roll Steel Wool; one 1-inch Chiseled Auto Painting Brush, Bear Hair; one ½-inch Bear Hair; one can Metal Polish to Polish Brass; one complete Set Instructions.

61R8576—Weight, 6 pounds. Price............**$2.65**

Gearless Differential

Eliminates all the faults of the differential gear—the one part of the automobile that has not been improved in 15 years.

Eliminates sideway slipping and tendency to skid. Gives a positive drive to both rear wheels—all the advantages of a solid axle in a straightway driving. Over soft or uneven ground, power is delivered only to wheel having traction. Pulls through bad spots where a car with the ordinary gear differential would be hopelessly stalled. Gives full power out of every atom of fuel. The saving in gas, oil and tires pays for it several times over. Think of the added comfort and safety. Exceptionally valuable for winter driving. Comes complete, ready to install. Weight, 20 pounds.

61R7723—Ford **$19.00**
61R7725—Chevrolet No. 490 .... 19.00
61R7727—Overland, any model.............. 23.75

You Can Use Every Ford Accessory on This Page

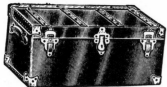

Rack Trunk

Built to carry on rack at the rear of Ford cars. Strongly made of kiln-dried basswood, and neatly covered with high-grade, extra quality black enameled duck material, making it water-proof. Has four wide, extra strong slats reenforcing the top. Corners covered with strong metal shields. A strong brass lock and two extra heavy trunk catches firmly attached. Strong leather handles furnished, making it easy to handle the trunk when moving or putting on the car. Neatly lined. A large, roomy trunk that will hold a great many articles necessary when touring. Size, 28x16x12 inches. Shipping weight, 24 pounds.

161R5759—Price, each **$5.70**

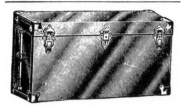

Running Board Trunk

A new type, for attaching to the running board of Ford touring cars. Well made, large and roomy. Made of basswood and neatly covered with black enameled water-proof duck. Strong metal corner guards greatly add to the appearance; protect corners. A strong lock and trunk catches, securely fastened. We furnish special quick detachable bolt fasteners, as illustrated, making it convenient to attach or detach quickly from car. Size, 33 x 9½ x 16 inches. Shipping weight, 24 pounds.

161R5760—Price, each **$5.75**

Slip Seat Covers

. By fitting your Ford car with a set of Slip Covers, you preserve the cushions, and add to the appearance of your car. Are neatly made of a very high-grade double texture, olive color Mackintosh cloth. Waterproof, bound and stitched. All seams reinforced with heavy fabric leather. Arm rests are of patent leather, which greatly adds to their appearance and wear. Are cool in Summer and warm in Winter. When soiled can be washed with soap and water. Outfit consists of a set of covers for seats, backs, arm-rests, and doors. Dust Hoods are made of same material as seat covers.

Either set can be easily and quickly fitted, as we furnish complete instructions, together with all necessary snap buttons and screw heads. Furnished only for 1913-14-15 models. Samples of material sent on request. State model desired.

Number	Price	Model	Year	Weight
61R5178	$8.20	Touring-Regular Dash	1915	12 pounds
61R5179	8.20	Touring-Cowl Dash	1915	12 pounds
61R5180	8.20	Touring	1914	12 pounds
61R5181	8.20	Touring	1913	12 pounds
61R5182	4.30	Roadster	1915	6 pounds
61R5183	4.30	Roadster	1914	6 pounds
61R5184	4.30	Roadster	1913	6 pounds
61R5185	2.15	Touring Top Dust Hood...	1914-15	3 pounds
61R5186	2.15	Touring Top Dust Hood...	1913	3 pounds
61R5187	2.15	Roadster Top Dust Hood...	1914-15	3 pounds
61R5188	2.15	Roadster Top Dust Hood...	1913	2 pounds

Note—For a lower priced Top Dust Hood, see 61R5464 or 61R5465 on this page.

Special Tire Trunk

Made to fit snugly inside of the spare tire for your Ford, taking no additional space. Finely made of basswood, covered with a high-grade water-proof enameled duck. The bindings are well sewed. Has three long harness leather straps for attaching to tire. As illustrated, the door revolves, making it more convenient than the old style. They fasten with a strong brass lock, which is securely attached to trunk. Will fit inside regular size Ford tires. Shipping weight, 14 pounds.

161R5761—Each **$3.95**

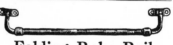

Folding Robe Rail

For Ford cars. Made of ⅝-inch steel tubing, highly nickeled or sheet brass covered, fitted with malleable end brackets. Folds back when not in use. Holds a robe, duster or coat. Length, over all, 31 inches. Weight, 2 pounds.
61R5555—Brass Finish **39c**
61R5556—Nickel Finish **41c**

Robe Rail for Fords

Attached to upper side of upholstery frame on front seat. Folds into small space in back of front seat. Will hold one large robe or several dusters. Made of rod iron, black ebony enameled. Width, 3¾ inches; length, 29½ inches.
61R5147—Weight, 3 pounds........**21c**

Anti-Rattling Door Check

When applied to the door frame in place of the regular Ford catch, they provide a sure means of silencing the rattle.

61R4739 — Set of three for Touring Car. Weight, 12 ounces.**63c**

61R4738—For Roadster. Weight, 4 ounces. Each **23c**

Curtain Cases
for Ford Cars

Its use will more than save its cost, as it will keep side curtains in perfect condition. Curtains that are kept in the tool box usually become damaged, and soon get dirty and unfit for use. Made of high-grade waterproof enameled duck, well bound and stitched. Has flap cover and glove fasteners. Is divided into two compartments. Sufficient in size to accommodate side curtains for Ford cars.

61R5772—Weight, 10 ounces.......**50c**

Door Cover With Pocket

A great convenience, and handy for carrying the many little things necessary to all motorists. Well made of pantasote, and bound with genuine leather, strongly stitched. There are two large pockets covered with flaps, which fasten with strap buttons. With each we furnish the necessary binding nails for fastening. Can be quickly and easily attached. Take up little space and greatly add to appearance of car. Always order by article number. State model desired. Average weight, 10 ounces.

Model	Year	Right Rear Door	Left Rear Door	Right Front Door	Left Front Door
Touring	1915	61R160	61R163	61R166	61R172
Touring	1914	61R161	61R164	61R167	61R173
Touring	1913	61R162	61R165	61R168	61R174
Roadster	1915	....	....	61R169	61R175
Roadster	1914	....	....	61R170	61R176
Roadster	1913	....	....	61R171	61R177

Price, each **75c**

Rear Curtain Window

A new attachable rear window. Made of celluloid firmly bound with black water proof enameled duck. Bottom is arranged slot fashion to fit over curtain making the window water-tight. Weight, 8 ounces.
61R4540—Rear Curtain Window. Each.**45c**

Top Cover for Ford Cars

When the top is down or not in use, its life and appearance can be greatly increased by the use of a top cover. It prevents fading and protects it from dust and dirt. This cover fits Ford top snugly. It has two straps as illustrated, which come down over back of rear seat and fasten underneath cushion. This keeps wind and dust from getting under cover, and prevents sagging of bottom part. Supplied with auto top fasteners. Furnished in high grade black enameled duck, which is water and dust-proof; or a fine quality of mohair. These covers are for 1913, 1914 and 1915 Ford cars only, but can make to order for previous models in ten days' time from receipt of order. Average weight, 4½ pounds.

Touring Model	Roadster Model	Price	Top Cover
61R5464	61R5465	$1.90	Enameled Duck
61R5466	61R5467	3.00	Mohair

ABOUT THE AUTHOR

Floyd Clymer literally grew up with the American automobile. For over half a century he has driven, tested, raced, sold, restored, and written about them. President Theodore Roosevelt called Clymer "the world's youngest automobile dealer" in 1906, when, at the age of eleven, Clymer sold 26 Reos, Cadillacs, and Maxwells. He also manufactured an automobile accessory, the Clymer Windshield Spotlight, which enjoyed considerable popularity over the years. His affection for the Model T is of long standing. He sold and raced Model T's for years and was a personal acquaintance of Henry Ford's.

Today Mr. Clymer writes a monthly column for *Popular Mechanics,* publishes two automotive magazines, and heads an automotive publishing concern which has produced over 125 books on his favorite subject. Mr. Henry Edmunds of the Ford Archives recently told Mr. Clymer that although thousands of books were in the library of Mr. Ford's home at Fairlane, among the very few books found in his personal desk when it was opened after his death was a complete set of Clymer's *Historical Motor Scrapbooks,* which the author considers a real tribute.

Two recent books of his own authorship are *Treasury of Early American Automobiles* and *Those Wonderful Old Automobiles,* both outstanding successes.

Mr. Clymer makes his home in Los Angeles.